THE CRISIS
IN CONTEMPORARY PREACHING

What Lessons can we Learn?

by

Rev. Prof. Dr. R. H. Creane

Professor of Systematic Theology

Urban Divinity Unit UK Limited

Affiliated to Canada Christian College and School of Graduate Theological Studies

Urban Divinity Ministries
11-13 Oughton Road, Highgate,
Birmingham, B12 0DF,
United Kingdom

"For the Word of God, and for the testimony of Jesus
Christ", (Rev. 1 v.9)

Urban Divinity Ministries Publications
P.O. Box 55, 57 Parkmore, Townland of Balteagh, Craigavon, County
Armagh, BT64 2AE

in association with
The Bible Christian Mission
and
RHC Consultancy Services

Scripture quotations are from the

Authorised Version of the Bible
(King James)

and

The Scottish Metrical Psalms

First published 2009
by
Urban Divinity Ministries Publications

ISBN -13: 978-0-9561911-3-7

Urban Divinity Ministries
Covenant School of Theology UDU Ireland

PSALM 119 V.9-16

By what means shall a young man learn
   his way to purify?
If he according to Thy Word
   thereto attentive be.

Unfeignedly Thee have I sought
   with all my soul and heart:
O let me not from the right path
   of Thy commands depart.

Thy Word I in my heart have hid,
   that I offend not Thee.
O Lord, Thou ever blessed art,
   Thy statutes teach Thou me.

The judgments of Thy mouth each one
   my lips declared have:
More joy Thy testimonies' way
   than riches all me gave.

I will Thy holy precepts make
   my meditation;
And carefully I'll have respect
   unto Thy ways each one.

Upon Thy statutes my delight
   shall constantly be set:
And, by Thy grace, I never will
   Thy holy Word forget.

SELECTED SAYINGS

"Preaching is something august, sublime, awe-begetting ----- a supernatural act, the transmission of a Person through a person to a company of persons, the Person so conveyed being the everlasting Jesus".

Ian Macpherson
Author of 'The Burden of the Lord', 1955

* * * * * *

"That which I was called to was to testify for God, to hold forth His name and ways to the dark world, and to deliver poor captives of Satan, and bring them to the glorious liberty of the children of God. This I was to make my only employment, to give myself to, and therein to be diligent, taking all occasions".

Richard Cameron
1648-1680
known as 'The Lion of the Covenant'
one of the great leaders of the Scottish Covenanters

* * * * * *

"Next to Christ I had but one joy ----- to preach Christ my Lord ----- serve Christ; back Him; let His Cause be your cause; give not a hairsbreadth of truth away, for it is not yours but God's".

Samuel Rutherford
1600-1661
warmly referred to as the 'Saint of the Covenant'
who has left the Church a rich legacy in his letters and writings

CONTENTS

An Appreciation of **JOHN CALVIN**

Date of Birth, 10th July 1509

by

Rev. Prof. Dr. R. H. Creane

John Calvin 1509-1564
The Geneva Reformer

"Separated unto the Gospel of God", (Rom. 1 v.1).

Writing on any aspect of the subject of 'Preaching', it is appropriate to refer to the Geneva Reformers. But in particular, hence this introductory article, the year 2009 marks the 500th anniversary of the birth of John Calvin, and the four hundred and fiftieth year of the third and final edition of his famous 'Institutes of the Christian Religion'. He was one of the principal figures and supreme Bible teacher of the Great Reformation in the sixteenth century. His grasp of profound theological issues and rediscovery of the Biblical doctrines of grace, greatly excelled throughout his ministry as a caring and compassionate pastor, and a faithful and powerful expositor of the Word of God.

With the publication of this book on 'Preaching', a number of conferences and lectures are also being arranged to celebrate Calvin's life and work as a gifted servant and instrument of God, the great preacher and leading theologian of the Reformation movement. The world today so desperately needs to hear of God's sovereignty and mercy, and few there are that can proclaim the Gospel of grace so distinctly and passionately as Calvin. We thank God for raising up such an eminent 'man of truth' who cleared away the pernicious errors and false teaching of Arminianism, Socinianism, Romanism, Marxism, and materialism. "Preach the Word" (2 Tim. 4 v.2), the Geneva Reformer exhorted his students with great fervency, and through their untiring labours in "holding forth the Word of life" (Phil. 2 v.16), many souls were converted and believed the Gospel.

Calvin's view of the Church's ministry, pastoral discipline, and proper freedom from state control created Presbyterianism as we know it today, restoring a Church government strictly patterned after the New Testament Early Church order of Pastors, Elders, and Deacons. He was an international figure in his own life time, advising and encouraging many Reformers throughout several European countries and elsewhere. The founding of a Christian University at Geneva was a haven and inspiration to thousands of Protestant students and refugees seeking religious liberty from the persecutions in other countries, "a model", says John Knox, "of the most perfect school of Christ since the Apostles".

Bible-centred in his living: as a Person, Pastor, Teacher, and Theologian

Calvin's achievements as pastor, teacher, scholar, theologian, and Christian character have influenced the Church profoundly over the past centuries. His basic standard that the Bible alone is the only ultimate authority for Christian belief and practice, is a Reformation principle that the Evangelical Church today needs to urgently repair and restore to its rightful place. By trusting in the promises of pardon and forgiveness, may we by Divine grace be enabled to glorify God in Christ, obey His Word, and seek to honour Him in all human relationships. Calvin's concept of the sacredness of all of life, when rightly understood, never ceased to produce humble, hardworking heroes of the faith, whose work ethic is to give glory to God. Well may we concur with his words, "There is no Power on earth but God, King of Kings, and Lord of Lords".

It is acclaimed John Calvin was, in fact, the finest exegete, the greatest systematic theologian, and the most profound Christian thinker that the Reformation produced. 'Bible-centred in his teaching, God-centred in his living, and Christ-centred in his faith', he integrated the confessional emphases of Reformation teaching:-

Sola Scriptura	:	By Scripture alone;
Christo Solum	:	By Christ alone;
Cruce Solem	:	By the Cross alone;
Sola Gatia	:	By Grace alone;
Sola Fide	:	By Faith alone;
Soli Deo Gloria	:	For the glory of God alone;

with supreme clarity, strength, and deep conviction that permeated his entire preaching life and ministry of the Word: God is all and man is nothing, battling for the Crown Rights of Christ the Redeemer in both Church and nation.

In God's good providence we pray for a fresh evidence of His mercy and favour upon the Church at large, and upon the nations, so that we may "give the more earnest heed to the things which we have heard, lest at any time we should let them slip", (Heb. 2 v.1). The Biblical principles and doctrines of God's grace that Calvin so ably proclaimed, and the fervent teaching of Divine truth during the great Covenanting and Puritan eras, are now no longer taught and largely forgotten throughout much of Christendom at the present time.

A Man of Humble Obedience contending Earnestly for the Faith

John Calvin was a man of simple faith, humble obedience, and rendered outstanding service of dedication and commitment to the true Cause of Christ's Church. He was very much a man of prayer, courage, and "not ashamed of the Gospel of Christ" (Rom. 1 v.16) he contended earnestly "for the faith which was once delivered unto the saints", (Jude v.3). The notion that Calvinism is a hindrance to evangelism and missionary enterprise is completely erroneous. Among the great preachers we have Jonathan Edwards (1703-1758), George Whitefield (1714-1770), Henry Cooke (1788-1868), Horatius Bonar (1808-1889), Robert Murray McCheyne (1813-1843), John Charles Ryle (1816-1990), Charles Haddon Spurgeon (1834-1892), Martyn Lloyd-Jones (1899-1981), and many others, who were staunch Calvinists, and their evangelical fervour in faithfully preaching the Word and expounding the doctrines of Divine grace, when rightly divided (2 Tim. 3 v.15), correctly understood, and properly applied, are most effective in the conversion of sinners and the edification of the saints: "as it is written, The just shall live by faith", (Rom. 1 v.17).

While appreciating the talents and piety to be found in many preachers and Christian workers, yet several of the truths and principles of Holy Scripture for which Calvin contended are ignored or forgotten by many Churches today that claim to be Evangelical. As servants of Christ we must obey the plain precepts of His Word, and endeavour to set God's glory and the Church's true prosperity above all else, with our eye singularly fixed upon our Exalted Lord, in the prayer that He will enable us to maintain a true witness in our profession and practice to spread abroad the message of the Gospel "in this present world", (Titus 2 v.12).

May the God of all grace so open our eyes to see His truth in the restitution of true religion and reformation of the Church in revival blessing, in the twenty-first century. With humility as well as gratitude we acknowledge that the power of the inspired, inerrant, and infallible Word is not of men, but of God, to Whom alone be "all glory and dominion for ever and ever. Amen", (Rev. 1 v.6).

Monumental Legacy of Christian Teaching

We owe a monumental debt of John Calvin for his long-lasting and massive legacy to the Church, albeit today somewhat lost in many places, and deeply appreciate the vast heritage of Christian writings he has left us, brilliantly written, of pure spiritual richness that are most enlightening, heart-searching, and convicting. These will continue to enrich and inspire all true believers in their walk with God. May we, in our day, be consumed with such passion to know, love, follow, and serve Christ.

In an era of growing apostasy when the Bible is considered of little relevance, the appeal of Calvin, even to the Church of today, is to restore to the pulpit the expository preaching of Scripture. He viewed the urgent work of preaching as the most noble and highest calling, the delivering of a Biblical message to men and women from God Himself. He greatly experienced the anointing of the Holy spirit upon his ministry in preaching, lecturing, and teaching of the Word as one who sought to speak "not with enticing words of man's wisdom, but in the demonstration of the Spirit and of power" (1 Cor. 2 v.4-5), so that his hearer's faith might not rest in the wisdom of men, but in the power of God.

The doctrines most emphasised by Calvin, among others, were the following;

(1) the holiness, majesty, and sovereignty of a glorious and gracious God;

(2) the sinfulness, helplessness, and total depravity of fallen man;

(3) the substitutionary atonement, death, and resurrection of the Lord Jesus Christ;

(4) the necessity of being born-again of the Holy Spirit, justification by faith alone, and His essential work in sanctification to live and witness as unto the Lord;

(5) the spiritual unity and eternal security of all true believers in the Lord Jesus Christ, and the responsibility of all the saints to live soberly, righteously, and godly in this present evil world;

(6) the glorious ascension of Christ, His mediatorial reign, His continual intercession at the Throne of God as the believer's Great High Priest and Advocate, His visible and personal return for His Church in glory and future judgment; and

(7) the expository, evangelical preaching, rightly dividing the Word of truth; the preservation and purity of doctrine, worship, and life, avoiding schism and heresy; and the encouragement of the exercise of all true gifts and graces in the extension of the Kingdom of Christ, to the glory of God.

Reformation and Revival in Contemporary Preaching

As true preachers of the Word, we ought to be concerned about the continuing rapidity of the declension, growing barrenness, and low spiritual state of the Church at large today. The only solution to the malady that presently obtains throughout much of Christendom ----- the crisis in contemporary preaching, the lethargy concerning the things of God, the moral decay in society, and the impotency of the Church generally to have any meaningful influence upon the world as a whole ----- is a fresh outpouring of the Spirit of God in reformation and revival. "Wilt Thou not revive us again: that Thy people may rejoice in thee? Shew us Thy mercy, O Lord, and grant us Thy salvation", (Psalm 85 v.6).

The Church today is facing a major cultural push to accept all persons regardless of beliefs, whether Roman Catholic, nominal Protestant, Hindu, Greek Orthodox, Jew, Muslim, or whatever, as brothers and sisters. The exclusivity of the Gospel is becoming more and more unpopular, "a stone of stumbling, and a rock of offence, even to them which stumble at the Word, being disobedient", (1 Peter 2 v.8). Sadly, many Evangelicals are embracing tolerance, but sacrificing truth.

Calvin being dead, yet speaketh; let us stand shoulder to shoulder with men of like passion in the truth of the Gospel for the defence of the faith. The Apostle Paul charges us as ministers and preachers of the Word to be diligent and faithful in the work of the Lord. "Take heed therefore unto yourselves, and to all the flock, over the which the Holy Ghost hath made you overseers, to feed the Church of God, which He hath purchased with his own blood", (Acts 20 v.28).

"Preach the Word", (2 Tim. 4 v.2).

"For Thy name's glory help us, Lord,
　　Who hast our Saviour been:
Deliver us; for Thy name's sake,
　　O purge away our sin.

Why say the heathen, Where's their God?
　　let Him to them be known;
When those who shed Thy servants blood
　　Are in our sight o'erthrown.

So we Thy folk, and pasture-sheep,
　　shall give Thee thanks always;
And unto generations all
　　we will shew forth Thy praise",

(Psalm 79 v.9-10,13).

The Reformation Monument, Geneva
William Farel, John Calvin, Theodore Beza, John Knox

18

FOREWORDS BY:

Dr. Wm. McCormack

There is absolutely no doubt that the Church today has lost sight of its true purpose and mission in the world. Many Church leaders become so immersed and occupied in social and political issues having "omitted the weightier matters of the law" (Matt. 23 v.23), and consequently have turned away from the fact that their true role should be the spiritual well-being of the nations.

In this book, Rev. Prof. Dr. Creane reviews the present situation at length. He has rightly emphasised many important issues by examining the deficiencies and weaknesses in a searching manner as to why the Church and its message are not being as successful as they once were. A very veritable point he makes is that all too often many of the modern-day preachers are but "blind leaders of the blind" (Matt. 15 v.14), and, alas, their 'message' is the presentation of 'another gospel'. He further states that preachers who are themselves believers and in possession of the truth, are greatly curtailed in their work by elders and congregations opposed to the teaching of the true Gospel in all its fullness. "The fear of man bringeth a snare", (Prov. 29 v.25). This being so, sermons are thus prepared, presented, and preached, tailored to suit audiences rather than proclaiming the whole truth of the Holy Scriptures ----- in fact, shunning to declare "all the counsel of God", (Acts 20 v.27).

Prof. Creane clearly shows the apostolic preaching and Biblical teaching of the true Evangel of Jesus Christ, whereby men and women, who are sinners by nature, "dead in trespasses and sins" (Eph. 2 v.1), "strangers from the covenants of promise, having no hope, and without God in the world" (Eph. 2 v.12), facing eternal separation and condemnation ----- can by faith in the saving atoning-work of Christ alone be "justified from all things" (Acts 13 v.39) and "have peace with God" (Rom. 5 v.1) for time and eternity.

In heaven, only the redeemed will be in the immediate presence of God, and will see Christ "as He is" (1 John 3 v.2). Heaven is God's house of "many mansions" (John 14 v.2), where the saved in Christ will dwell with Him for evermore. (Rev. 21 v.3). The preacher's ministry is distinctively that of the propagation of "the Gospel of God", (Rom. 1 v.1). This high calling must be regarded as a sacred trust (Gal. 2 v.7), and we must become servants of the Gospel by the gift of God's grace (Eph. 3 v.7), which Prof. Creane rightly emphasises.

Eternal issues are at stake, and the author emphatically states that the Holy Scriptures are the only infallible authority in all matters of faith and practice. The Bible alone is the inerrant Word of God and the only source of all truth and the final court of appeal. No other source or opinion of man can be substituted.

This is the Gospel that the great Apostle Paul took to the pagan inhabitants of the Roman world. He saw it triumph over the wisdom and philosophy of men in Athens, the terrible immorality of the people in Corinth, the power of Satan in Ephesus, and the multi-religious people of Rome, the metropolis of the world. It is this Gospel, the pure teaching of the Word of God, that Prof. Creane urges men to preach "in all the world for a witness unto all nations", (Matt. 24 v.14).

Preachers today should read this book and seek to benefit from its many challenges and profitable exhortation to "preach the Word", (2 Tim. 4 v.2).

W. McCormack

Dr. William McCormack
Bible Preacher and Teacher
City of Lisburn

Rev. Dr. R. J. Coulter

This is a timely book, for many in the Church believe that those who occupy our pulpits in the 21st century have lost the art of preaching. The questions are often asked – "Where are the Spurgeons of today"? Where are the orators in our Churches who enhance the Word of God?"

Prof Creane in addressing the issue states that "the real problem, the true fault, of what is wrong with preaching in our Churches today is failure in the man who preaches and in the spurious message he communicates".

This book makes it clear that the superlative need of the Church today, is not for more preachers, but for better preachers. Those who are committed to expounding the unsearchable riches of Christ in the Gospel of salvation for a dying, sinful world, must be personally prepared before God, before preaching to others.

The message of Prof. Creane in these pages is that the true preacher of the Gospel who is doctrinally sound and Spirit-controlled ----- will be effective in making God's living Word alive to the people. Preaching for such exponents of the Gospel will always be, as John Piper says, "a Scripture-founded and a Scripture-saturated event".

However, effectiveness in preaching is found, not only in the performance of the preacher but in his life. "Powerful preaching as patterned after the prophets and apostles is rooted in the soil of the preacher's own heart and life". Prayer, study of the Word, a genuine love for lost men and women, but above all, an unswerving loyalty to the Lord Jesus Christ, is the undergirding the preacher must have.

It is cogently summed up by the Author when he writes, "A return to Biblical exposition and application of Scripture truth is the dire need of the hour. Our Churches are swamped with all kinds of innovations, and it is imperative, therefore, that we deal honestly, truthfully, and faithfully in our preaching of the 'whole counsel of God' (Acts 20 v.27). We must pray fervently, walk worthily, watch diligently, and 'obey from the heart that form of doctrine which was delivered to us', (Romans 6 v.17)".

Prof. Creane goes back to the Greek of the New Testament to explain the foundation meaning of the preacher's message. The "Good News", the "proclamation", the "teaching", the "exhortation", are all part of this glorious statement of truth. This is true preaching since the word "preach" simply means, "to tell thoroughly".

This book is a challenge to all who hear the call of the Holy Spirit to expound the Gospel message. When I read this book I felt so inadequate as a preacher and it drove me to a new awareness of the awesome responsibility of preaching the Word of Truth. If preaching is an awesome responsibility, it should be for the preacher an unequalled privilege to have a private, personal interview with God before preaching.

I congratulate Rev. Prof. Dr. Creane on giving us a well researched book and I pray that those who read its pages will be brought to a new inner place with God, a better awareness of the need for preparation to preach, and a superior knowledge of the privilege of preaching.

The message of this book can be summed up in the words of the greatest preacher of the New Testament Church, the Apostle Paul – "Preach the Word". (2 Timothy 4 v.2).

R. J. Coulter

Rev. Dr. Robert J. Coulter MLA
Glarryford
formerly Broughshane Presbyterian Church
Ballymena
County Antrim

Rev. Dr. Wm. J. Malcolmson

This book, by Rev. Prof. Dr. Robert Creane, has as its Sub-title – "What lessons can we learn"? The answer is found in this remarkable book, which covers a very wide spectrum concerning the subject of preaching, and the preacher himself.

Professor Creane's approach is direct, it is wide-ranging, and thoroughly un-compromising from a Reformed and Evangelical stand-point.

Here is writing at its best which is Biblically-based, and therefore God-exalting, rather than man-centred. This book deals with much of the inefficiency in the pulpit today due to "indiscipline in the reading and study of the Scriptures, and failure in the private place of prayer. These things lead to a lack of personal morality, integrity, and purity of life". In much of the preaching today there is a departure from the great Formularies and Confessions of Faith which preachers undertook at Ordination to uphold.

Dr. Creane, in this fresh and gripping exposition of preaching, defect in preachers, and the present perilous situation inside and outside the Visible Church, writes both as theologian and pastor.

<u>"It is uniquely a tract for our times"</u>

His aim is that Churches and their spiritual leaders will recognise the problems and tensions inherent in being God's people and His ministers in the increasingly secular world of today, creating a deep need for the return to preaching "the Bible, the whole Bible, and nothing but the Bible". This book seeks to bring back to the Churches the desire and intent to express the total Lordship of Christ to a world becoming increasingly godless. Professor Creane seeks to bring to the surface, by a Biblical Theology, the rich resources for Christian Ministry and Mission, that are already there in the Churches, but which have sadly been neglected for many years.

This book endeavours to wean the Evangelical Church away from worldliness, and spiritual sleeping-sickness.

In this we have "<u>a wake-up call</u>"

It also calls for Christian Doctrine to be brought to the fore for the building up of believers in their "most holy faith".

Professor Creane must be congratulated in providing "Extracts from the Great Confessions of the Reformation", accounts of the Scottish National Covenant 1638, details of The Westminster Assembly, the Solemn League and Covenant 1643, and quotations from George Whitefield and Jonathan Edwards.

The urgency of the challenges before us, the weakness of much of Evangelical Christianity, the characteristics of false preachers, and the nature of true worship and reverence for God are all emphasised, as well as the need for preaching the whole counsel of God.

The great merit of this Book is that it does not merely deal with all the errors, but positively shows the way forward to the revival of true worship and the spiritual recovery and reformation of "The Glorious Body of Christ".

W. J. Malcolmson

Rev. Dr. W. J. Malcolmson
Congregational Reformed Church
Belfast

PREFACE

"Preach the Word", (2 Tim. 4 v.2).

This book began its life as a special series of lectures and the contents of these pages is really a brief synopsis of what was given in the lecture theatre. Ministers, lay preachers and all those who are called to the task of delivering God's Word in today's world, will find this vital work of preaching the Gospel of God in all its fullness with faithfulness and power, immensely challenging.

The crisis in contemporary preaching is attributable in large measure to the deficiency of the man, the weakness of the message he brings, and incompetency in the pulpit. Because of:

(1)   a lack of personal morality, integrity and purity;

(2)   failure in the private place of prayer;

(3)   indiscipline in the meditation and study of God's Word;

(4)   negligence in duty, broken vows to uphold the truth, and a failure to maintain a daily devotional experience of Christ;

(5)   barrenness in spiritual reformation;

(6)   a mere outward formality in the public worship of God;

(7)   greed of filthy lucre and materialism; and other weaknesses in the preacher,

the so-called sermons in public worship are not actual preaching.

No preaching is worthy of the name that does not contain a real, vital message from the Word of God. The message we are commissioned to preach can be summed up in one word, "which is Christ" (Col. 1 v.27): "Christ in you, the hope of glory". Our message is not just a philosophy, or merely a creed, a cold doctrine, or merely about ethics and a new reformed way of life ----- but a

Living Person, Christ: "Christ the power of God, and the wisdom of God", (1 Cor. 1 v.24).

Robert Murray McCheyne (1813-1843) declared, "What a man is alone on his knees before God", especially a preacher, "that he is, and no more". Due to a dearth of intimate personal fellowship and a deeper knowledge of God and of His Word on the part of many contemporary preachers, their preaching will inevitably be lacking and ineffective in bringing any lasting renewal, reformation, or genuine revival in the personal, family, and corporate life across the nation.

If the sermon fails to open up the Scriptures, or fails in the application of the Word, it falls very far short of being true preaching. The need for preaching sermons that properly teach and adequately apply the message of Scripture cannot be questioned for one moment. They are the Lord's message to men and women with the purpose to inform, persuade, and call forth an appropriate response to God in repentance, faith, and new "obedience unto righteousness" (Rom. 6 v.16) ----- having "obeyed from the heart that form of doctrine which was delivered you", (Rom. 6 v.17).

Just as God's Word must keep on reforming our theology, ethics and conduct to a fuller understanding of the truth, so also it must reform our prayer habits, the priorities we should adopt, and the beliefs and practices that should shape and mould our lives. Prayer is the measure of the man, spiritually, in a way that nothing else is, and therefore it is imperative to heed the injunction of Holy Scripture to "Pray without ceasing", (1 Thess. 5 v.17).

The main thrust and purpose of this book then, is to call preachers back to God, and back to the Bible, in repentance and faith, so that with the unction of a Spirit-filled exposition, we may proclaim and publish the truth of God far and wide.

God has revealed His mind and will in the Holy Scriptures. "Thy Word is true", (Psalm 119 v.160). By the power of the Holy Spirit, every true preacher must set forth faithfully the Divine truths of the Word that are by some denied, and that are by many ignored. May God give us grace to stand against every perversion of Scriptural doctrine, every corruption of Scriptural ordinance, and all disobedience to the revealed will of God.

Christian doctrine cannot be ignored or set aside. To do so would be at our peril, for it is only by seriously studying the Word of God and meditating upon the doctrines of grace, that we can hope to build up ourselves on our "most holy faith" (Jude v.20), grow spiritually, and be fit vessels for effective Christian service.

"The doctrine of God our Saviour" (Titus 2 v.10) has been largely jettisoned, deemed impractical, and considered irrelevant by the Church. In these days of word-spinning, the root cause of the crisis in preaching is not so much the desire for modernity, but rather the rejection of Biblical teaching. The aim of this book is that it might have a profoundly sobering effect upon ministers, pastors, preachers and all evangelists and Christian workers, so that with renewed concern for the glory of God and for the well-being of man, we may have greater faithfulness and steadfastness in proclaiming the great truths of the "Everlasting Covenant, ordered in all things, and sure", (2 Sam. 23 v.5).

In our preaching of the Gospel of free and sovereign grace, may we be motivated by the desire to glorify God and to magnify Christ by a faithful declaration of the Word of truth. "The Word of the Lord endureth for ever. And this is the Word which by the Gospel is preached unto you", (1 Peter 1 v.25).

Our preaching must be concerned above all things to honour Christ, the only King and Head of the Church, and to declare the whole counsel of God to needy men and women. May all who preach the Gospel of salvation in these evil days, do so with profound solemnity and concern to exalt our glorious and mighty Saviour: "that in all things He might have the preeminence", (Col. 1 v.18).

We need to pray fervently that the Evangelical Church will be delivered from worldliness, corruption and spiritual malady. May "the light of the glorious Gospel of Christ" (2 Cor. 4 v.4) shine forth with power, and may the recovery of the doctrines of grace that shook the world in the Great Reformation be embraced with open arms. In our service for God, may we know Christ more intimately, may we preach Him more effectively for the good of all, and may we live more triumphantly to the glory of God.

As we endeavour by Divine help to articulate the Bible's teaching concerning the truths of God, may He graciously use our efforts and influence, feeble though they be, to give greater understanding of the Gospel to those who hear us. Let us earnestly tell the story, "By grace are ye saved through faith" (Eph. 2 v.8), so that many may come to "taste and see that the Lord is good: blessed is the man that trusteth in Him", (Psalm 34 v.8). We cannot in human terms measure the richness and greatness of His manifold grace and bountiful mercy bestowed upon undeserving sinners like ourselves.

The exhortation of this book is forceful, terse, frank, simple, yet profound as we would endeavour to preach the wonder, marvel, and majesty of God's grace to men, who by nature are totally lost, "dead in trespasses and sins", (Eph. 2 v.1). In these days of widespread compromise and growing apostasy, may every true preacher "give attendance to reading, to exhortation, to doctrine ----- for in doing this thou shalt both save thyself, and them that hear thee", (1 Tim. 4 v.13-16).

This book will have served its purpose if it whets the appetite of preachers and others to a more detailed study of the Word, and a greater commitment to proclaim the Gospel of truth in all its fullness. "And we know that the Son of God is come, and hath given us an understanding, that we may know Him that is true, and we are in Him that is true, even in His Son Jesus Christ. This is the true God, and eternal life", (1 John 5 v.20).

I would like to express my grateful thanks and praise to the God of all grace, Who giveth strength to lecture, preach, and write; to my Theological Seminary colleagues and all other staff, fellow workers, friends and students who have helped to stimulate conviction and discussion; to Dr. W. McCormack, Rev. Dr. R. J. Coulter and Rev. Dr. W. J. Malcolmson for writing the Forewords; to Mr. George W. Patton, Chief Executive Officer, for permission to use pictures from the Ulster-Scot paper; to Mr & Mrs Kenny (George and Helen) for their untiring and skilful use of the computer, editing, and placing on disk the final text of this book; and not least to my wife and family for all their love, support and encouragement in the Lord.

"Neglect not the gift that is in thee", (1 Tim. 4 v.14).

"Preach the Word", (2 Tim. 4 v.2).

R. H. Creane

Principal
Covenant School of Theology UDU Ireland
Urban Divinity Ministries
Birmingham

THE CRISIS
IN CONTEMPORARY PREACHING
What Lessons can we Learn?

2 Timothy 4 v.1-5

I charge thee therefore before God, and the Lord Jesus Christ, Who shall judge the quick and the dead at His appearing and His kingdom;

Preach the Word; be instant in season, out of season, reprove, rebuke, exhort, with all longsuffering and doctrine.

For the time will come when they will not endure sound doctrine; but after their own lusts shall they heap to themselves teachers, having itching ears;

And they shall turn away their ears from the truth, and shall be turned unto fables.

But watch thou in all things, endure afflictions, do the work of an evangelist, make full proof of thy ministry.

INTRODUCTION

Throughout our land and further afield, most people today are out of touch with the Christian message of the Gospel of God's Word. "How shall they hear without a preacher?", (Rom. 10 v.14).

Contemporary preaching is in great turmoil and crisis at the present time. I would direct your attention to some aspects of this particular subject so that we might in all earnestness, think seriously and soberly about the task of preaching. We pray that the Holy Spirit will enlighten our hearts and minds by drawing us closer to God, and as we contemplate on this important matter let us seek His deliverance from all lethargy and failure on our part in fulfilling our calling as preachers and teachers of the Word. "We are ambassadors for Christ" (2 Cor. 5 v.20) who must go forth with implicit faith, and as the prophet Jonah was directed, to preach unto the people "the preaching that I bid Thee", says the Lord, (Jonah 3 v.2).

Our Scripture reading at the beginning is from one of the Pastoral Epistles in which the Apostle Paul charges Timothy, in very strong language, regarding the importance and relevance of preaching. With these stirring verses before us, the Word of God confronts us as we attempt to think Biblically about our task in proclaiming the Word. I think most of us who are preachers have enough sense of logic to reason from this passage of Scripture (2 Tim. 4 v.1-5) to ourselves and therefore to conclude that this will be an attempt to expose the weaknesses and failures in our own preaching. "Buy the truth, and sell it not; also wisdom, and instruction, and understanding", (Prov. 23 v.23).

At this juncture I would point out that one would have to be omniscient and be vested with infallible gifts of analysis and global oversight to be able to make final and accurate pronouncements as to what is wrong with much of the preaching today. I make no such claim to any of these things. I do, however, trust that the comments and observations made will be nevertheless valid, correct, and to the point. As we survey the Church, it would seem that preaching is in a state of grave crisis, increasing declension, and much decay.

The Old Paths Forsaken

The turning away of many Churches and preachers from "the old paths" (Jer. 6 v.16) of Divine Truth is in freefall all around us, and there is great barrenness and backsliding almost everywhere, the rapid pace of which is most alarming. Pure Gospel preaching is being

31

diluted, so much so that the centrality of the Bible is no longer regarded as the only infallible rule in all matters of faith and practice. In this so-called post-modern, post-enlightenment age, the absolute authority of the Word of God is no longer adhered to in many of the Protestant denominations.

In the Acts of the Apostles, Chapter 2, we have the account of the descent of the Holy Ghost upon the disciples of Christ on the day of Pentecost. The outpouring of the Holy Spirit had a mighty influence upon the preachers of the Gospel and upon the hearers of the Gospel. By the preaching of the Word, thousands were saved from sin and brought unto obedience of faith in Christ by the power of God. They received the Word, embraced it, and "continued steadfastly in the apostles' doctrine and fellowship", (Acts 2 v.42). In our day and generation we need to be diligent and constant in our attendance upon the preaching of the Word and continue in the apostles' doctrine and creed. We must never disown nor desert the teaching of Scripture. May we continue instant in prayer, ever abounding in piety and devotion with thanksgiving and praise to God. "Thanks be to God, which giveth us the victory through our Lord Jesus Christ. Therefore, my beloved brethren, be ye steadfast, unmoveable, always abounding in the work of the Lord, forasmuch as ye know that your labour is not in vain in the Lord", (1 Cor. 15 v.57-58).

The Scriptures show fallen man by nature in a dead and desperate state ----- "dead in trespasses and sins", (Eph. 2 v.1). Being totally depraved and unable to effect his own salvation, he needs to be saved by the sovereign grace of God, (Eph. 2 v.8-9). We thank God for the gift of salvation and deliverance from sin, through the Person and Work of Christ, and by the operation of the Holy Spirit giving assurance of eternal life to His people (Acts 4 v.12). The only merit upon which a sinner may be saved is Christ's merit (Rom. 5 v.18-19). Even the act of faith (Acts.16 v.31; and Rom. 5 v.1), by which a man reaches out and receives Christ, is a Divine gift, given on the grounds of His righteousness, (2 Peter 1 v.1). He purchased our redemption by the sacrifice of Himself on the Cross of Calvary (Heb. 9 v.12), and assures us of eternity with Himself in heaven which He has gone to prepare (John 14 v.1-3). The Scripture speaks of lost sinners being saved, but never of saved sinners being lost (John 10 v.28).

For many decades now one is exposed to great sections of the spectrum of Evangelical life throughout these Islands and further afield. From a Biblical perspective there is among my peers, colleagues, and others, a strong indication of unease, concern, and deep reflection upon the inferior quality and poor state of preaching in many of the Churches today. In all honesty we have to admit to our great shame that throughout vast swathes of Christendom world wide at the present time, preaching is of a very low standard. "Where there is no vision, the people perish", (Prov. 29 v.18).

In the realm of what is effective Biblical preaching, I believe we can glean from the Scriptures an accurate standard of what good and sound preaching is by examining the preaching of the prophets, of the apostles, and of our Lord Jesus Christ. As we look also at the lives, ministries, and sermons of the great men of God of past ages, worthy servants, mighty in the Gospel, who where instruments of God to bring sinners to Christ, men such as Rutherford, Edwards, Whitefield, McCheyne, Spurgeon, Baxter, Bunyan, and others, we cannot but be moved by their loyalty, courage and single-hearted devotion to Christ Jesus, the King and Head of the Church. In their day each of them "earnestly contended for the faith which was once delivered unto the saints", (Jude V.3).

The Reformers, Covenanters, Puritans and others over the centuries were men of great vision, deep conviction, firm resolve, steadfast in the faith, and unmoveable in the cause of civil and religious liberty. They stood firm for the Gospel without wavering or compromise, holding forth the Lamp of Scripture truth with untiring perseverance, and even in the face of fiery opposition and persecution, continued to uphold, maintain, and defend the blessed doctrines of the manifold grace of God. May we in our day be committed by the grace of God to the fidelity of the Word which is the best security against apostasy.

"Remove not the ancient land mark, which thy fathers have set", (Prov. 22 v.28).

The Laodicean Disease

The most exciting and amazing experience anyone can have is to be "born again" (John 3 v.3) and become a member of God's family. Sadly, today, such preaching is ridiculed, not only by the secular world, but also by many within the Christian Church. As preachers who desire to love, obey and serve the Lord in communicating the message of salvation to others, may we run the race to obtain the crown with renewed passion and zeal for the Gospel that marked the early preaching of the apostolic Church of the New Testament. There is always the great danger of yielding to compromise, negligence of the means of grace, indifference to the Gospel, even giving way to open hostility and outright rejection of the authority of God's Word.

There is no doubt that the Laodicean phase is now with us, and that the same lukewarmness and failure of that early Church have deeply infected the Church of today. The inroads of worldly standards, apathy and materialism have dimmed our vision of the lost and their eternal doom. The preaching of the Gospel of God (Rom. 1 v.1), evangelism, worship, discipline, Church government, and personal witness, are matters that contemporary preachers no longer consider important. With the help of the Holy Spirit I trust we shall see the widespread dearth, barrenness and famine of great preaching in our day, and discover more deeply the causes of this deplorable condition. May God awaken us and equip us by His Spirit as we learn from Holy Writ the remedy of this dreadful plight that is blighting the Church at the present time.

How then are we to approach this vast subject? As we look out upon the Church at large today, what are the distinguishing marks of such a crisis? How would we recognise such a problem? How do we identify the characteristic elements of such a malaise? And how do we measure the gravity of what is wrong with preaching today?

Is it by the dropping attendance in the Churches? Is it by the decreased attention in the pew? Is it by the declining standards of the modern day cultural appeal of preaching? Is it by the compromising and declining social status of preachers? Or might the reality be far more radical and devastating than this?

As we look further at the plight of the situation before our very eyes, might the true evidence of the crisis in preaching be instead, immature and even ignorant Christian leaders falling prey to false doctrine? Might it be a worldly Church proclaiming an increasing worldly message? Might it be confusion, disorder, and an increasing secularity of religion? Might it be lack of instruction giving way to a state of flux and continuous change in doctrine and morals? Might it be lack of discipline in our Churches? Or might it also be the development of party-factions and seditious cliques given over to spurious disputes which result in contentious divisions with all kinds of false teaching, unlawful actions, and hurtful behaviour that tend to be injurious and damaging to the Cause of Christ?

From time to time we also hear about some of the concert-styles of organised 'praise' elements and the contemporary 'prayer' modes which give rise for deep concern in some parts, but what if such a crisis in our Churches were more fundamentally evidenced by the substance of what we preach or fail to preach?

The minimising approach of ministers and pastors to the task of preaching Christian truth leads only to emptying the Gospel of its doctrinal content, thus nullifying the effectiveness of its practical application. All the weaknesses, failures and crisis in preaching today are basically two things ----- the man who preaches, and the message he brings. As we draw due attention to the teaching and exposition of Holy Scripture, and apply the spotlight of the Word of God to this crisis, we shall see that the real problem, the true fault, of what is wrong with preaching in our Churches today is failure in the man who preaches, and in the spurious message he communicates. "And who is sufficient for these things? For we are not as many, which corrupt the Word of God: but as of sincerity, but as of God, in the sight of God speak we in Christ", (2 Cor. 2 v.16-17).

Defining the Gospel of God

We need to be "stirred up" (Isaiah 64 v.7) by the Spirit of the Lord and aroused afresh as to what are the essential elements of true Gospel preaching. In this context we would rightly ask, What is the Gospel of God? The comprehensiveness of the Gospel is well defined by the great Puritan, Thomas Manton, in the following words: "The sum of the Gospel is this, that all who, by true repentance and faith, do forsake the flesh, the world, and the devil, and give themselves up to God the Father, Son, and Holy Spirit, as their Creator, Redeemer, and Sanctifier, shall find God as a Father, taking them for His reconciled children, and for Christ's sake pardoning their sin, and by His Spirit giving them His grace; and, if they persevere in this course, will finally glorify them, and bestow upon them everlasting happiness; but will condemn the unbeliever, impenitent, and ungodly to everlasting punishment. That this is the sum of the Gospel appeareth by Mark 16 v.15-16, 'go ye into all the world, and preach the Gospel to every creature. He that believeth and is baptised shall be saved; but he that believeth not shall be dammed' ----- where you have all the Christian religion laid before you in one short view and prospect".

A close examination of THE SCRIPTURE leads us to the conclusion that the deficiencies in today's preaching of the Gospel largely ignore the great doctrines of sovereign and saving grace, the attributes of God, original sin through the Fall, total depravity and utter ruin of mankind, the holy law of God, repentance, and faith. Calling on people to bow to the enthroned Christ of God (Luke 9 v.20) as Lord and King of all of life, is no longer taught in our Churches: "that in all things He might have the pre-eminence", (Col. 1 v.18).

The scribes and Pharisees of old had corrupted the Word of God, and Scripture warns us not to "add unto the Word which I command you", (Deut. 4 v.2). Corrupting the authority of Scripture, perverting the doctrines of the true Church of Christ and distorting the Biblical teaching of assurance of salvation in Christ Jesus, are enormous deceptions. The obscuring of "the doctrine of God our Saviour in all things" (Titus 2 v.10) goes right to the very heart of the crisis of contemporary preaching in our time.

All is not well in the Churches. Throughout our land and further afield, we deeply lament and deplore the weaknesses that exist at the present time, and lameness in Gospel ministry is deepening yet more and more. Sinners are not turning to Christ in great numbers. Christians are not being fed on the strong meat of the Word. Churches generally are lukewarm and dead. The preaching by and large, is hollow and shallow. The worship of God "in spirit and in truth" (John 4 v.24) is substituted by gimmicks and entertainment. And the Church services generally are human-centred rather than God-centred, which robs the Lord God Almighty of His glory.

We need God's mighty power to return to the preaching of today. We need to pray for reformation and revival in the pulpit. We need an awakening of the Spirit of God and an outpouring of His grace to deliver us from the dangers that surround us. We long for the spiritual vitality and fruitfulness of earlier days, with the prayer that God might revive and restore us yet again: "Wilt Thou not revive us again, that Thy people may rejoice in Thee? Shew us Thy mercy, O Lord, and grant us Thy salvation", (Psalm 85 v.6-7).

Sin causes us to loose many blessings. The devil is the great disrupter, and the Church has become a spiritual desert. The crucial mistake with major errors is that evangelicals are co-operating and merging with liberals and others hoping to revitalise and strengthen a weakened Church through relevance, respectability, fashion and especially unity. From the human point of view organisational unity based on the lowest common denominator must be found to suit everybody and not offend anyone. The result is the wholesale surrender of Divine truth and labelling the doctrinal preciseness of Holy Scripture as unessential, unimportant, and therefore not necessary.

This landslide compromise is precisely the root problem of the crisis in preaching today. This evil influence goes on spreading yet more and more to the point that the local Church must not get too specific about truth either, as it may affect its harmony with the denomination. To define the Gospel of God and to expound the doctrines of grace carefully in a Biblical manner will bring conflict and friction, and therefore unity on the lowest common denominator, at the expense of truth, is deemed to be the key to success. That is the devil's lie.

Sola Scriptura

We are now approaching the 400th anniversary in 2011 of the Authorised Version of the English Bible, and we thank God for our Reformation heritage. Let us ever pray for grace to yield our supreme allegiance to the Lord Jesus Christ, and in obedience to His Word may we justly claim the principle of the Reformers and Covenanters ----- Sola Scriptura, Scripture Alone ----- as the only infallible rule in all matters of faith and practice. "All Scripture is given by inspiration of God, and is profitable for doctrine, for reproof, for correction, for instruction in righteousness: That the man of God may be perfect, throughly furnished unto all good works", (2 Tim. 3 v.16-17).

Sadly, many of our present-day Protestant Churches who claim to be evangelical are saturated with doctrines and practices which have no Biblical foundation or warrant whatsoever. In the central issue of the way of salvation, they have inherited methods and systems of so-called evangelistic preaching which are unBiblical, and which cannot be traced back to the Reformers and Covenanters. But worse still, they cannot be traced to the Scriptures. The resulting product is a dangerous conglomerate of superficial exegesis, human intellectualism, and worldly reasoning, in a so-called modern package that twists Bible verses and uses half-truths to "bring in damnable heresies ----- when many shall follow their pernicious ways", (2 Peter 2 v.1-2). The devil delights in this sort of thing which he uses to maximum advantage to delude and damn the souls of sinners ----- men, women, and children ----- in hell for ever.

Casting doubt upon God's Word has been Satan's strategy from the beginning: "Yea, hath God said?" (Gen. 3 v.1), and the great deception continues to this day by selling another 'gospel' to our generation. The apostasy and delusion advances as the arch-enemy is employing more and more men in preaching a dethroned Christ. Such men do not adhere to the authority and infallibility of the Word of God, nor do they give careful attention to the study and exposition of the truths of Scripture, thus distorting the doctrines of grace and perverting the preaching of the true Gospel of God as revealed in Holy Writ. The tragedy is that the majority of those who supposedly 'make decisions for Church membership' continue to live like the world with no evidence of the grace of God in a transformed life. In reality they are still travelling on the broad road that leads to destruction, death, and hell. "For the wages of sin is death; but the gift of God is eternal life through Jesus Christ our Lord", (Rom. 6 v.23).

Repentance and faith become real and lasting among the redeemed of the Lord, only when God the Holy Ghost comes down with mighty convicting power and converting soul-saving grace. Many who have come forward at various times to sign 'decision' cards in our modern campaigns and Church rallies, sadly, are being deluded and lulled by a perverted 'gospel', and greatly misled by a false confirmation of salvation. On the shallow ground of man's logic, large numbers have been given an 'assurance' which does not belong to them. "From the prophet even unto the priest everyone dealeth falsely. They have healed also the hurt ----- of my people slightly, saying, Peace, peace; when there is no peace. Were they ashamed when they had committed abomination? nay, they were not at all ashamed, neither could they blush: therefore they shall fall among them that fall: at the time that I visit them they shall be cast down , saith the Lord", (Jer. 6 V.13-15).

The message and methods of preaching employed by many preachers today are unBiblical and therefore misleading and misdirecting souls, and it is no wonder then that so-called 'converts' remain as carnal as ever. There is no sign of godliness in their lives like the Saviour they 'profess', they are not zealous for His Cause, nor do they study the Bible to seek His will or pray. Such empty profession is a complete sham, and in this situation the devil is having a field-day!! Unless our preachers and Church leaders approach the way of salvation by obeying God's Word, and preaching God's Word in all its fullness, evangelicalism will continue to be choked yet more and more in the morass of human tradition, shackled in ignorance, and misguiding souls for eternity. The current trends and modern changes in today's preaching are extremely serious, contrary to the Scripture, which grieves the Holy Spirit and yields empty nets. So grave and dangerous is the crisis in preaching today that it means the eternal death of souls, the sterility of the Churches, and above all dishonour to the Lord God Almighty by ignoring the teaching of His inspired and inerrant Word. "Fear thou the Lord . . . and meddle not with them that are given to change", (Prov. 24 v.21).

The Urgency of the Challenge

With deepest urgency and conviction the challenge comes to all of us to follow the Christ of Scripture, and lay hold of "the everlasting Gospel to preach unto them that dwell on earth, and to every nation, and kindred, and tongue, and people, Saying with a loud voice, Fear God, and give glory to Him", (Rev. 14. v.6-7). We are still living in the Day of Grace and opportunity, but the world is rushing onward regardless of the peril and doom that awaits her. There is no sense of urgency to prepare for the world to come among people. They are void of any thought of eternity and with indifference, contempt, and scorn, they despise the preaching of the Gospel. Yet, they need to hear about sin and its consequences, and to be convicted of the need to be saved by the sovereign grace of God. The Scripture speaks of the "deceivableness of unrighteousness in them that perish; because they received not the love of the truth, that they might be saved", (2 Thess. 2 v.10).

The Apostle Paul speaking to the Corinthians, said, "I declare unto you the Gospel which I preached unto you ----- by which also ye are saved ----- for I delivered unto you first of all that which I also received, how that Christ died for our sins according to the Scriptures; And that He was buried, and that He rose again the third day according to the Scriptures", (1 Cor. 15 v.1-4). Again, in giving his last address to the Church at Ephesus, Paul stressed, "I kept back nothing that was profitable unto you, but have shewed you, and have taught you publickly, and from house to house, Testifying both to the Jews, and also to the Greeks, repentance toward God, and faith toward our Lord Jesus Christ", (Acts 20 v.20-21). And yet again he declares, "For by grace are ye saved through faith; and that not of yourselves: it is the gift of God: Not of works, lest any man should boast. For we are His workmanship, created in Christ Jesus unto good works, which God hath before ordained that we should walk in them", (Eph. 2 v.8-10).

The essence of true Biblical Gospel-preaching in which the following elements are outlined, emphasised and proclaimed, are:-

(1) The sovereignty, wisdom, and holiness of God;

(2) The Person and Work of Christ: His life, death, burial, and resurrection;

(3) The question of sin and the need for repentance toward God;

(4)   The necessity of faith alone by grace alone through our Lord
       Jesus Christ alone for salvation.

This kind of language and presentation of doctrine are fast disappearing from today's preaching. In regard to teaching from the pulpit on the fundamental truths of the Bible, many preachers are too afraid and scared of offending their people, and so the doctrines of grace are relegated and banished to a place of unimportance: "the fear of man bringeth a snare", (Prov. 29 v.25). Instead, they trot out stuff that is perhaps academic, literary, philosophical and sophisticated, but which does not reflect the true exposition of the Word accurately and faithfully. As well as being boring much of the time, such preaching is not distinctive, clear, plain, or easy to understand. It is void of Biblical authority and content, and does not spell out the truth of the infallible Word, so much so that the souls of men continue to flounder and remain in ignorance of salvation, ignorance of progress in sanctification, ignorance of dying to sin more and more, and ignorance of living unto righteousness more and more. We are not to allow ourselves to be conformed to this world. A transformed spirit and a renewed mind dispose the soul to receive the revelation of the Divine will, saturated and controlled by the Word of God. "And be not conformed to this world: but be ye transformed by the renewing of your mind, that ye may prove what is that good, and acceptable, and perfect, will of God", (Rom. 12 v.2).

A major crisis that is all too common among today's preachers is the absence of the doctrine of the resurrection. Sadly, the passion that once marked the preaching of the Word in the past has largely disappeared. Dry-eyed sermons are presented as a matter of form without a tear of concern at the prospect of a soul being consigned to the wrath of God for ever. Many ministers have abandoned and deserted the core-elements of the Gospel by casting doubt upon the Word of God and rejecting the central truth of the resurrection.

The Compromise of a Changing Church

In Second Timothy, Chapter. 4, we are warned about false teachers and those who live contrary to the truth deeply resent and resist the teaching of sound doctrine. Many Churches today are filled with those who want their ears tickled with the myths of easy-believism, to have their egos fed and to feel good in the many variations of selfism. Tragically, such religious myths insulate people from the true Gospel and drive them away still further from the Lord.

The faithful preacher is to be stable, unwavering and steadfast in the truth. He refuses to be trendy or compromising to please men, rather he endeavours to be a God-pleaser. "For we preach not ourselves, but Christ Jesus the Lord; and ourselves your servants for Jesus' sake", (2 Cor. 4 v.5). Following the example of the Apostle Paul in the midst of a changing world, a changing Church, and even a changing 'gospel'----- which is not really the Gospel but a distortion of "the Gospel of Christ" (Gal. 1 v.7; 2 Cor. 11 v.4) ----- we as servants of Christ are to remain committed to the changeless truths of God's Word. "For our exhortation was not of deceit, nor of uncleanness, nor in guile: But as we were allowed of God to be put in trust with the Gospel, even so we speak; not as pleasing men, but God, which trieth our hearts. For neither at any time used we flattering words, as ye know, nor a cloke of covetousness; God is witness", (2 Thess. 2 v.3-5).

The doctrine of the resurrection gives life to every other area of Gospel truth. "I am the resurrection, and the life", says Jesus, "he that believeth in Me, though he were dead, yet shall he live: And whosoever liveth and believeth in Me shall never die", (John 11 v.25-26). True New Testament Christianity is a religion of the resurrection. Because the resurrection is the cornerstone of the Gospel, it has been the target of Satan's greatest attacks against the Church. The devil has many willing agents who distort or deny this great truth.

If the resurrection is eliminated from preaching, the life-giving power of the Gospel is eliminated, the deity of Christ is eliminated, salvation from sin is eliminated, and eternal life is eliminated. Without the resurrection salvation could not have been provided, and without belief in the resurrection salvation cannot be received. It is impossible to claim to be a Christian preacher and not believe in the resurrection of Jesus Christ. The way to be saved and to secure the righteousness God requires is the supreme essential. There is great confusion in much of the Church today about God's way of salvation. Salvation and its attendant righteousness are appropriated by confession and by faith. Only the person who is righteous before God is truly saved. "If thou shalt confess with thy mouth the Lord Jesus, and shalt believe in thine heart that God hath raised Him from the dead, thou shalt be saved. For with the heart man believeth unto righteousness; and with the mouth confession is made unto salvation", (Rom. 10 v.9-10).

In our modern age of scepticism, humanism and heresies, the doctrine of Christ's resurrection is questioned, ridiculed and denied. A 'professing' Christian preacher claiming to hold to orthodox doctrine and godly living, but who fully rejects the resurrection proves that his own salvation was never real. His message, therefore, is empty, void of any genuine substance, and without any real worth. Those who forsake Christ and undermine His Holy Word prove that they never really belonged to Him or members of His true Body. (1 John 2 v.19). "If ye continue in My Word", says Christ, "then are ye My disciples indeed", (John 8 v.31). "Examine yourselves, whether ye be in the faith", (2 Cor. 13 v.5). "Whosoever transgresseth, and abideth not in the doctrine of Christ, hath not God", (2 John v.9).

Throughout the Western world many of our modern preachers appear to be so lethargic and spiritually moribund. "If the blind lead the blind, both shall fall into the ditch", (Matt. 15 v.14). "Can the blind lead the blind? Shall they not both fall into the ditch?" (Luke 6 v.39). If we are shallow in our understanding of the tenets of the Gospel and unfruitful in our discipleship, we are in great need to be awakened by the Spirit of God to the glories of a renewed life in Christ. "And be renewed in the spirit of your mind; And that ye put on the new man, which after God is created in righteousness and true holiness", (Eph. 4 v.23-24).

The Weakness of Evangelical Christianity

Our 'evangelical' Christianity today is so weak which for far too long has been subjected to a feeble proclamation of the Word. It is no wonder then that so-called evangelicals are indistinguishable from the ungodly and unregenerate people surrounding them, and why the Churches are failing to make any appreciable impact upon society. We are ineffective because many who consider themselves to be Christians are not saved and know not the power of the grace of God in their lives. "For whosoever shall call upon the name of the Lord shall be saved", (Rom. 10 v.13).

Scripture teaches us that man by nature is utterly depraved, but how often do we hear the depravity of mankind discussed? How often do we hear sermons on the atonement, propitiation, predestination, vicarious substitution, redemption, reconciliation, justification, repentance, or faith? How many of our preachers today walk in the footsteps, not only of the prophets and the apostles, but of such theological stalwarts and pastoral giants as Martin Luther, John Calvin, John Knox, James Guthrie, Samuel Rutherford, Charles Hodge, Louis Berkhof, Martyn Lloyd-Jones, and others. By the grace of God these men greatly abounded with steadfastness and constancy in obedience, dedication, commitment, and continuous faithfulness to the Word. Fervent in the faith they were "labourers together with God" (1 Cor. 3 v.9), who could say with Paul, "Yet not I, but the grace of God which was with me", (1 Cor. 15 v.10).

Preaching today has veered away from "the Gospel of God" (Rom. 1 v.1), and people are encouraged to become 'Christians' without raising the question of sin, the holiness of God, or any mention of repentance whatsoever. To preach anything other than the pure Word of God, or anything less, is another 'gospel'.

The New Testament speaks of two general categories of people whom God reserves to destruction. The first category is "If any man love not the Lord Jesus Christ, let him be Anathema Maranatha", (1 Cor. 16 v.22). The second is false teachers who "would pervert the Gospel of Christ ----- if any man preach any other gospel unto you than that ye have received, let him be accursed", (Gal. 1 v.6-9). Christ warned His disciples that "there shall arise false Christ's, and false prophets, and shall shew great signs and wonders; insomuch that if it were possible, they shall deceive the very elect", (Matt. 24 v.24).

False preachers and false teachers are the children of their "father the devil" (John 8 v.44) who willingly carry out his designs to destroy the faith of the Church. One way to deny the truthfulness of the Word is to deny the authority of the One Who gave us His special revelation as embodied in Holy Scripture. The Bible is inspired by God, infallible, complete and invariable, and contains the authoritative revelation of His Mind and Will. It reveals the plan of God for the redemption of sinners and of the world, and the way in which this plan is realised. It is instrumental in renewing man, illumines his mind, and inclines his will to prepare him for heaven. The Bible shows us the message of redemption, enriches us with the knowledge of the great truths of the Gospel, and transforms our lives to enjoy all the benefits and rights which the Redeemer, as our Surety, has purchased for His people, to have fellowship with Him in grace and glory, and fellowship with one another as believers together in the Body of Christ: "for ye are all one in Christ Jesus" (Gal. 3 v.28); "ye are the Body of Christ", (1 Cor. 12 v.27).

The Characteristics of False Preachers

In his rebuke to those who opposed the preaching of Paul and Barnabas (Acts 13 v.7-10), the Apostle exposes four characteristics of false preachers. They are:-

(1)   full of all subtlety and all mischief, deceitful;

(2)   children of the devil;

(3)   enemies of all righteousness; and

(4)   perverters of the right ways of the Lord.

Even today within the Church there are many who oppose the preaching of the Gospel. But the marks of a Spirit-filled preacher, is one who walks in obedience to the will of God. Since God reveals His will in the Holy Scriptures, the faithful preacher must be committed to the Word of God. In comparing the reading of Ephesians 5 and Colossians 3 reveals that being filled with the Spirit and letting the Word richly dwell in one's life produce the same effects. Being doctrinally sound and Spirit-controlled, the true preacher of the Gospel will be effective in making God's living Word alive to the people. Many in the ministry today are busy with shallow activities and empty programmes which do not lead to a clear understanding of Biblical truth. God chooses men for further ministry who are already active in serving Him. He is not likely to take idle Christians down from the shelf, dust them off, and entrust them with important work. They will be proven men, called of God, with appropriate gifts and qualifications as specified in Scripture (1Tim. 3 and Titus 1), "sent forth by the Holy Ghost", (Acts 13 v.4).

When God's servants seek to advance His purposes and mission, satanic opposition will always mount against the preaching of the Gospel. Leading souls to Christ involves an all-out war against the forces of Satan and hell. The devil will continue to disrupt the work of God, even within the Church, by internal dissension, division, disbelief, disunity, deceit and fraud: "Full of all subtlety and mischief", (Acts 13 v.10). The word "subtlety" in the Greek is "dolos" meaning "snare", and the word "mischief" is "radiourgias" meaning "ease or facility in doing", hence readiness in turning the hand as the "enemy of all righteousness", constantly seeking to twist and pervert the Gospel of God. "O full of all subtlety and all mischief, thou child of the devil, thou enemy of all righteousness, wilt thou not cease to pervert the right ways of the Lord", (Acts 13 v.10).

All who oppose the truth of God are agents of hell and adversaries of heaven. It follows that those who are enemies of righteousness and perverters of the truth, become not only so hardened in their unjust prejudices but also mislead others against the light of the Gospel. Those who are in any way instrumental to prejudice people against the truths of the Word of God and the doctrines of grace, are doing the devil's work. As preachers we should be filled with a holy zeal against the enemies of Christ, not from personal resentment but from a strong commitment and firm stand upon the Word of God. Those who are enemies of the doctrine of Christ are enemies to all truth and righteousness. "Wherefore take unto you the whole armour of God, that ye may be able to withstand in the evil day, and having done all, to stand", (Eph. 6 v.13).

Satan's messengers and greatest aids are often religious leaders, posing as 'Christians', and 'ministers' of Christ whom Paul describes as "false apostles, deceitful workers, transforming themselves into the apostles of Christ", (2 Cor. 11 v.13). "And no marvel", he goes on to explain, "for Satan himself is transformed into an angel of light", (2 Cor. 11 v.14). Through the activities of such evil men, Satan effectively accomplishes his most destructive work, using human agents who describe themselves as God's 'servants', but really they are the spokesmen of the devil and of hell. They weaken the Church, wreck spiritual havoc on the people, and turn Biblical truth into various forms of modernism and liberalism. "As the serpent beguiled Eve through his subtlety, so your minds should be corrupted from the simplicity that is in Christ", (2 Cor. 11 v.3).

Every faithful minister cannot but be afraid and concerned for his flock, lest they should lose that which they have received, especially when deceivers have crept in among them. False doctrine is the underlying source of ungodly practice and behaviour. In regard to the Ephesian elders, Paul issues the warning, "Take heed therefore unto yourselves, and to all the flock, over the which the Holy Ghost hath made you overseers, to feed the Church of God, which He hath purchased with His own blood. For I know this, that after my departing shall grievous wolves enter in among you, not sparing the flock. Also of your own selves shall men arise, speaking perverse things, to draw away disciples after them", (Acts 20 v.28-30). The Apostle commanded these elders to mind the work to which they were called, overseers of the flock, that is, under-shepherds, that they be true to their trust. We today, likewise, must be faithful in the discharge of our duties as "ministers of the Word", (Luke 1 v.2) and pastors of the flock under our charge.

Ministers in Christ's service have no authority to propagate their own fancies, but are charged to declare the Gospel and spread the Christian faith according to the Scriptures. They are to be stewards of the things of God, and preach His Word with faithfulness and steadfastness.

Preachers must not feed the Church with the chaff of their own inventions thus depriving the congregation of the wholesome food of Christian doctrine and Biblical truth. Ministers of the Gospel should make it their hearty calling and continual endeavour to approve themselves trustworthy that will receive the acceptance and approbation of our sovereign Lord and Judge. It is imperative, therefore, that we lead the sheep of Christ into green pastures, lay the strong meat of the Word before them, and feed them with solid Biblical doctrine: "stewards of the mysteries of God", (1 Cor. 4 v.1). "Moreover it is required in stewards, that a man be found faithful", (1 Cor. 4 v.2). As well as feeding the Church of God, such a responsibility also carries with it tender evangelical discipline among the wayward and see to it that nothing is lacking in offering all necessary spiritual support and nourishment to their eternal well-being. "And now, brethren, I commend you to God, and to the Word of His grace, which is able to build you up, and to give you an inheritance among all them which are sanctified", (Acts 20 v.32).

It is very regrettable that in many Churches today, false teaching is rife concerning the doctrine of salvation. Consequently, when the heart of the Gospel is undermined people are confused, and they have no way of coming to God but remain in ignorance under Satan's influence and lies about the Church, the Christian Gospel, justification, sanctification, and many other things. Our great concern should be that the Gospel of salvation by the sovereign grace of God, made possible through the Person and Work of the Lord Jesus Christ, is fully proclaimed according to the Scriptures.

In all ages of the Church when God sends forth His true servants and heralds of the Word, earnestly contending for the faith (Jude v.3), the devil launches his emissaries to do their deceptive work. Sadly, "some depart from the faith, giving heed to seducing spirits, and doctrines of devils; Speaking lies in hypocrisy" (1 Tim. 4 v.1-2), as Satan lures them to turn away from following God's truth. The tragic reality is, even today, there are many who act like Judas, who have abandoned the Divine revelation God has given to us in His Word. The Apostle Peter solemnly warns us against the destructive elements of all such seducing preachers. "There shall be false teachers among you, who privily shall bring in damnable heresies, even denying the Lord that bought them, and bring upon themselves swift destruction. And many shall follow their pernicious ways; by reason of whom the way of truth shall be evil spoken of", (2 Peter 2 v.1-2).

False teachers are more interested in popularity than in truth. "As many as desire to make a fair shew in the flesh" (Gal. 6 v.12), "speaking perverse things" (Acts 20 v.30), constrain others to gain a following for themselves. They shall "with feigned words make merchandise of you" (2 Peter 2 v.3), preaching a salvation of works, ceremonialism, and ritualism. In their greed for money "with covetous practices" (2 Peter 2 v.14), they "walk in lies" and "strengthen also the hands of evildoers" (Jer. 23 v.14). Such accursed servants and false prophets are a menace and a plague to the Church. It is deeply grieving that the truth of God's sovereign and gracious offer of redemption through the atoning sacrifice of Christ is being greatly corrupted. Many are not only being confused and weakened in their confidence to live by grace, but are actually deserting the ways of God altogether.

God's Unmerited Favour

The only true "Gospel of God" (Rom. 15 v.16) is "the Gospel of grace" (Acts 20 v.24), which is the Gospel of Divine redemption apart from any works or merit of man. "For by grace are ye saved through faith ----- not of works" (Eph. 2 v.8-9). "Therefore being justified by faith, we have peace with God through our Lord Jesus Christ: By Whom also we have access by faith (continually) into this grace wherein we stand, and rejoice in hope of the glory of God", (Rom. 5 v.1-2). From the moment of the New Birth by the Holy Spirit we live in grace, "created in Christ Jesus unto good works, which God hath before ordained that we should walk in them", (Eph. 2 v.10). Salvation is the free gift of God to the sinner by grace alone through faith alone in the Lord Jesus Christ alone. The grace of Christ is God's free unmerited favour by His sovereign act of love and mercy in granting to us everlasting life through the death and resurrection of our great Redeemer and only Mediator, Christ Jesus, our Lord. "In Whom we have redemption through His blood, the forgiveness of sins, according to the riches of His grace", (Eph. 1 v.7).

Preachers who promote a different 'gospel' through human works and endeavours, is totally foreign and contrary to the teaching of Holy Scripture. True Christians should have nothing to do with false teachers, no matter what their qualifications or credentials. It is unScriptural to stay in a Church that denies the authority, infallibility and inerrancy of the Bible. Preachers who distort the Gospel of Christ cannot glorify God or exalt the Saviour. They should have no place in the assembly Christ. The Word of God warns us to stay away from error and to concentrate entirely on the pure truth of God. "If thou put the brethren in remembrance of these things, thou shalt be a good minister of Jesus Christ, nourished up in the words of faith and of good doctrine, whereunto thou hast attained. But refuse profane and old wives fables, and exercise thyself rather unto godliness ----- give attendance to reading, to exhortation, to doctrine", (1 Tim. 2 v.15). "Study to shew thyself approved unto God, a workman that needeth not to be ashamed, rightly dividing the Word of truth", (2 Tim. 2 v.15).

The present-day crisis in preaching, with its disobedience and compromise have greatly weakened the testimony of the Church. To tolerate distortion of the Word, and to "pervert the Gospel of Christ" (Gal.1 v.7), discredits our Lord and Saviour and brings dishonour to God. We need seriously to renew our vows to the Lord and earnestly engage our energies to maintain the truth of God and to publish it far and wide. The great commission exhorts us to "go into all the world and preach the Gospel to every creature", (Mark 16 v.15). The whole Church has a corporate responsibility in making known to mankind the Glad Tidings of the Gospel of Christ. God's believing people are to be "the salt of the earth" and "the light of the world", (Matt. 5 v.13-14). "Let your light so shine before men, that they may see your good works, and glorify your Father which is in heaven", (Matt. 5 v.16). May God give us that deep conviction of spirit, and burden of heart for the lost, so that with godly concern and passion we shall go forth to be vibrant witnesses where Providence allows, in the extension of His kingdom, to Whom be all praise, honour, and glory.

Apostasy, Authority and Submission

Writing in his Second Epistle to Timothy, the Apostle Paul knew he was coming to the end of his ministry. His words, therefore, carry great weight because we know these are his last words to the Church. This Epistle contains a chastening word for all of us. This is the Word from God addressed to Timothy in the presence of the Lord Jesus Christ, Who shall judge the living and the dead: "Preach the Word", (2 Tim. 4 v.2). The context of this passage is very clear in describing the problems of the Church, warning young Timothy to beware of the enemies of the truth. They will cause injury to the Church, "evil men and seducers", who "shall wax worse and worse, deceiving, and being deceived", (2 Tim. 3 v.13).

But then comes the primary issue as Paul writes so eloquently, passionately, and pointedly about the authority of the Word of God. He underlines the fact that the Holy Scriptures are powerful, truthful, trustworthy, and are the only rule of faith and practice. God is the Author of every Word of Scripture, and the whole Bible is the inspired, infallible, and inerrant Word of God. "But continue thou in the things which thou hast learned and hast been assured of, knowing of whom thou hast leaned them; And that from a child thou hast known the Holy Scriptures, which are able to make thee wise unto salvation through faith which is in Christ Jesus. All Scripture is given by inspiration of God, and is profitable for doctrine, for reproof, for correction, for instruction in righteousness: That the man of God may be perfect, throughly furnished unto all good works", (2 Tim. 3 v.11-17).

"All Scripture is given by inspiration of God" which we may depend upon as infallibly true. It is profitable for teaching and doctrine, for reproof, for correction of all errors in judgement and practice, and for instruction and training in truth and righteousness. It instructs us in that which is true, reproves us for that which is amiss, and directs us in that which is good. THE SCRIPTURE is the perfect rule of faith and conduct. By it we are thoroughly furnished and equipped for every good work. By it we shall be made men of God, complete, adequate and mature in His service.

We are commanded to preach the pure Word of God. We are to hold fast the Scriptures of the Old and New Testaments as our authoritative text, our witness, the deposit of faith. When the light of Scripture is darted into the blind mind and dark understanding of man by the Holy Spirit of God, then the spiritual day dawns and the day-star arises in the soul. We are to preach the Word of light, the truth of the Gospel, the whole Gospel, the purity of the Gospel, the power of the Gospel ----- no other 'gospel': "Preach the Word", (2 Tim. 4 v.2).

Such a solemn charge means that we must preach the Word in all its fullness, "in season" and "out of season", (2 Tim. 4 v.2). The link between the preaching of the Gospel and the preaching of the Word is indissoluble and unbreakable. We are charged to preach the Gospel of God (Rom. 1 v.1), not to invent a 'message' that will be well received. If we are to preach with Divine authority, with Divine power, we must submit to the Word of God ----- preachers of the Word: "Preach the Word", (2 Tim. 4 v.2).

We are to be servants of Christ and of His Word, not to be lords over the Scriptures. As John Piper says, "Preaching is a Scripture-founded and a Scripture-saturated event". This is where many preachers go wrong. There is the temptation in many churches to separate Scripture from preaching, but in the true Christian Church, preaching cannot be severed from the Bible. The true purpose of preaching is not that we ourselves as preachers might be heard, or be impressive, but that the text of the Word of God might be heard and makes its impression on the human heart. "So they read in the book in the law of God distinctly, and gave the sense, and caused them to understand the reading", (Neh. 8 v.8).

There are those, sadly, many of them around, as the Apostle warned, who preach 'messages' designed to satisfy "itching ears", (2 Tim. 4 v.3). We are living in an age of itching ears with a self-centred focus, persuasive individualism, subjectivism, relativism, and deadly spiritual sickness. On every hand, even within the Church at large, there is a revolt against God and against His Word. The cause of this apostasy is deeply spiritual and the stark reality of such a decline is an outright rejection of the teaching of the Word of God.

The gravity of this crisis in contemporary preaching is rebellion against God and failure to submit to the authority of Scripture. But we are not to lose hope, for our God can raise up champions to speak the truth and defend His Cause as in the days of Moses, Elijah, John the Baptist, Luther, Calvin, Latimer, Knox, Guthrie, Renwick and Rutherford. The Lord's Cause is invincible, and those who fight against God are engaged in a losing battle. Even though preachers of the Gospel may suffer wrong for righteousness sake, yet as in the case of the early disciples we should persevere to publish the name of Jesus as the Christ, the Anointed King and Saviour of mankind. "And they departed from the presence of the council, rejoicing that they were counted worthy to suffer shame for His name. And daily in the temple, and in every house, they ceased not to teach and preach Jesus Christ", (Acts 5 v.41-43).

By refusing to obey and submit to Biblical authority cannot but have tragic consequences for both Church and society. The arrogance of the Christ-rejecters who impugn and malign the Scriptures is thunderous. The true Preacher must learn to be urgent in proclaiming the Word in all its fullness in all seasons. He must study how to reprove and confute the gainsayers, as well as how to instruct those who are willing to hear. When so many are turning away from the truth, it is more incumbent upon the preacher to be diligent and to be earnest in faithfully declaring the Word. We are commanded to preach the Gospel with fidelity, zeal, and diligence as willing servants of Christ. Those who are slothful, lazy, and unwilling will be made accountable on that great Judgement Day at the bar of Christ. "Woe is unto me, if I preach not the Gospel", (1 Cor. 9 v.16).

The Prevalence of Corrupt Society

In the Corinthian Church there were many serious problems, factionalism, worldliness, immorality, corruption and other idolatrous practices. Like many Christians today the Corinthian believers had great difficulty in disassociating themselves from

55

the unbelieving and corrupt society around them. They wanted to have what they thought was the best of both worlds, to be in God's kingdom while at the same time hang on to the pleasures of this world. "No servant can serve two masters: for either he will hate the one, and love the other; or else he will hold to the one, and despise the other. Ye cannot serve God and mammon", (Luke 16 v.13).

Christian principles were knocked on their head by the Corinthians, which nullified and made their witness ineffective to society around them. Today likewise there is much religious uncertainty, ambiguity, and confusion that is reaping a harvest of unrest, disharmony, disunity, carnality, and quarrelling in many of our Churches when they fall far short of the Lord's standards in matters of faith, conduct, and discipline. "Continue in the faith grounded and settled, and be not moved away from the hope of the Gospel, which ye have heard, and which was preached to you", (Col. 1 v.23).

In true Biblical unity lies the joy and strength of Christian ministry and the credibility of Christian testimony. We are to serve the Lord in truth and in unity. With diligence and constancy in our attendance upon the preaching of the Word, we are to continue "steadfastly in the apostles' doctrine and fellowship, and in breaking of bread, and in prayers", (Acts 2 v.42). Such unity bears great fruit not only in our ministry one with another, but also in our witness to the world, that will be most pleasing and glorifying to God.

The true preacher is one sent by Christ "to preach the Gospel: not with wisdom of words, lest the Cross of Christ should be made of none effect. For the preaching of the Cross is to them that perish foolishness; but unto us which are saved it is the power of God", (1 Cor. 1 v.17-18). Paul ever gloried in the fact that he was sent by Christ to preach the Gospel. His preaching was not with "wisdom of words" to impress men with oratory or rhetoric. "My speech", he says, "and my preaching was not with enticing words of man's wisdom, but in demonstration of the Spirit and of power: that your faith should not stand in the wisdom of men, but in the power of God", (1 Cor. 2 v.4-5).

The Apostle clearly shows in his writings that Divine wisdom centres in the doctrine of the atonement, that Christ is the complete answer to the need of mankind. What he emphasises is not the act of preaching but the content of the message, the truth of the Gospel embedded in the Cross. The saving force of His message did not lie in "wisdom of words", but in the Christ of the Cross. There are no mistakes or errors in the Word of God. "Thy word is true", declares the Psalmist, (Psalm 119 v.160). God protected the writing of the Scripture from error, the Bible is the Word of God, Divinely inspired, infallible, and inerrant. Our calling as preachers is to teach the Word, proclaim the Gospel of God, and expound the doctrines of grace to bring men to trust in Jesus, and to establish oneness in "the household of faith" (Gal. 6 v.10) according to the Scriptures, under the rule of Christ, Who is the sole King and Head of the Church. "And He is the Head of the Body, the Church: Who is the firstborn from the dead; that in all things He might have the pre-eminence" (Col. 1 v.18).

Vigilance and Courage in Witness

As preachers we should acquit ourselves with vigilance and courage, and with eternity always in view, we should strive to excel in the preparation and proclamation of God's truth. The Apostle Paul earnestly exhorts the faithful, the true servants of Christ, to "preach the Word", (2 Tim. 4 v.2). It is imperative, therefore, that we ask ourselves, 'Are we faithful every time we preach that it is actually Gospel, Biblical, and absolutely Scriptural preaching we deliver on every occasion?' All too often many evangelicals are so easily seduced and co-opted by the surrounding culture and immersed in entertainment and other things rather than being God's mouthpiece to the people. "Be it known unto you therefore, men and brethren, that through this Man is preached unto you the forgiveness of sins: And by Him all that believe are justified from all things, from which ye could not be justified by the law of Moses", (Acts 13 v.38-39).

We should be reminded that the principle of the Reformers and the Covenanters ----- Sola Scriptura, Scripture Alone ----- was intended to guard the Church lest it return to vain tradition, human authority, and the lure of modern culture and worldly fashion. In his day the Apostle Paul and the early disciples were not concerned with poll ratings, popular tastes, and cultural trends. "But we preach Christ crucified, unto the Jews a stumbling block, and unto the Greeks foolishness; But unto them which are called, both Jews and Greeks, Christ the power of God, and the wisdom of God", (1 Cor. 1 v.23-24). We are to "preach the Word" (2 Tim. 4 v.2), so that we:-

(1)   convince the sinner and make the case for the faith;

(2)   rebuke the wayward so as to correct error and confront falsehood;

(3)   exhort the saint, the believer, to use the Scripture as the infallible standard of right and wrong; and

(4)   encourage the man of God unto truth and righteousness and complete fitness for every good work in Christ Jesus.

In Second Timothy, Chapter 4, the warning is given that "the time will come when they will not endure sound doctrine; but after their own lusts shall they heap to themselves teachers, having itching ears; And they shall turn away their ears from the truth, and shall be turned unto fables", (2 Tim. 4 v.3-4).

Genuine preaching will continue to weaken and go out of vogue, and instead, "itching ears" will look more and more to be tickled and scratched. Why is it that sound preaching no longer commands the attention and engage the interest of the masses it once did? Biblical preaching is such a high calling, and its responsibility weighs so heavily upon us, that we must take it seriously and make Scripture central as our authority. It is THE SCRIPTURES that bear witness of Christ. "Search the Scriptures; for in them ye think ye have eternal life: and they are they which testify of Me", (John 5 v.39).

When a preacher who is "apt to teach" (1 Tim. 3 v.2), and whose soul is on fire for the Lord and having his "loins girt about with truth" (Eph. 6 v.14), the power of the Spirit will be so evident as to influence character, life, and destiny for His glory. Our sacred duty and solemn task in teaching the Word of God should be to set forth the truth of Scripture and "preach among the Gentiles the unsearchable riches of Christ", (Eph. 3 v.8). We must study, interpret, and apply the Word to the conscience of men in accordance with its true meaning. May God give us grace and raise up from amongst us a great army of preachers, men of true piety, men who are "mighty in the Scriptures" (Acts 18 v.24), to do battle for the Lord.

We are commanded in Scripture to show faithfulness in our stewardship of the Gospel. Preachers who live carelessly, luxuriously and worldly in disobedience to Christ, are unclean vessels: "be ye clean, that bear the vessels of the Lord", (Isaiah 52 v.11). Paul describes Christian preachers, Christian ministers, as stewards of God over His Church and family: who "must be blameless, as the steward of God; not self-willed ----- not given to filthy lucre ----- holding fast the faithful Word", (Titus 2 v.7-9). All believers are described as stewards of God's gifts and graces to dispense the benefits of them to the world. "As every man hath received the gift, even so minister the same one to another, as good stewards of the manifold grace of God", (1 Peter 4 v.10). The exhortation then is that we should manage our worldly goods and material benefits wisely and with such liberality and generosity as will promote the Cause of the Gospel, true piety, Christian charity, and enlightened benevolence. To be fit vessels for the Master's use, we need to have that sense of constraint and compelling responsibility which the apostle Paul articulates in the words of 1 Cor. 9 v.16, "For though I preach the Gospel, I have nothing to glory of".

Paul chose God's call in the sense that he was not "disobedient unto the heavenly vision" (Acts 26 v.19), he was under compulsion: "for necessity is laid upon me; yea, woe is unto me, if I preach not the Gospel", (1 Cor. 9 v.16). God had set him apart even from his "mothers womb" (Gal. 1 v.15), called and ordained him to be "made a minister, according to the dispensation of God which is given to me for you, to fulfil the Word of God", (Col. 1 v.25). Failure to obey that call and failure to preach the pure Word of God would result in his suffering serious chastisement. In the third chapter of his Epistle, James teaches us that the sternest and severest judgements are promised on unfaithful ministers. "My brethren, be not many masters, knowing that we shall receive the greater condemnation", (James 3 v.1). Stewardship of the Gospel is a responsibility that we are to care for properly. That is the case in every call to preach, and woe, if we fail, for stern discipline is promised to the one who falls short: "lest that by any means, when I have preached to others, I myself should be a castaway", (1 Cor. 9 v.27).

It should be emphasised that the soil out of which powerful evangelical preaching and warm Biblical exposition grow, is in the preacher's own heart and life. It is possible that 'great' men may appear in the pulpit but who are devoid of the saving and sanctifying grace of God in their daily lives. "And why call ye Me, Lord, Lord, and do not the things which I say"? (Luke 6 v.46). Powerful preaching as patterned after the prophets and apostles is rooted in the soil of the preacher's own heart and life. Many preachers are only too aware that their performance falls far short of what they would wish. The secret of the preaching of such men as Rutherford, Whitefield, McCheyne and others is found in their lives. They lived with such vital communion with God that the truth became a living principle when it came through such vessels to their congregations. By the grace of God their anointed lives became the soil of their anointed ministries which bore much fruit. Under God their preaching was effective and fruitful in reaching souls with the message of salvation and building up the Body of Christ "on their most holy faith", (Jude v.20). The more we are known by our people, as godly or otherwise, our influence among the flock will increase or diminish according to the spiritual tenor of our lives. "For our Gospel came not unto you in word only, but also in power, and in the Holy Ghost, and in much assurance; as ye know what manner of men we were among you for your sake", (1 Thess. 1 v.5).

The true preacher must go forth as a live brand from the altar of God's Throne bearing the Glad Tidings of Jesus Christ as Saviour and Lord. Being called, commissioned and consecrated to the service of the Master, he must be a living embodiment of the power of the Word of God, so that when he speaks that Word and preaches the truth of the Gospel of God in all its fullness, it comes with power, authority, and conviction to his hearers. "God forbid that I should glory, save in the Cross of our Lord Jesus Christ ----- that I might preach Him", (Gal. 6 v.14, and 1 v.16).

A Conscience Void of Offence

As preachers we should have a conscience that is both "good" (1 Tim. 1 v.5, Heb. 13 v.18, 1 Peter 3 v.16, 21) and "pure" (1 Tim. 3 v.9, 2 Tim. 1 v.3): "have always a conscience void of offence toward God, and toward men", (Acts 24 v.16). In conduct and in attitude we should be an example to the people. "In all things shewing thyself a pattern of good works", (Titus 2 v.7). We are not only to proclaim right things by precept, but also to embody those right things in a right example. Insincerity, deceitfulness, guile, and a flippant manner are things that should not characterise one who is a teacher and preacher of the Word of God. The exhortation of the Epistle of Paul to Titus is that we should "adorn the doctrine of God our Saviour in all things", (Titus 2 v.10).

The exemplary life of the preacher will give impetus and momentum to his words of counsel and promote goodwill and openness of mind towards the faith and sound doctrine. A degenerate lifestyle only serves to malign the Word of God. In all our teaching and preaching, the importance of integrity, sincerity and seriousness in the life of the preacher is most vital, because the matters the Christian message deals with are weighty, and they carry eternal consequences for the men, women, boys and girls who hear them. These qualities are the marks of the true servant of Christ, especially those who are entrusted with the teaching and preaching of the Word of God. All Christian workers and helpers, even in the most lowly forms of service and duty, have the opportunity and privilege to promote the Cause of Christ among men and to glorify God.

In the Gospels we read of the conversion of Simon, Andrew, James and John. (Matt. 4, Mark 1). No doubt they had heard John the Baptist preaching the message of repentance. When Jesus came into Galilee, He engages in conversation with them by the lakeside and brings them into discipleship. Not only was our Lord a great and powerful preacher, He had compassionate evangelistic concern when He was not preaching or delivering a sermon. By means of individual conversation, all Christians must engage in witness for the Lord. Sadly, many preachers do not minister in this way, believing that their responsibility is in the pulpit only and that it is up to everyone else to advance Christ's Kingdom by personal evangelism. We are to "walk worthy of the Lord unto all pleasing, being fruitful in every good work, and increasing in the knowledge of God", (Col.v.10).

The Bible clearly teaches that "all have sinned, and come short of the glory of God", (Rom. 3 v.23). By nature "there is none righteous, no, not one ----- there is none that seeketh after God", (Rom. 3 v.10-11). The Westminster Shorter Catechism gives us an accurate summary of the teaching of Scripture on this point: "All mankind by their fall lost communion with God, are under His wrath and curse, and so made liable to all miseries in this life, to death itself, and to the pains of hell for ever", (No. 19).

Under the burden of sin, the unconverted are in a terrible plight. They do not enjoy God, their conscience condemns them, and they know nothing of the comfort and assurance of His grace. They are "without

Christ ----- and strangers from the covenants of promise, having no hope, and without God in the world", (Eph. 2 v.12). In reaching out the hand of mercy to sinners, the Saviour invites us: "come unto Me, all ye that labour and are heavy laden, and I will give you rest", (Matt. 11 v.28). The invitation is not to come to Christianity, or to a Church, or to some particular religious activities, but to Christ. "But as many as received Him, to them gave He power to become the sons of God, even to them that believe on His name: Which were born, not of blood, nor of the will of the flesh, nor of the will of man, but of God", (John 1 v.12-13).

Throughout our land, many who claim to be great Christian servants, Church workers, and Gospel preachers, not only have the Bible and may boast of a great Christian heritage, but for the most part their Christianity is only a pretence and a sham. "Beware of false prophets" says the Bible, "which come to you in sheep's clothing, but inwardly they are ravening wolves", (Matt. 7 v.15). What a fearful thing that it is possible to be a minister of the Church and yet be a unconverted man. You must come to Christ: "Except a man be born again, he cannot see the Kingdom of God", (John 3 v.3). He alone has the words of eternal life. "I give unto them eternal life; and they shall never perish, neither shall any man pluck them out of My Father's hand", (John 10 v.28-29). "For Christ also hath once suffered for sins, the Just for the unjust, that He might bring us to God", (1 Peter 3 v.18).

The unconverted 'preacher', first and foremost, needs to call out to God to be saved, in the knowledge "that whosoever shall call on the name of the Lord shall be saved", (Acts 2 v.21) (Rom. 10 v.13). We are to be owned by Another, even Jesus, and to walk in newness of life in Him by coming under the rule of Christ as Lord and Saviour. "Take My yoke upon you, and learn of Me; for I am meek and lowly in heart: and ye shall find rest unto your souls", (Matt. 11 v.29). To be saved from the estate of sin and misery means life everlasting. It means to be free from the terrors of the law, justified by faith in Christ alone, accepted and adopted into the Body of Christ to become children of God. "There is therefore now no condemnation to them which are in Christ Jesus, who walk not after the flesh, but after the Spirit. For as many as are lead by the Spirit of God, they are the sons of God", (Rom. 8 v.1,14).

Sanctification, Orthodoxy and Reform

To all who repent and believe the Gospel have their whole nature changed by the indwelling power of the Holy Spirit, (1 Cor. 12 v.3). "If any man be in Christ, he is a new creature: old things are passed away; behold, all things are become new", (2 Cor. 5 v.17). By God's grace they will continue to grow in holiness and sanctification, and when they die the souls of believers will enter the glory of heaven. At the resurrection their bodies will be raised unto the likeness of Christ's own glorious body, "shall be openly acknowledged and acquitted in the Day of Judgement, and made perfectly blessed in the full enjoying of God to all eternity", (WSC No 38). "When the Son of man shall come in His glory ----- He shall set the sheep on His right hand, but the goats on the left. Then shall the King say unto them on His right hand, Come, ye blessed of My Father, inherit the Kingdom prepared for you from the foundation of the world ----- Then shall He say also unto them on the left hand, Depart from Me, ye cursed, into everlasting fire, prepared for the devil and his angels: And these shall go away into everlasting punishment: but the righteous into life eternal", (Matt. 25 v.31,33-34, 41, 46). "So shall we ever be with the Lord", (1 Thess. 4 v.17).

These are the exceeding great and precious promises that the true preacher must handle and present to those who will come to Christ. God has "given to us the ministry of reconciliation" to be "ambassadors for Christ, as though God did beseech you by us: we pray you in Christ's stead, be ye reconciled to God. For He hath made Him to be sin for us, Who new no sin; that we might be made the righteousness of God in Him", (2 Cor. 5 v.18, 20-21). Many of the preachers today talk about 'modern theology' and 'new theology', but one of the chief points of difference between Biblical Theology and much that is called 'modern theology' or 'new theology', is that in the Bible we have an infinitely great God, a gracious God, a sovereign God, an all-powerful God, and a very small man; whereas in much that is called 'modern theology' or 'new theology' we have a very small God, and a very big man.

God is not controlled by the will of man. He is omnipotent, omniscient, and omnipresent. The Bible says that God is truth, life, light, love, righteousness, and so on. As a true soldier of Jesus Christ it is imperative to expound and proclaim the greatness and glory of God, the wonder and power of the Gospel, and veracity and authority of Biblical truth. In the frontline service of spiritual warfare we need to "be strong in the Lord, and in the power of His might. Put on the whole armour of God, that ye may be able to stand against the wiles of the devil", by taking "the helmet of salvation, and the Sword of the Spirit, which is the Word of God", (Eph. 6 v.10-11, 17).

The present sad state of ministry, preaching and evangelism seems to be a continual endeavour to reduce all that is dear to Biblical Christianity in order to accommodate 'modern man'. All deceitful and profane workers who dare to corrupt or change the Word of God, either by adding to it or taking from it, draw down upon themselves everlasting punishment, (Rev. 22 v.18-19). The practical test of a man's orthodoxy and holiness of life will be shown by his love for and obedience to the truth (1 Peter 1 v.22). The eternal truth of God is both living and life-giving, and as true ambassadors of Christ we must not fail to declare "all the counsel of God", (Acts 20 v.27). "The Word of the Lord endureth for ever. And this is the Word which by the Gospel is preached unto you", (1 Peter 1 v.25).

The greatest need in the Church today is for men called, equipped, and made preachers by God to "reprove the world of sin, and of righteousness, and of judgement", (John 16 v.8). It is only by "the Spirit of truth" (John 16 v.13) that we are guided, instructed, and given the understanding that will enable us to explain, defend, and teach "the deep things of God", (2 Cor. 2 v. 10). The testimony of the Spirit always concurs with Holy Scripture. Our great Gospel duty is to walk uprightly, worthy of the Lord, in accordance with the teaching of the Holy Bible. "For this cause also thank we God without ceasing, because, when ye received the Word of God which ye heard of us, ye received it not as the word of men, but as it is in truth, the Word of God, which effectually worketh also in you that believe", (1Thess. 2 v.13).

It is an awesome privilege and solemn responsibility for the true servant of the Gospel to be called of God to preach the glorious message of salvation. By prayer ever seeking Divine help, he will earnestly "contend for the faith" (Jude v.3) and "to make known the mystery of the Gospel", (Eph. 6 v.19). We believe that the preaching of the Word in all its fullness in the power of the Holy Ghost will regenerate, reform, and revive at a time when many preachers have compromised the truth. The passionate teacher will be determined by God's grace to preach and "adorn the doctrine of God our Saviour in all things" (Titus 2 v.10), and among others, he will sound forth the sovereignty of God the Father, the sufficiency of Christ the Son, and the saving power and conviction of the Holy Spirit in the plan of redemption. "Take heed to the ministry which thou hast received in the Lord, that thou fulfil it", (Col. 4 v.17).

In our responsibility as preachers and teachers of God's Word, we must be faithful in our calling and we must perseveringly explain its contents and duties without fear or favour to all mankind. By encouraging the weary traveller heavenward and rebuking the wayward we must with passion and conviction apply and enforce the Biblical message in the lives of our hearers so as to promote an honest response to its demands. If the preacher is to be heard and heeded by his people, he must not only insist on the trustworthiness of his message, he must also show himself to be worthy of respect by the quality of his faith, conduct and leadership. Workmen that are unskilled, unfaithful and lazy in the preparation, and consequent failure in the preaching and duty of "holding forth the Word of life" (Phil. 2 v.16), have need to be ashamed. "Study to shew thyself approved unto God, a workman that needeth not to be ashamed, rightly dividing the Word of truth", (2 Tim. 2 v.15). It is our duty, not only to hold fast, but to hold forth the Word of life, not only for our own benefit, but also for the benefit of others. We are to divide and preach the Word of truth faithfully, not to invent a new 'gospel'. We are charged to rightly divide the Gospel that is committed to our trust.

The Consequences of Indiscipline and Falsehood

Scripture clearly affirms that God is truth and that He speaks truth and cannot lie. "Thy Word is truth", (John 17 v.17). Satan is a liar and the father of lies (John 8 v.44), and if it were possible, he would "deceive the very elect", (Matt. 24 v.24). Sadly, God's own people have not escaped the plague of falsehood. False preachers, false teachers, have always been the bane of the Church, and this situation will continue worse and worse until our Lord returns. The devil attempts to obliterate God's truth and cause confusion and division in the Church. False teaching about God, about Christ, about the Bible, and about spiritual reality is perverting and corrupting the saving and sanctifying truth of God's written Word, the Holy Scriptures. It is distorting and misrepresenting the message of His living Word, His Son, the Lord Jesus Christ. Many of our congregations are suffering serious spiritual and moral decline, and as always, ungodly teaching leads to ungodly living.

Carelessness and indiscipline in the personal life of the preacher will result in shoddiness, delinquency and failure in the discharge of his responsibility to the souls over whom he is overseer. Such impairment, weakness, and omission of duty quenches the Spirit (1 Thess. 5 v.19) and will result in failure to see the saving purpose of God wrought in the hearts of those to whom he ministers. May the Lord give us hearts to comply with the call and Word of God to make us preachers and witnesses in His name among the people, and with

Paul be able to say with resolute conviction, "I was not disobedient unto the heavenly vision", commanding people everywhere "that they should repent and turn to God, and do works meet for repentance", (Acts 26 v.19-20).

Performing deeds appropriate to repentance involves a change of mind that results in a change of behaviour. Those who truly repent and turn to God will "bring forth therefore fruits meet for repentance", (Matt. 3 v.8; 7 v.16,20; James 2 v.18). In true repentance we are to forsake our sin by turning away from our sinful ways with sorrow, and turning to God with definite purpose and desire to love, obey, and serve Him. Repentance is a grace, imparted by God to the sinner as a gracious gift in Christ Jesus, and wrought in the individual heart by the Holy Spirit through His Word. In his sense of guilt and helplessness, the sinner grieves and shows deep remorse for his sin committed against a holy and just God. Under positive conviction (Acts 2 v.37) and a disposition to seek pardon (Isaiah 55 v.7) and cleansing (Jer. 33 v.8), leadeth him to repentance (Rom. 2 v.4), saving faith in Christ (Acts 16 v.31), and trust in God for salvation (Acts 4 v.12).

The evidence of this change of mind and will to follow Christ is more properly termed regeneration, created by the gracious sovereign action of the Holy Spirit, which transforms the disposition of fallen man into one of trust, of repentance for past rebelliousness and unbelief, and loving obedience to God (Rom. 6 v.14; Col. 1 v.9-18). Regeneration is the cause of conversion, of our turning to God in faith and repentance, and the "new-birth" or "birth from above", "birth of the Spirit" (John 3 v.3-8) signifieth the beginning of the new life in the believer. Only the regenerate receives Christ and enters into the privileges of God's children (John 1 v.12-13). "Therefore if any man be in Christ, he is a new creature: old things are passed away; behold, all things are become new", (2 Cor. 5 v.17). With the understanding being enlightened (2 Cor. 4 v.6; Eph. 1 v.18), and the will renewed (Phil. 2 v.13), this new life in Christ will proceed to bring forth fruit consistent with God's demands, not only of faith and repentance, but also of the diligent use of all the means of grace, continuing "stedfastly in the apostle's doctrine and fellowship, and in breaking of bread, and in prayers", (Acts 2 v.42).

The term "preacher" derives from the Greek word "kerusso", which means "to herald, proclaim, or speak publicly". To promote and lead "a quiet and peaceful life" (1 Tim. 2 v.2), it is vital that preachers pursue godliness, dignity, honesty, and moral earnestness. We are not promised that the Christian life will be a bed of roses free from trouble or problems, for "all that will live godly in Christ Jesus shall suffer persecution", (2 Tim. 3v.12). If we are persecuted, it must be for Christ's sake, for the sake of righteous living. (1 Peter 2 v. 13-23). In serving the Lord we must show due reverence toward our Maker, and live for the majesty, holiness, love, and glory of God. It is true, as the Scriptures confirm, that trials bring about spiritual maturity. (James 1 v.2-12).

In the Sermon on the Mount, we are told by Christ Himself, that it is the duty of Christians to love their enemies. "But I say unto you", says Jesus, "Love your enemies, bless them that curse you, do good to them that hate you, and pray for them which spitefully use you, and persecute you", (Matt. 5 v.44). We must have a compassion for them, a goodwill toward them, and pray that God will forgive them. "Look unto Me", says the Lord, "and be ye saved, all the ends of the earth: for I am God, and there is none else", (Isaiah 45 v.22).

Prerequisites for Effective Preaching

The reality of ministry is that preachers often struggle in sermon preparation and due diligence in presentation. When staleness and rut set in, the people become bored, and in order to revive our waning enthusiasm and ineffectiveness in the pulpit, we need to gain an added dimension of the power of the Spirit and authority of the Word of God. All too often the preacher insists on throwing Scripture verses at their congregations without due attention or adequate explanation, with no passion or warmth whatsoever. They come across to the congregation as cold-hearted and uncaring with boring dullness and drained of all life. Those "who labour in the Word and doctrine" (1 Tim. 5 v.17) must teach by their life, and be examples both in speech and conduct. "Give attendance to reading, to exhortation, to doctrine. Neglect not the gift that is in thee, which was given thee by prophecy, with the laying on of the hands of the presbytery", (1Tim. 4 v.13-14).

We must study hard in order to expound the Scriptures correctly, and in faithfulness to the Word teach others what to do and what to believe. Preachers must be much in prayer and meditation otherwise their usefulness will wither away. We must pay due and proper attention to personal devotion, to doctrine, to learning, always aiming at the salvation of the lost and the building up of the people of God on their most holy faith. "Go after that which is lost" (Luke 15 v.4), "for the Son of man is come to seek and to save that which was lost" (Luke 19 v.10) ----- "being confident of this very thing, that He which hath begun a good work in you, will perform it until the day of Jesus Christ", (Phil. 1 v.6). Let us meditate on the great trust committed to our charge, on the worth and value of immortal souls, and on the account that we shall give to the Great Judge on the Last Day. "Obey them that have the rule over you, and submit yourselves: for they watch for your souls, as they that must give account, that they may do it with joy, and not with grief: for that is unprofitable for you. Pray for us: for we trust we have a good conscience, in all things willing to live honestly", (Heb. 13 v.17-18). We have a great God Who loves us, and calls us to this difficult task, the task of preaching, but He has also promised to equip us for it, and never to leave us nor forsake us along the way (Matt. 28 v.19-20).

By having a fresh encounter with God every time before we preach, the message should have a clear purpose and be aimed for the hearers' with great precision, tenderness, faith and truth, and so teach them clearly its implications for their lives. It was for this precise cause that Paul was appointed by God to be a preacher of the Word.

"Whereunto I am ordained a preacher, and an apostle, I speak the truth in Christ, and lie not; a teacher of the Gentiles in faith and verity", (1 Tim. 2 v.7). This refers to the great truths that God is our Saviour, Christ is our Mediator Who gave Himself as a ransom for our sin, and the Holy Spirit applieth to us the redemption purchased by Christ, enabling us to embrace Jesus Christ freely offered to us in the Gospel. "Now then we are ambassadors for Christ" (2 Cor. 5 v.20) sent out into the world to proclaim the Gospel of Jesus Christ. As messengers "in Christ's stead" we are to "speak the truth", "and lie not". A holy life and earnestness in fervent prayer, are prerequisites for effective preaching. "If I regard iniquity in my heart", says the psalmist, "the Lord will not hear me", (Psalm 66 v.18). Do we have the passion that inspired John Knox to cry out, "Give me Scotland or I die?" Let us pray with Paul, "that utterance may be given unto me, that I may open my mouth boldly, to make known the mystery of the Gospel", (Eph. 6 v.19).

The great danger of false preachers is not only in the evil of their teachings of themselves, but in their being taught supposedly as the truth of God. "Evil men and seducers shall wax worse and worse, deceiving, and being deceived", (2 Tim. 3 v.13). False and deceptive teachers, who claim to preach in the name of the Lord, are not only destructive but their evil influence greatly weakens and destroys the Church. For the saving of sinners, for the strengthening of believers in the faith, and the building up of the Church in the Word and doctrine, it is so important that preachers are careful and consistent in declaring "all the counsel of God", (Acts 20 v.27). A congregation that is untaught in the Scriptures is vulnerable to all kinds of innovations and practices contrary to the teaching of the Bible. Holy Scripture is not only the food but also the armour we need as soldiers of Christ, (Eph.6 v.10-17). "Wherefore take unto you the whole armour of God, that ye may be able to withstand in the evil day, and having done all to stand", (Eph. 6 v.13).

Large swathes of the Church today that once held to orthodox teaching have now so much declined and lost credibility that they no longer can be deemed evangelical. They need to be reformed and revived by the power of God to effect a re-affirmation of belief and commitment to Biblical truth emphasising the immutability of the purpose of God, the centrality of the Bible in worship and doctrine, and the certainty of salvation of all the elect. Evangelicalism can only remain evangelical if it is passionate and serious about truth and theology. The Scripture teaches the sovereignty of God in creation, providence, and redemption, revealed in the Lordship of the Lord Jesus Christ, the only Mediator between God and men. "For there is one God, and one Mediator between God and men, the man Christ Jesus; Who gave Himself a ransom for all", (1 Tim. 2 v.5-6).

Distinctive Principles and Spiritual Authority

We are greatly indebted to the Early Church fathers, the Reformers, Covenanters, Puritans, and other Heroes and Martyrs of the faith, whose manuscripts, sermons and writings have come down to us and enriched our understanding of Biblical theology by their faithful preaching of the Word of God, by their examples of principled living, and by their spiritual authenticity. We pray for renewal of evangelical theology in our Churches today, not only to appreciate the rich heritage and stock of Christian literature that is now available to us, but also that we in our day may contribute positively to the proclamation of the Gospel of Jesus Christ to which He gave His life: "Preach the Word", (2 Tim. 4 v.2).

It is vitally imperative that the cardinal truths so essential to the Christian Gospel are upheld and maintained in our generation. Without them Christianity ceases to be the teaching of the Bible. As the Scriptures declare, we must "be ready always to give an answer to every man that asketh you a reason of the hope that is in you with meekness and fear: Having a good conscience; that, whereas they speak evil of you, as of evildoers, they may be ashamed that falsely accuse your good conversation in Christ", (1 Peter 3 v.15-16). Remarkably enough, Pilate asked the question of all questions when, in the presence of Jesus, "What is truth?" (John 18 v.38). In that great Chapter, Hebrews 11, the writer declares, "By faith we understand". As opposed to liberalism, modernism and all other 'isms', we gladly confirm our loyalty and allegiance as Biblical fundamentalists to the Holy Scriptures, firmly believing without reservation the distinctive principles of the Christian faith:

(1)   the eternal Being and Works of God;

(2)   the full and final authority of Holy Scripture;

(3)   the Deity, Humanity, and Atonement of our Lord Jesus Christ;

(4)   the saving power of the Gospel of salvation;

(5)   the mediating ministry of the Holy Ghost;

(6)   the Divine institution of the Church, purity of worship and the means of grace; and

(7)   the supreme Lordship and mediatorial Reign of Jesus Christ over the Church and nations: "that in all things He might have the pre-eminence", (Col. 1 v.18).

It is through the Church, patterned and operating according to the Word of God, the Bible, that "the Gospel of Jesus Christ" (Mark 1 v.1) is to be taught, and His saving grace announced and proclaimed.   As heralds and messengers of the Cross, we have "the everlasting Gospel to preach unto them that dwell on the earth, and to every nation, and kindred, and tongue, and people", (Rev. 14 v.6).   Faith in Jesus Christ as a saving grace cannot be known except by experience of the New Birth (John 3 v.3), through trusting and believing in Him for salvation.   In Him "we have redemption through His blood, the forgiveness of sins, according to the riches of His grace", (Eph. 1 v.7).

The Gospel, of course, is for the whole world. In Romans Chapter 1, we have the most important statement of the Epistle. It is the heart of Biblical religion and the very essence of Christianity. Paul was ready to preach the Gospel at Rome. He says, "For I am not ashamed of the Gospel of Christ: for it is the power of God unto salvation to every one that believeth; to the Jew first, and also to the Greek. For therein is the righteousness of God revealed from faith to faith: as it is written, the just shall live by faith", (Rom. 1v.16-17). These verses tell us how it is possible for sinful men and women, boys and girls, to become right with God. God has provided a perfect righteousness in Christ Jesus which is imputed to us as we embrace Him in saving faith. Only by faith in Jesus Christ can we be right with God. Paul appeals to believers to walk "uprightly according to the truth of the Gospel", (Gal. 2 v.14).

It is a great indictment to the Church that many of its preachers today are totally void of conviction and do not have the courage and loyalty to stand for the truth of God's Word. Their best so-called services, however polished and disguised, neither please God nor profit mankind. They are not conscientious in their duty to God nor in their duty to men. The Scripture clearly exhorts us to a strong and constant desire for the Word of God: "the sincere milk of the Word, that ye may grow thereby", (1 Peter 2 v.2). This milk of the Word must be sincere, not adulterated by the innovations and mixtures of men. Such preachers are content to take a passive and lethargic role for fear of the criticisms of men and the sneers of the world, so they play along as social-climbers for acceptance into the high stratum of society. They are glad to have much religious trappings, pomp and ceremony, but too little sense of commitment and responsibility of conforming to Gospel standards and obeying the commands of the Word of God in matters of faith and practice. "Beware lest any man spoil you through philosophy and vain deceit, after the tradition of men, after the rudiments of the world, and not after Christ", (Col. 2 v.8).

We are exhorted by Paul to "walk worthy of the vocation wherewith ye are called, with all lowliness and meekness", (Eph. 4 v.1-2). Right doctrine is essential to right living and service for the Master. "No servant can serve two masters: for either he will hate the one, and love the other; or else he will hold to the one, and despise the other. Ye cannot serve God and mammon", (Luke 16 v.13). Those who set Biblical theology aside also set aside sound Christian living. Church renewal, reform and revival do not come with new programmes, new buildings, or new external measures. But rather as the Scripture says, "be renewed in the spirit of your mind; And that ye put on the new man, which after God is created in righteousness and true holiness", (Eph. 4 v.23-24). May God give us "the spirit of wisdom and revelation in the knowledge" of Himself, (Eph. 1 v.17). Along with our ministry of proclaiming Christ "Whom we preach", may we warn every man, and teach every man "in all wisdom; that we may present every man perfect in Christ Jesus", (Col. 1 v.28). That is why our call to preach is a high calling, and why all faithful preachers are determined to serve the Lord to the best of their ability through their preaching, teaching, writing, exhortation, and other ministries in Christ's vineyard.

True Worship and Reverence for God

Much modern preaching is deeply anaemic, with the life-blood of the Nature and Works of God absent from the message, but centred instead upon man. True worship and reverence for God, the Almighty, Who is infinite, eternal and unchangeable, has largely vanished. He is the Creator, Preserver, and Governor of all things, the one true and living God. "Great is the Lord, and greatly to be praised; and His greatness is unsearchable", (Psalm 145 v.3). The prophet Isaiah describes Him as "the High and Lofty One that inhabiteth eternity", (Isaiah 57 v.15). In the prophecy of Jeremiah, the verity of God is made very plain. He is the God of truth; He is God in truth. Our God, the great Jehovah is truth upon Whom we may depend, Who cannot lie and will not deceive. He is life itself; has life in Himself;

and He is the source and fountain of life to all creatures. He is the everlasting King; He is King of eternity; and He shall reign unto all generations and for evermore. "But the Lord is the true God, He is the living God, and an everlasting King: at His wrath the earth shall tremble, and the nations shall not be able to abide His indignation", (Jer. 10 v.10).

No theme in Scripture is more fascinating and rewarding than that of the Names and Titles by which God has made Himself known to men throughout the ages. When preachers and Christian workers have made an in-depth study of the titles and metaphors through which God's character and activities are made to shine, they will have a greatly enlarged vision and appreciation of the greatness and majesty of God, Who is Creator, Sustainer, Redeemer, and Judge, thus giving them a much more rich and deeper knowledge of the "Name that is above every name", (Phil. 2 v.9).

Yet, generally, men today will readily use the name of God lightly, or even worse, as a swear word, or curse. Telling men that God is Almighty, Holy, Wise, Just, Omniscient, Omnipresent, Loving, Merciful, Gracious and Sovereign is deemed unnecessary. To preach on the great Biblical doctrines of grace is considered unessential, divisive, and may cause conflict. So 'do not rock the boat' is the plea from many Church councils and missionary boards. Surely something is gravely amiss in the Church when the message of the Gospel of grace and the truth of Scripture have to be greatly diluted and weakened. "Let no man deceive you with vain words: for because of these things cometh the wrath of God upon the children of disobedience. Be not ye therefore partakers with them", (Eph. 5 v.6-7).

In consequence of the entrance of sin into the world at the Fall (Gen. 3), all mankind are born in a state of guilt. "By one man sin entered into the world and death by sin; and so death passed upon all men, for that all have sinned", (Rom. 5 v.12).

So we "are all under sin" (Rom. 3 v.9), destitute of original righteous-ness and unable to save ourselves. We are "by nature the children of wrath" (Eph. 2 v.3), under sin's dominion, subject to death and liable to everlasting punishment. We can do nothing of ourselves to merit the favour of God "because the carnal mind is enmity against God"(Rom. 8 v.7) and "that which is born of the flesh is flesh" (John 3 v.6). "Salvation belongeth unto the Lord" (Psalm 3 v.8) and comes to us by faith alone through Christ alone. "Neither is there salvation in any other: for there is none other name under heaven given among men, whereby we must be saved", (Acts 4 v.12).

The Bible assures us of complete deliverance that, through the Person and Work of Christ, and by the operation of the Holy Spirit, gives pardon and forgiveness to His believing people. We are delivered from a state of sin into a state of salvation by the means and merit of the ransom paid by Christ on the Cross of Calvary on our behalf. He "put away sin by the sacrifice of Himself", (Heb.9 v.26). "For Christ also hath once suffered for sins, the Just for the unjust, that He might bring us to God, being put to death in the flesh, but quickened by the Spirit", (1 Peter 3 v.18). The only merit upon which a sinner may be saved is Christ's merit. "Believe on the Lord Jesus Christ, and thou shalt be saved, and thy house", (Acts 16 v.31). This is the message we are commissioned to preach to a lost world. Proper and just views of the present moral state of man are essential to a right understanding of the Gospel, and a right relationship with God. God "hath reconciled us to Himself by Jesus Christ ----- not imputing their trespasses unto them; and hath committed unto us the word of reconciliation", (2 Cor. 5 v.18-19).

The only Infallible and Authoritative Rule

The enemies of the Divine Word pervert the truth of God and contemptuously disregard the plain teaching of the Most High. The Word of God stands like a rock, immovable from generation to generation, amid the tumultuous waves of human hostility. "The

Word of the Lord endureth forever", (1 Peter 1 v.25). True preaching is the Word of God in the sense that it is an exposition and interpretation of the Bible as the only infallible and authoritative rule of faith and practice. The Christian preacher needs to assert that the Scriptures are the living Word of God, and not be distracted or attracted to programmes of entertainment, drama and musicals for those who "will not endure sound doctrine; but after their own lusts shall they heap to themselves teachers, having itching ears; And they shall turn away their ears from the truth", (2 Tim 4 v.3-4). This becomes all the more prevalent as preachers fail to proclaim the full counsel of God. The assertion, "Thus saith the Lord" (Jer. 2 v.2) is absent from today's preaching, and more and more with increasing opposition, the malice of wicked men rages against the Bible. But the Psalmist reminds us that the word of the Lord "is true from the very beginning", and every one of His "righteous judgements endureth for ever", (Psalm 119 v.160).

With failure of preaching in the pulpit, weakness of witness and discipline in the Church, corruption and unbelief among the people, "the devil, as a roaring lion, walketh about, seeking whom he may devour", (1Peter 5v.8). The Gospel is ridiculed, despised, scorned, derided, and sneered at by the world. No matter how much preachers and ministers apostatise and abandon the truth of Scripture, or how decadent and barren the Church may become, the Bible tells us that "the just shall live by faith", (Rom. 1 v.17). This was Martin Luther's text, and as he was summoned before the Imperial Diet at Worms refusing to recant his faith, he said "Unless I am convinced and persuaded by the testimony of Scripture, my conscience is bound by the Word of God, I cannot and I will not retract, for it is unsafe for a Christian to speak against his conscience. Here I stand. I can do no other. May God help me. Amen". Thus did the German monk, who shook the world, utter the words that still thrills the heart of the believer after some five hundred years.

Luther, the great Reformer, spoke out against the corrupt religious practices and abuses of his day. His demand that the authority for doctrine and practice be SCRIPTURE, not Popes or Councils, roared across the face of the world when he nailed up his Ninty-five Theses upon the Church door at Whittenberg, which ignited the Great Reformation of the sixteenth century. He was accused of heresy by the Roman authorities and threatened with excommunication and death. Maintaining his bold stand for truth, he refused to recant or compromise. He said "If the doctrine of justification by faith alone is lost, then all Christian doctrine is lost at the same time. On this premise the Church stands or falls. It alone begets, nourishes, builds, preserves, and defends the Church of God, and without it the Church of God cannot exist for one hour". What a rebuke against the weakness, barrenness and declension of present-day Christianity.

Many so-called preachers, teachers and ministers today will discourse very eloquently and intellectually on various subjects to show off their cleverness and education in a religious ritualistic manner to impress the unwary and unenlightened. The absence of doctrinal content in teaching and lack of Biblical exposition in preaching are the chief factors for the lamentable ignorance and rapid decline in the Church at the present time. The Bible is criticised and rejected by the modernist, who wants to abandon Biblical theology, to be replaced by secular theology to accommodate modern man by fitting into modern culture and other things that are "contrary to sound doctrine", (1 Tim. 1 v.10). "This people honoureth Me with their lips, but their heart is far from Me. Howbeit in vain do they worship Me, teaching for doctrines the commandments of men", (Mark 7 v.6-7). (See also Isaiah 29 v.13).

Let us pray that God will save us and deliver us from the plague of false preaching. "But there were false prophets also among the people, even as there shall be false teachers among you, who privily shall bring in damnable heresies, even denying the Lord that bought them, and bring upon themselves swift destruction. And many shall follow their pernicious ways; by reason of whom the way of truth shall be evil spoken of", (2 Peter 2 v.1-2). False preachers lull the people by leaving them with a vague impression to the effect that being a 'Christian' is a good thing, without any express exposition of what faith really is. Salvation is by faith alone in Christ alone, and because of the urgency of the message, it is highly important to tell people who want to be saved just what faith really means. If a 'preacher' cannot do that, he is not a true servant of the Lord Jesus Christ, and he should therefore step away from any position of leadership within the Church. "Wherefore by their fruits ye shall know them", (Matt. 7 v.20).

The decline in the Church today is due in great measure to the failure, compromise and faulty teaching of our contemporary preachers, large numbers of whom are false servants that do not understand, appreciate, or live by the truth of God: being yet "aliens from the commonwealth of Israel, and strangers from the covenants of promise, having no hope, and without God in the world", (Eph. 2 v.12).

The doctrine of justification by faith "through the redemption that is in Christ Jesus" (Rom. 3 v.24), is that by which the Church in all ages stands or falls, as Martin Luther rightly maintained. We need men of that calibre to lead the Church today who are not ashamed to stand up for truth and righteousness. It is to be lamented that large sections of the Church in our day no longer stand tall before the world. Her witness to maintain the truth of God and to publish it far and wide has greatly diminished. "A true witness delivereth souls: but a deceitful witness speaketh lies", (Prov. 14 v.25). The Scripture goes on to say, "A false witness shall not be unpunished, and he that speaketh lies shall perish", (Prov. 19 v.9).

The Current Religious Scene Perilous

Throughout our nation and further afield, it is evident that the Church at large has lost the vision and the will to serve the Lord according to His Word. Fifty years ago the word 'evangelical' described those Christians who, accepting the Scriptures as God's infallible and authoritative Word, stress man's fall and his redemption through the atoning substitutionary death of the Lord Jesus Christ, along with the necessity for the New Birth, repentance and faith and who therefore endeavour by God's grace to live godly lives. It is by no means the same today. Vast numbers of Church members have little or no understanding of the privileges and responsibilities of the Gospel for themselves, and therefore are not concerned about the need of their countrymen around them. The ministers are muted because they have absorbed the modernism as taught at universities and theological colleges which have corrupted the teaching of the Holy Scriptures, with the tragic result they lost sight of the vitality and urgency of the Christian message in the Church. "Where there is no vision, the people perish", (Prov. 29 v.18).

We cannot seriously consider the dire religious situation in the world at the present time, without realising that the Church is passing through a momentous crisis, probably the greatest in its history since the days of the Reformation. Surely it must grieve the Holy Spirit of God that the Church is impotent to edify and minister grace unto the hearers, lacking in the vision that she may reasonably hope to be graciously used in saving sinners, and in manifesting the glory of God's Kingdom. Instead she is bowing to the world, adopting worldly standards, methods, customs and culture with a veneer of religious tolerance at the expense of Biblical truth. Many of her ministers would call themselves 'new evangelical' scholars and portray themselves as more 'enlightened' preachers. Their liberalism and rejection of the inerrancy and authority of Scripture only serve to further the cause of the enemy, "and to destroy souls, to get dishonest gain", (Ezek. 22 v.27). Let us rather give heed to the call of the Psalmist, exhorting us to praise God, "For His merciful kindness is great toward us: and the truth of the Lord endureth for ever", (Psalm 117 v.1-2).

Sadly, many preachers and Church members no longer hold to the infallibility and Divine inspiration of the Bible. Rather than face up to the ridicule, opposition and persecution of the world they go into apostasy and 'shipwreck' concerning the faith. They do not "war a good warfare; Holding faith, and a good conscience; which some having put away concerning faith have made shipwreck", (1 Tim. 1 v.18-19). They know not the truth of God in Christ Jesus, nor the blessing of salvation and what it is to be clothed in His Divine righteousness. "For He hath made Him to be sin for us, Who knew no sin; that we might be made the righteousness of God in Him", (2 Cor. 5 v.21). The Church will never be strong unless it is united in grace to stand up for God and for His truth around faithful preachers of the Word, and ministers of firm conviction and courage, who are "not ashamed of the Gospel of Christ: for it is the power of God unto salvation to every one that believeth", (Rom. 1 v.16).

The Scriptural requirement for a man aspiring to the office of minister, preacher, or teaching elder, is both experimental and doctrinal. He must be a man whose faith and walk of life is known by His consistency and constancy in practical godliness and holiness. His personal and family life must be exemplary and above reproach, (1 Tim. 3 v.7). "If a man desire the office of a bishop, he desireth a good work", (1Tim. 3 v.1). He "must be blameless, the husband of one wife, having faithful children not accused of riot or unruly", (Titus 1v.6). Furthermore, as well as knowing the grace of God in his heart and the call of the Lord upon his life to be a preacher of truth and righteousness, he must be one who holds "fast the faithful Word" (Titus 1 v.9), practically adorning "the doctrine of God our Saviour in all things", (Titus 2 v.10).

As we look out upon the Church at large today, it is not surprising from the Biblical perspective to find that the standard of contemporary preaching has greatly fallen. Because of false teachers, carnal leadership, and rejection of God's truth, the faith is shipwrecked. In the Bible, faith and a good conscience are often repeated together. The faith is a reference to the Christian faith, the Gospel, the Word of God. Keeping the faith means holding fast to that revealed truth. The faith is indeed the content of Holy Scripture as revealed truth. A preacher must hold to it with a clear conscience: "Holding the mystery of faith with a pure conscience", (1 Tim. 3 v.9). It is not enough merely to believe the truth, but also to live it.

The true preacher must be a man of firm faith, integrity, and loyalty to the Word of God. The stronger the theological knowledge of truth, and Biblical obedience to it, the stronger will be the affirmation of conscience and deeper the conviction of assurance, peace, and joy of serving the Lord. Every preacher should be able to say with Paul the Apostle, "For our rejoicing is this, the testimony of our conscience, that in simplicity and godly sincerity, not with fleshly wisdom, but by the grace of God" (2 Cor. 1 v.12), the constant course and tenor of our faith and life.

The Minister's Personal Piety

As well as ability in theological matters concerning ministerial requirements for preachers of the faith, it is of the highest importance that the candidate's advancement in personal and domestic piety are factors which must be placed at the top of the list. Moral and spiritual example is an absolute necessity that the true preacher should possess. The humble preacher must take great care to remain "strong in the Lord" (Eph. 6 v.10), and be constantly "nourished up in the words of faith and of good doctrine" (1 Tim 4 v.6) in relation to moral character, home life, spiritual maturity, and public leadership.

It should be emphasised at this point that contemporary preaching is defective because of a failure, and carelessness, even daily, to be watchful of one's personal devotional life before the Lord, resulting in coldness of heart and devotion to the Lord Jesus Christ and marked by doctrinal imbalance. It is no wonder then that there is so little application of Scripture truth from the pulpit whenever the private reading and study of the Book of God and prayer are neglected as regards the personal illumination and daily sanctification of the preacher's own heart and life. Chapter three of Second Timothy, demonstrates in a powerful way the great truth of the inspiration and authority of the Holy Scriptures. It contains a very serious word to us today. As servants of God and preachers of the Word, this chapter is most striking and heart-searching. It says in verse 15, "And that from a child thou hast known the Holy Scriptures, which are able to make thee wise unto salvation through faith which is in Christ Jesus". But that is not the only function of Scripture. It goes on to tell us in clear language, "All Scripture is given by inspiration of God, and is profitable for doctrine, for reproof, for correction, for instruction in righteousness: That the man of God may be perfect, thoroughly furnished unto all good works", (v.16-17).

There is an explicit statement in verse 17 to which we must give earnest heed. It states very emphatically that the inspired Scriptures are for the perfecting and maturing of the man of God. We see here that Divine revelation has as its primary function the personal sanctification of the preacher so as to equip him unto every good work. A preacher is not furnished to preach simply by merely possessing gifts of speech, eloquence and oratory. He needs first of all to be indoctrinated and instructed in the Word of God unto sanctification of life and holiness, otherwise he is not a fit person to declare it unto others. It is necessary to take heed unto ourselves before we can apply the Word with effectiveness to others. "For I determined not to know any thing among you, save Jesus Christ, and Him crucified", says Paul, "And my speech and my preaching was not with enticing words of man's wisdom, but in demonstration of the Spirit and of power", (1 Cor. 2 v.2,4).

It is a Biblical imperative that we should, first of all, nourish and build up ourselves in truth and righteousness, and then, apply the truth to those that hear us. The weeping prophet, Jeremiah, in setting us a good example could say, "Thy words were found, and I did eat them; and Thy Word was unto me the joy and rejoicing of mine heart: for I am called by Thy name, O Lord God of hosts", (Jer. 15 v.16). That is precisely what the Apostle Paul is exhorting us to do in his Pastoral Epistles to Timothy, First and Second, and to Titus. We are to let the Word of God teach us in all wisdom and understanding. Let us get our doctrinal instruction on our knees before the Lord with an open Bible, and pray, so that the principles of truth and doctrines of Scripture are not just icy propositions, but rather may go forth from our hearts as conscious living truths of the Word of God burning deeply within the very fibres of our souls by the power of the Holy Spirit. "Be not thou therefore ashamed of the testimony of our Lord", (2 Tim. 1 v.8). "Faith comes by hearing, and hearing by the Word of God" (Rom. 10 v.17), ----- by the Word preached (Titus 1 v.3).

The Burden and Passion of a Preacher's Heart

With the desire to know God more and to take delight in Him, may He incline our hearts increasingly toward Him and to His Word so that we might employ our time and efforts more effectively in serving Him in the ministry of His Church. As preachers of the Word with the burden of a teacher's heart and a passion for souls, may the Holy Spirit enable us to declare the truth aright and to show forth the glory of God. Whatever we do in the service of Christ, we must be humble, for we are all God's servants. We must take great care to grid ourselves to serve Him (Luke 17 v.8), and keep ourselves free from everything that is entangling and encumbering. Though we should do "all those things which are commanded you ----- which was our duty to do" (Luke 17 v.10), yet, in many things we come very far short of this. The best servants of Christ must humbly acknowledge that they are but "unprofitable servants", (Luke 17 v.10).

In our service of Christ, the King and Head of the Church, we are bound by that first and great commandment to "love the Lord thy God with all thy heart, and with all thy soul, and with all thy mind", (Matt. 22 v.37). As servants of the Lord Jesus Christ, let us encourage each other, as did David of old "in the Lord his God", (1 Sam. 30 v.6). Hezekiah, in his day, commanded the priests and the Levites, "that they might be encouraged in the law of the Lord", (2 Chron.31 v.4). So he set the priests in their charges, "and encouraged them to the service of the house of the Lord", (2 Chron. 35 v.2). In the midst of all the confusion and compromise of the Church in our day, we must likewise let the Word of God teach us. Let it reprove us. Let it correct us. Let it instruct us in the way of righteousness and true holiness.

As we endeavour by the help of the Holy Spirit to glorify God and serve His people, we must sanctify ourselves and prepare ourselves according to the Word of the Lord, (2 Chron. 35 v.6). While the minister's work must begin at home, it must not end there, we must do what we can to encourage each other and to prepare each other by admonishing, instructing, exhorting, quickening, and comforting each other in the service of the Lord. May God equip us and grant us that power from on High to be vessels "meet for the Master's use" (2 Tim 2 v.21), "thoroughly furnished unto all good works" (2 Tim. 3 v.17), to His eternal glory. "Be ye clean, that bear the vessels of the Lord", (Isaiah 52 v.11).

The best preaching practice in declaring the truth of God's Word is that it should be illustrated and applied with other Scripture. It is always refreshing for the preacher to have deep communion and fellowship with the Lord in the understanding of His Word, and then out of that experience go forth to explain and to teach what a passage of the Bible really means. "So they read in the book of the Law of God distinctly, and gave the sense, and caused them to understand the reading", (Neh. 8 v.8).

The dominant thrust of our ministry, as preachers, should be to make God's living Word alive to the people, so that they might understand and know His Word of truth. "Study to show thyself approved unto God, a workman that needeth not to be ashamed, rightly dividing the Word of truth", (2 Tim. 2 v.15). We must preach it with faithfulness as before the Lord to the souls of men, and allow it to dwell in them richly, with the prayer that the Holy Spirit may lodge it deep in the hearts and minds of His people and bring forth greater obedience, confidence, and trust in God. " Let the Word of Christ dwell in you richly in all wisdom: teaching and admonishing one another in psalms and hymns and spiritual songs, singing with grace in your hearts to the Lord", (Col. 3 v.16).

In Psalm 60 v.4, we read, "Thou hast given a banner to them that fear Thee, that it may be displayed because of the truth". In the midst of the current crisis and failure of contemporary preaching at this time, our hope is in God to lift up a standard as a rallying point for those who would unite in testimony for Him. We must gather to God's banner in the cause of truth, and maintain a witness among the nations. As in the days of our Covenanting and Reformation forefathers, may God again in this our twenty-first century, raise up ministers and preachers who are prepared to maintain a consistent witness and an undiluted testimony to the great truths of the Everlasting Gospel of Christ. Real preaching is precisely the communication of the Word of the Everlasting Lord. There is plainly no work in all the world that can possibly compare or compete with it in value and importance.

Of the early Covenanters, William Blakie writes, "One of the lessons for preachers in every age, very specially derived from Scottish experience, that to be effective, preaching must not be hard and cold, however able, but warm and hearty, glowing in every sentence with the warmth of the preacher's soul ----- for real efficiency, for attracting interest, producing impression, and moulding the character of the people, the pulpit of the seventeenth century hardly knows a rival". The Church of the Blue Banner for Christ's Crown and Covenant, emphasised the doctrine of the supremacy of the Lord Jesus Christ and the abiding obligation to pay supreme regard to His will as expressed in His Word. As Alexander Henderson expressed it, her great endeavour is "that all things be done in God's house according to God's will".

As Christ Himself was the Divine Word made flesh, so, designing to employ human agency for the promotion and extension of His Kingdom among men, He made a special appropriation of man's distinguishing faculty of speech by appointing it as the primary and principle means of diffusing God's Word of truth and message of salvation throughout the world. "Go ye into all the world, and preach the Gospel to every creature", (Mark 16 v.15). Preaching is designed to enlighten and quicken the consciences of men as a means of affecting their earthly character and their eternal destiny.

Addressing his divinity students, Ian Macpherson is on record as saying, "Having discharged your duty aright, you are not like a professor who has just given a lecture on obstetrics: you are like a woman who has just given birth to a child ----- exhausted, yet exultant". What a marvellous privilege, having paid the price in due and earnest preparation and prayerfully borne and brought forth the message of Christ, to see men and women, not on their feet in acclamation of the sermon, but bowing in humility, homage, and adoration to the Lord. What a tremendous task to be thus filled with a fresh sense of God's presence and power in the preaching of His Word. To preach the Gospel is none other than the manifestation of the Incarnate Word, from the Written Word, by the spoken word.

The ultimate end which all elements of true preaching serve is the glory of God and the good of men, women and children in their salvation and edification. The enemy of the souls of men will do everything he can to distract and hinder the reception of the Word preached. Nothing should take away from the preaching of the Word. Preaching is a serious business. To make of the pulpit a platform for the display of one's wit or repartee is to debase it and to prostitute it to unholy ends. When the Word is really on the preacher's heart and soul to deliver, he does not feel in the least like jesting. We should use humour sparingly and judiciously, lest with a joke we damn a soul. May it please God to revive preaching in our day for the glory of God and the good of the Christian Church.

Today, sadly, the meaning of the word 'Christian' has been reduced to practically nothing. As a symbol of Christendom in that part of the world in which Christianity is the perceived religion, it has been made to mean so little in modern usage, even amongst our contemporary preachers. It can mean anyone who is not Jewish, anyone who lives in a so-called 'Christian' nation, anyone who claims some sort of connection to a Church however vague that may be, or anyone who claims any kind of 'allegiance' to Jesus Christ. The term 'evangelical' is following the same trend without any precise definition of what truth is. The world may be confused about what a Christian is. But the Bible is clear, and states, very plainly that Christians are those who are savingly called out of the world and united to God through Jesus Christ as our Mediator and Redeemer, those whom "God hath from the beginning chosen to salvation through sanctification of the Spirit and belief of the truth", (2 Thess. 2 v.13).

The Distinguishing Marks of Church Testimony

In the Book of the Revelation, Chapters 2 and 3, Christ is speaking to the seven Churches in Asia Minor. Each of which had a distinct feature or characteristic:

(1)   Ephesus, lost first love, 2 v.1-7;

(2)   Smyrna, persecuted, 2 v.8-11;

(3)   Pergamos, doctrinal falsehood, 2 v.12-17;

(4)   Thyatira, lack of holiness, 2 v.18-29;

(5)   Sardis, deadness, 3 v.1-6;

(6)   Philadelphia, faithfulness, 3 v.7-13; and

(7)   Laodicea, lukewarmness, 3 v.14-22.

While not precisely duplicated, the above characteristics also represent the types of Churches that are generally present throughout the entire Church today. Five of the seven were rebuked for tolerating sin in their midst, ranging from waning love at Ephesus to total apostasy at Laodicea. Many Churches today have a mixture of sins that greatly plague them, and our failure to love, follow, serve and worship God with all our heart, soul, mind, and strength, is to sin. "Thou shalt love the Lord thy God with all thy heart, and with all thy soul, and with all thy mind. This is the first and great commandment. And the second is like unto it, Thou shalt love thy neighbour as thyself. On these two commandments hang all the law and the prophets", (Matt. 22 v.37-40).

The Lord of the Church universal, the Almighty and Omniscient One, knows everything there is to know about the Church, both good and bad. Before rebuking the Church at Ephesus for their failures, the Lord Jesus Christ first of all addresses them with a word of commendation. He speaks of their doctrinal correctness and of their faithfulness in discipline, they hated "the deeds of the Nicolaitans, which I also hate", says Christ, (Rev. 2 v.6). But their service had degenerated into mechanical orthodoxy. Typical of many Churches and pastors today, the current generation of contemporary preachers, like the Ephesians, are maintaining in theory the doctrine handed down to them, but they have left their first love. "Nevertheless I have somewhat against Thee, because thou hast left thy first love. Remember therefore from whence thou art fallen, and repent, and do thy first works; or else I will come unto Thee quickly, and will remove thy candlestick out of his place, except thou repent", (Rev. 2 v.4-5).

It is clear from the Biblical record that the Ephesian Church had lost their love for God and Christ, lost their love for His Word of truth, lost their love for each other, and lost their love for lost sinners. The same is true of many Churches today. Their hearts become cold in affection, devotion and fellowship, and while correct doctrine in the head and busy hands in Church activity are important, the maintenance of the burning heart glowing in righteousness and holiness is an indisputable necessity. Nothing it appears, as far as the Ephesian Church was concerned, had been defective in the head or the hands. The defect, the weakness, the failure, the crisis, was in the heart. This is a very apt description of many Churches, pastors, preachers and ministers today. The call of Scripture to all of us is that we should be found often in the Holy Writ, meditating upon God's Word, and praying, that all our preaching and service in what we say and do for the Master, is shaped and moulded by the living Word of the living God. "I beseech you therefore, brethren, by the mercies of God, that ye present your bodies a living sacrifice, holy, acceptable unto God, which is your reasonable service. And be not conformed to this world: but be ye transformed by the renewing of your mind, that ye may prove what is that good, and acceptable, and perfect, will of God", (Rom. 12 v.1-2).

The example of rebuke to the Ephesian Church warns us that doctrinal correctness and orthodoxy, and outward service and activity, cannot make up for a cold heart. All believers, including ministers, pastors and preachers, must carefully heed Solomon's counsel, "Keep thy heart with all diligence; for out of it are the issues of life", (Prov. 4 v.23).

The Remedy for Spiritual Malady

There is in the Word of God a proper remedy for all our spiritual maladies, failures and backslidings. Preachers must keep a watchful eye and a strict hand upon all the motions of the inward man. Out of a heart well kept will flow living issues, good products, to the glory of God and the edification of others. We must act with steadfastness, steadiness, caution, and consistency. "Let all thy ways be established. Turn not to the right hand nor to the left: remove thy foot from evil", (Prov. 4 v.26-27). There are errors whether to the right or left hand, and Satan gains control if he prevails to draw us aside either way. "See that ye walk circumspectly, not as fools, but as the wise", (Eph. 5 v.15). We are called to walk, labour, and serve Christ, the great King and Head of the Church, in humility, unity, separation, love, and light of the truth of God's Word "to make known the mystery of the Gospel", (Eph 6 v.19).

The Church at large, today, has greatly strayed from the path of truth, innovations without Scriptural warrant have been rampant, preachers have compromised to accommodate 'modern' man, and ministers have failed in their duty and responsibility in "holding forth the Word of life", (Phil. 2 v.16). We would do well to heed the exhortation of the prophet Hosea to "return unto the Lord thy God; for thou hast fallen by thine iniquity. Take with you words, and turn to the Lord: say unto Him, Take away all iniquity, and receive us graciously: so will we render the calves (praises) of our lips", (Hosea 14 v.1-2). In His grace and mercy, God has promised to heal our lukewarmness, deadness, unfaithfulness, falsehood, and lack of holiness and love. "I will heal their backsliding, I will love them freely: for Mine anger is turned away" from them. (Hosea 14 v.4). "And I will restore to you the years that the locust hath eaten", (Joel 2 v.25).

The daily private reading of God's Word, the study and meditation of Biblical truth, and prayer, go together, and a preacher best serves the Lord when his gifts and graces are in good order. "Take heed unto thyself, and unto the doctrine; continue in them: for in doing this thou shalt both save thyself, and them that hear Thee", (1 Tim. 4 v.16). John Owen, the great Puritan, says, "No man preaches his sermon well to others if he doth not first preach it to his own heart". It would be calamitous for a preacher to be spiritually out of order, and worse still to be a minister of the Gospel and yet be unconverted. True piety is necessary as a first indispensible requisite of a pastor: "Brethren, give diligence to make your calling and election sure: for if ye do these things, ye shall never fall", (2 Peter 1 v.10).

In his book 'Lectures to My Students on the art of Preaching'. C. H. Spurgeon writes, "Inferior preaching not only comes from the failure of the minister in the personal application of the Word of God to his own heart, but also in the matter of secret prayer. If he is not familiar with the mercy-seat in communion with God, all else is mere emptiness. Prayer is the tool of the Great Potter by which He moulds the vessel, and nothing can so gloriously fit us to preach as descending fresh from the altar of prayer with God to speak with men, having wrestled with God on their behalf. The preacher becomes another man when clothed by the Spirit". "How much more shall your Heavenly Father give the Holy Spirit to them that ask Him?" (Luke 11 v.13). Spurgeon goes on to say "To face the enemies of truth, to defend the bulwarks of the faith, to rule well in the house of God, to comfort all that mourn, to edify the saints, to guide the perplexed, to bear with the froward, to win and nurse souls ----- all these and a thousand other works beside are not for a Feeble-mind or a Ready-to-halt, but are reserved for Great-heart whom the Lord has made strong for Himself. Seek then strength from the Strong One, wisdom from the Wise One, in fact, all from the God of all".

We must earnestly plead with God upon our knees to make real to us that the very people we speak to may savingly hear the words of eternal life, turn from sin to follow and serve the living Lord. In our consideration of what is lacking in contemporary preaching today, the root of the problem lies in the fact that preachers are not on their knees in prayer before God pouring over the Scriptures. They are duped and snared by Satan into a lazy attitude that any 'old mash' will do by pursuing the wisdom of the world, accepting its standards, and utilising its methods. Oh that we as preachers might repair our personal devotional lives, and thus be enabled by the Holy Spirit to study and preach the Word of God with the glow and fire of heaven upon our souls to the souls of men with results following. We need to repent of our worldliness, recover the great doctrines of Holy Scripture as did the Reformers and Covenanters five hundred years ago, and live a life transformed by the essential truths and testimony of "the Gospel of the grace of God", (Acts. 20 v.24). In obedience to the Lord may we go forth "in the fullness of the blessing of the Gospel of Christ" (Rom. 15 v.29), "preaching and shewing the Glad Tidings of the Kingdom of God" (Luke 8 v.1) with confidence to the world.

It is important to underline that an area of hindrance which greatly hampers the witness of the Church is the absence of practical piety in the domestic, marital and family life of the preacher. He "must be blameless, the husband of one wife, vigilant, sober, of good behaviour ----- One that ruleth well his own house, having his children in subjection with all gravity; For if a man know not how to rule his own house, how shall he take care of the Church of God?" (1 Tim. 3 v.2, 4-5); ----- "having faithful children not accused of riot or unruly", (Titus 1 v.6).

The preacher, the minister, the pastor, the elder, whose wife gossips with a wagging, ferocious and vicious tongue, whose children are worldly, promiscuous and wayward, and who faileth to rule well his own house are marks of disqualification, and he has no right to remain in office. If he cannot show a godly example, exercise proper discipline in his own house, and gives way to disorderly government and misrule of his own home and family, how can he rule well the House of God? "Even so must their wives be grave", that is, the wives of preachers and Church officers, "not slanderers, sober, faithful in all things", (1 Tim. 3 v.11). The women must "be in behaviour as becometh holiness, not false accusers, not given to much wine, teachers of good things", (Titus. 2 v.3).

Another area of potential weakness and great danger for the preacher is to become a showman, comedian, entertainer, and a joker. Such pretentious behaviour is usually an endeavour to cover up the shortcomings and fruitlessness of his life and ministry. A clown and a preacher do not sit well together, they are contrary the one to the other, nor can a lazy minister occupied with non-essential trivials who lacks discipline and spirituality be regarded as giving himself "continually to prayer, and the ministry of the Word", (Acts 6 v.4). In fact he is boxed into a corner, so much so that he will not address his congregation on situations that arise and apply the Word for fear of offending someone. "The fear of man bringeth a snare: but whoso putteth his trust in the Lord shall be safe", (Prov. 29 v.25)

God is looking for willing workers, dedicated preachers, that will go where in providence He would send them, to declare what He would command them. "As we are allowed of God to be put in trust with the Gospel, even so we speak; not as pleasing men, but God, which trieth our hearts", (1 Thess. 29 v.25). Preachers of the Word must walk in the fear of the Lord amongst men, as servants of God in a hostile world, willing to answer and submit to the call of Jehovah as did Jeremiah the prophet: "for thou shalt go to all that I shall send thee, and whatsoever I command thee thou shalt speak. Be not afraid of their faces: for I am with thee, saith the Lord", (Jer. 1 v.7-8).

Proclaiming Truth and Righteousness

Looking out over the past half-century it is a sad fact that true Biblical preachers, Church leaders and teachers in the true Scriptural sense have greatly diminished. Those called to preach, teach, and lead God's flock in truth and righteousness, are entrusted with proclaiming the Gospel of grace to unbelieving sinners, and to build up the saints to maturity ----- "unto the measure of the stature of the fullness of Christ", (Eph. 4 v.13). The false teaching of the opponents of the Gospel and detractors of the faith in our day need to be counteracted by vigorous preaching, upholding, maintaining, and defending the truth of God's Word. To do so, we must show our confidence in God's power, commitment to God's truth, as dedicated preachers commissioned by Divine authority to do His will to the glory of God.

Today false preachers not only seek to gain power and influence through their "flattering words", but are also motivated by greed under "a cloke of covetousness", (1 Thess. 2 v.5). Our aim and object as true heralds of the Cross is to present and proclaim the truth of the Gospel in all its fullness to mankind, to the honour, praise, and glory of God. "Now unto Him that is able to do exceeding above all that we ask or think, according to the power that worketh in us, Unto Him be glory in the Church by Christ Jesus throughout all ages, world without end. Amen", (Eph. 3 v.20-21). May God give us that humility, tenacity and integrity to speak "the truth in love"

(Eph. 4 v.15) on the authority of the Word as commanded by Christ (Matt. 28 v.18-20), to Whom we shall "give account thereof in the Day of Judgement", (Matt 12 v.36).

To experience power in the pulpit we need to be motivated by the fear of the Lord, devotion to Christ, love for the truth of God's Word, and fired by the Spirit. Our passion for the souls of men must be such that we are willing to communicate the fullness of the truth of the Gospel with heartfelt compassion, which they do not relish, but which is for their eternal salvation and well-being, to the glory of God.

By showing compassion for the lost and a desire to build up the people of God in the faith, the Prince of Darkness will endeavour to distract us and have us running here and there doing a thousand good little things in order to keep us from doing the two most important works ----- "prayer, and the ministry of the Word", (Acts 6 v.4). In the midst of all the business of a preacher's life, those who hold a high view of Scripture are often tempted and mistakenly think they do not need to do the diligent work of preparation. So they just throw out the message 'ad libitum' to the people in whatever shape or form it first comes to them, without any careful thought or deep study of the Word, (2 Tim. 2 v.15).

Too many preachers are caught in the vicious circle of last-minute sermon preparation, and worse still, many yield to the temptation of drawing down sermons from the internet. Such a habit and preoccupation with other things not only wastes talents and brings tension, but is destructive in all sorts of ways and harms the people of God. Our personalities, as we preach, ought to adorn the truth rather than obscure it. Because sermons are ill-prepared, much of the energy is spent on worry rather than on the message itself. It is necessary to get to work early in preparation and be guided as the Spirit enables us to do it well. Each day will add more input and energy to the message and people will notice the difference, freshness, and appeal of the sermon. The ministry of preaching is a trust, and those who are appointed and called by God are charged to "preach the

Word", (2 Tim. 4 v.2). God "hath in due times manifested His Word through preaching, which is committed unto me", says Paul, "according to the commandment of God our Saviour", (Titus 1 v.3).

Shallow, shoddy, and half-hearted preaching produces no lasting fruit or benefit to the hearers. It only serves to bore people with the Bible. Inspiring preaching is the need of the hour in the Church, and we must not allow ourselves to be side-tracked in that noble and worthy duty. Only by God's grace and the reviving power of the Spirit can real enthusiasm and effectiveness in preaching be restored unto us. Let us then enter the pulpit each time having had a fresh encounter with Christ Who has promised to equip us and never leave or forsake us along the journey. (Matt. 28 v.19-20).

Many contemporary preachers are appallingly weak and woefully lacking in an effective and powerful preaching ministry. Failure in the place of prayer, preparation, and the meditation and study of God's Word means disaster, not only in the life of the preacher, but also in the congregation as well. There is the problem, too, that some men seek the status and position of a minister, pastor, preacher, who are not called and equipped with the requisite gifts for a teaching and preaching ministry. Such men are a stumbling-block to the people and a hindrance in the advancement of Christ's Kingdom, and they should leave and find some other form of useful employment. Is it any wonder then that much of the preaching today is greatly lacking in substantive Biblical content and deeply defective in solid doctrinal teaching. Sermons that are not ringed with Divine truth are powerless and useless. The so-called 'address' is dull and boring with no sense of urgency or earnestness to impel sinners to seek refuge in Christ or instruction in godliness and holiness. When the Word of God is not being conveyed to the hearers in the pew, they go away unmoved, and their minds and spirits remain unchallenged in the truth of Holy Scripture.

The Whole Gospel for the Whole World

It is no light matter to preach "the Gospel of God", (Rom 1 v.1). The Apostle Paul was ready to preach the whole Gospel to the whole world, to wise people, ordinary people, religious people, to everybody everywhere, wherever in providence God placed him. His Epistle to the Romans is the best treatment of the whole Gospel in all of Scripture. "I am ready", he says, "to preach the Gospel to you that are at Rome also. For I am not ashamed of the Gospel of Christ: for it is the power of God unto salvation to everyone that believeth; to the Jew first, and also to the Greek. For therein is the righteousness of God revealed from faith to faith: as it is written, The just shall live by faith", (Rom.1 v. 15-17). These three verses, in short, sum up the heart of true Biblical religion.

The whole world needs the Gospel, and the Gospel it needs is the whole Gospel of God's grace to sinners through the atoning death of the Lord Jesus Christ. Men and women in themselves are not right with God. When the first man, Adam, sinned, in the Garden of Eden (Gen. 3), the whole human race, except Christ, fell with Him in his first transgression, which corrupted our whole nature, commonly called Original Sin. By nature we are in rebellion against God and because of our own evil hearts we are in captivity and bondage to sin. We are polluted and totally depraved with a positive inclination to do wrong. "We are all as an unclean thing, and all our righteousnesses are as filthy rags" (Isaiah 64 v.6) in God's sight. "For all have sinned, and come short of the glory of God", (Rom. 3 v.23). "All we like sheep have gone astray; we have turned every one to his own way", (Isaiah 53 v.6). The Scripture declares, "There is none righteous, no, not one", (Rom 3 v.10).

Contemporary preachers shy away from the doctrine of the utter ruin of mankind at the Fall. We read in Romans 1 v.18-3 and 20 where the Apostle Paul is writing by the inspiration of the Holy Spirit, and these verses very specifically give us God's description of the total depravity of the human race. The end of fallen man is death, not only physical death, but spiritual death, which is the death of the soul and spirit in hell. Death means separation, not only separation of the soul and spirit from the body, but separation of the soul and spirit from God for all eternity. "The way of peace have they not known: There is no fear of God before their eyes", (Rom. 3 v.17-18). All are "guilty before God" (Rom. 3 v.19) and "sold under sin" (Rom. 7 v.14).

Man cannot be justified before God by good works. "Therefore by the deeds of the law there shall no flesh be justified in His sight: for by the law is the knowledge of sin", (Rom. 3 v.20). Yet we must all appear before the Judgment Seat at the Last Day, from which there is no escape (Rom. 2 v.3). "We are sure that the Judgment of God is according to truth against" (Rom. 2 v.2) the ungodly, the unrighteous, and the wicked. "The natural man receiveth not the things of the Spirit of God: for they are foolishness unto him: neither can he know them, because they are spiritually discerned", (1 Cor. 2 v.14). Sinful man has no defence, he cannot save himself, nor can he of himself approach unto a holy God. His only saving answer is to plead for mercy and forgiveness through the shed blood of the Lord Jesus Christ. "Christ died for the ungodly", (Rom. 5 v.6).

It is important therefore to set our minds to the serious study of Christian doctrine and apply rigorous Christian principles to evangelism, worship, discipline, Church government, and our own personal belief and witness. Many modern preachers today are sceptical and cynical in regard to the great doctrines of grace, and are greatly lacking in the tenets of the Christian faith with an inferior understanding of the Biblical reasons for believing in the Deity of Christ, life after death, and many of the other great truths of Scripture. "Christ died for our sins ----- was buried ----- and rose again the third day according to the Scriptures", (1 Cor. 15 v.3-4). In God's great plan to redeem fallen man, all our sins were laid upon Christ, the Sinless One, and willingly He bore the punishment for our iniquity, in our stead, on the Cross of Calvary.

The 'lovey-dovey gospel-preaching' of many in our day is far removed from the truth of the Word of God. The Scriptures show the enormity of the plight of fallen man in a dead and desperate state of sin: "by nature the children of wrath", (Eph. 2 v.1-3). He needs to be saved (Acts 4 v.12), or he must perish (John 3 v.3). Being totally depraved and dead in sins, man cannot do a single thing to effect his own salvation (Eph. 2 v.9). "Not by works of righteousness which we have done, but according to His mercy He saved us, by the washing of regeneration, and renewing of the Holy Ghost", (Titus 3 v.5).

We must pray for "the sound of a going in the tops of the mulberry trees" (2 Sam. 5 v.24; 1 Chron. 14.15), as we confidently commit ourselves and our cause to Him Who "searcheth all hearts" (1 Chron. 28 v.9) and "judgeth righteously" (1 Peter 2 v.23). With the Psalmist our prayer should be, "Arise, O God, plead Thine own cause", (Psalm 74 v.22). May we keep our eye fixed upon our Sovereign Lord, for "Thou shalt arise, and have mercy upon Zion: for the time to favour her, yea, the set time, is come", (Psalm 102 v.13). By His grace, may there arise a thorough revival in preaching that is faithful to the Word of God and to the whole of His revealed counsel. May God's hand of power be increasingly manifested so that we may experience "times of refreshing from the presence of the Lord", (Acts 3 v.19). "When the Lord shall build up Zion, He shall appear in His glory", (Psalm 102 v.16).

The Uniqueness of True Christianity

Preaching on the atonement and the provision which God in His sovereignty and mercy has made for the salvation of man is strikingly manifold and exhibits the superabundance of His goodness, wisdom, love and grace." "For God so loved the world, that He gave His only begotten Son, that whosoever believeth in Him should not perish but have everlasting life", (John 3 v.16). Christ "gave Himself a ransom for all" (1 Tim. 2 v.6), "that He might redeem us from all iniquity" (Titus 2 v.14), to secure complete deliverance, that God, through the Person and Work of His Son, and by the operation of the Holy Spirit, gives to His elect people. Our redemption was purchased at tremendous cost, so that we might go at last to heaven, saved by His precious blood. "Forasmuch as ye know ye were not redeemed with corruptible things, as silver and gold, from your vain conversation received by tradition from your fathers; But with the precious blood of Christ, as of a lamb without blemish and without spot: Who verily was foreordained before the foundation of the world, but was manifest in these last times for you, Who by Him do believe in God, that raised Him from the dead, and gave Him glory; that your faith and hope might be in God", (1 Peter 1 v.18-21).

Our concern for a dying Church is that God may hear our prayers of repentance and faith to raise up preachers of the Word of God in the power of the Holy Spirit that will regenerate, reform, and revive its impoverished adherents to the truth of the Gospel. Because of sin, rebellion, and disobedience, the showers of blessing have been withholden, "and there hath been no latter rain", (Jer. 3 v.3). "Turn, O backsliding children, saith the Lord; for I am married to you ----- And I will give you pastors according to Mine heart, which shall feed you with knowledge and understanding", (Jer. 3 v.14-15).

Sinners are dying every day, having no hope, and without God in the world", (Eph. 2 v.12). Few there are to warn them and to tell them the Good News of the "Everlasting Covenant, ordered in all things, and sure", (2 Sam. 23 v.5). Lost souls need to be made aware by the preaching of the Word, that when we die we will be judged by a Holy God. The natural man still in that state of sin and rebellion will be banished from His presence to hell forever. In an age of shallow teaching, men and women, boys and girls, are left confused and bewildered, and need to be taught the precious truths and fundamental principles of the Gospel. They need to be awakened by the convicting power of the Holy Spirit to their need of salvation in Christ, and be enabled by the grace of God to live out these truths to the glory of God. "Whatsoever ye do in word or deed, do all in the name of

101

the Lord Jesus, giving thanks to God and the Father by Him", (Col. 3v.17).

Humanly speaking there is no hope and nothing can be done by man to rescue the sinner from the bondage of sin. The only remedy for man's redemption and deliverance from the penalty of sin is clearly set out by the Apostle Paul in the Epistle to the Romans. There we read how God has done precisely what needs to be done. He has provided a Divine gift, on the ground of Christ's righteousness, and imputed to believers (Rom. 3 v.21-26). By His perfect obedience and vicarious atonement, Christ paid the debt of the believer's sin, satisfied Divine justice on our behalf, and thereby renders it possible for God to be just and to justify the sinner (Rom. 5 v.1-2; 1 Peter 3 v.18). This Divine gift is received, not by doing good deeds and works (Rom. 3 v.28) which we can never achieve, but by simple faith (Eph. 2 v.8). It is received by believing what God tells us in His Word. "The Word of the Lord endureth for ever. And this is the Word which by the Gospel is preached unto you", (1 Peter 1 v.25).

How vital, then, it is that we should preach the Word of God clearly and faithfully. The discrepancies, differences, and falsehoods within the vast range of our contemporary preaching issue from Satan, who, "as a roaring lion, walketh about, seeking whom he may devour", (1 Peter 5 v.8). With unspeakable malignity toward God and men, the devil amasses a host of willing agents to advance his evil activities and deception to distort the truth: "And no marvel; for Satan himself is transformed into an angel of light", (2 Cor. 11 v.14).

The Good News of the Gospel is when we, who are by nature hell-deserving sinners, have been made alive to inherit eternal life by God through the Everlasting Covenant ----- turn from our sin, and turn from our own attempts at self-righteousness, which can only condemn us ----- and embrace the Lord Jesus Christ by saving faith as our Lord and Saviour, God declares all our sins to have been punished in Christ and imputes His righteousness to our account. This righteousness is by the grace of God alone through faith alone in Christ alone, which comes to us only by the operation of the Holy Spirit in the hearts and lives of His elect people. By believing and trusting God in regard to the Person and Work of the Lord Jesus Christ as revealed in Holy Scripture, is the only way anyone can be saved. This emphasis underlines the utter uniqueness of Christianity in this fundamental matter. It is at this very point that the crisis in our contemporary preaching arises, and which falsely teaches a human way to achieve eternity, and a man-made ladder to bliss and happiness. It is, as Paul wrote to the Ephesians, "Not of works, lest any man should boast", (Eph. 2 v.9).

It is not popular today to proclaim a Biblical message and to tell men they are lost sinners by nature. Robert Murray McCheyne (1813-1843), the celebrated Scottish preacher and evangelist, said, "The man who loves you most is the man who tells you the most truth about yourself". We too need to follow the example of Paul who rebuked the people of Corinth for the sin and scandal that was found among them, and the great grief they had caused to others. "For though I made you sorry with a letter", he writes, "I do not repent, though I did repent: for I perceive that the same Epistle hath made you sorry, though it were but for a season. Now I rejoice, not that ye were made sorry, but that ye sorrowed to repentance: for ye were made sorry after a godly manner . . . . for godly sorrow worketh repentance to salvation", (2 Cor. 7 v.8-10). Men do not like the truth, yet the Apostle did not neglect his duty to them. "I will very gladly spend and be spent for you; though the more abundantly I love you, the less I be loved", (2 Cor. 12 v.15).

Sadly, contemporary preachers lack conviction of the power and truth of the Gospel and are not able, and not willing to be forthright, straitforward and fearless in their preaching of the Word for fear of offending people or wounding their feelings and self-esteem. As a consequence such preaching is hugely faulty and deficient. It is marked by glaring defects and falsehood, lacking in Biblical content, and dishonourable to the Lord. "With lies ye have made the heart of the righteous sad", saith the Lord, "and strengthened the hands of the wicked", (Ezek. 13 v.22). Furthermore, the doctrinal content is so weak and warped that they fail completely to proclaim "all the counsel of God", (Acts 20 v.27).

Scripture that is exegetically mistreated, textually mishandled, and falsely proclaimed, are ploys of Satan to mislead so that souls may perish in hell for evermore. With little or no application of any Biblical truth, sinners remain "dead in trespasses and sins" (Eph. 2 v.1) and continue to walk in darkness "according to the prince of the course of this world, according to the prince of the power of the air, the spirit that now worketh in the children of disobedience", (Eph. 2 v.2).

Servants of God and Shepherds of the Flock

Many of the preachers today fall very far short of the truth according to the Word of God, and fail miserably to emphasis the necessity and nature of repentance and faith. There is no teaching of the Biblical doctrine of man's utter inability to achieve salvation from sin apart from the direct intervention of the sovereign work of God. So intense and earnest was Paul's preaching, and his passion and concern for the lost, that he cried out, "woe is unto me, if I preach not the Gospel", (1Cor. 9 v.16). His fervency and zeal for preaching the Gospel compelled him to make his preparation of it thorough and complete. His presentation of truth was never shallow, shoddy or partial, but detailed, exhaustive and comprehensive. "And how I kept back nothing that was profitable unto you, but have shewed you, and have taught you publicly, and from house to house, Testifying both to the Jews, and also to the Greeks, repentance toward God, and faith toward our Lord Jesus Christ", (Acts 20 v.20-21). A Biblically-sound Gospel address and presentation must contain these two elements ----- repentance toward God, and faith in our Lord Jesus Christ. (2 Peter 3 v.9; Phil. 3 v.9).

The true preacher of the Word will see himself as a servant of God, as a shepherd feeding the household of faith, and as a herald of Christ announcing to sinners the Good News of salvation. In Acts 26, we read how the Jews were zealous to persecute Paul, even plotting to kill him, and the Apostle in making his own defence before king Agrippa has this to say, "I was not disobedient unto the heavenly vision: But shewed first unto them of Damascus, and at Jerusalem, and throughout all the coasts of Judaea, and then to the Gentiles, that they should repent and turn to God, and do works meet for repentance", (Acts 26 v.19-20). Preaching in this manner largely no longer prevails in our Churches today.

The duty, the nature, and the fruits of true Biblical preaching as that of "repentance toward God, and faith toward our Lord Jesus Christ" (Acts 20 v.21) are not spelled out before our people. Because of this neglect and failure in preaching, the people do not see, yet alone be convicted and convinced, of the need and necessity to repent, and to put their trust in Christ. When Jesus began His public ministry, His message was urgent: "The time is fulfilled and the Kingdom of God is at hand: repent ye, and believe the Gospel", (Mark 1 v.15). The apostles preached the same message with the same urgency. "And they went out, and preached that men should repent", (Mark 6 v.12). On the day of Pentecost, Peter, "standing up with the eleven", urged "pricked" hearts to "repent, and be baptized every one of you in the name of Jesus Christ for the remission of sins", (Acts 2 v.14,37-38). The only account of our Lord's Great Commission which records the doctrinal content of the message to be preached, is Luke 24 v.46-47. Here Christ insisted "that repentance and remission of sins should be preached in His name, among all nations, beginning at Jerusalem".

The gravity of the crisis in contemporary preaching is compounded, intensified, and made worse by the increasing failure to expound and apply the whole Gospel to the whole man. Preaching in the full Biblical sense of the term is no longer the norm in today's Church. The great body of truth based on the authority and veracity of Holy Scripture as handed down to us by the Reformers and Covenanters is forsaken, abandoned and deemed irrelevant. Modern so-called preachers think they must overhaul the principal requirements made to mankind, and there is little doubt the rich young ruler, that we read of in Mark 10, would have received today's 'version' of the 'gospel' joyfully. Without the requirement of repentance he would have accepted the free gift of eternal life 'with no strings attached'. These are the kind of people that largely populate the Church in our time, still in their sin and peddling a different 'gospel' for the twenty-first century. No wonder the Church is ineffective in the world at large. It is time to re-establish the true content of the Gospel and the necessity of preaching the truth Christ delivered to His disciples. We must rise by the grace of God above a deadening Church, and "earnestly content for the faith which was once delivered unto the saints" (Jude v.3), to His glory.

The Biblical Teaching of the Great Reformation

These are not good days for the Church and the more we evaluate our contemporary preaching, the more we find that Biblical theology and practice have been surrendered to pursue instead worldly wisdom, worldly doctrines, and worldly methods. Whenever the core principles of the Great Reformation statement are set aside ----- by Scripture alone, by Christ alone, by the Cross alone, by Grace alone, by Faith alone, and for the Glory of God alone ----- we do not have a true Church. Having ceased to be committed to a Biblical Gospel in all its totality, and compromised the essential truths of the Word of God, the Church at large has lost the power and the reality of Holy Scripture: "the Word of the truth of the Gospel", (Col. 1 v.5).

It is imperative that we recognise the seriousness of the ongoing decline and crisis in the Church, and that we understand the urgency of the call to rediscover the true meaning and message of the Gospel of grace. Only as we recover the Reformation principles that shook the world in the Sixteenth Century can the Church again be reformed and revived. We must pray for its survival, and by repenting of its rampant worldliness, let us return to God, and summit to His truth. By the quickening power of the Word (Psalm 119 v.25,50,107,154) may we experience that strength and courage from on High to live out the teaching of the Gospel in every area of life. May the Holy Spirit enable us to confess the truth of Holy Scripture as did the Reformers, Covenanters, Puritans, and other Heroes of the faith, and see that truth embodied in doctrine, worship, discipline, life and witness of the Church to the glory of God.

Our forefathers were faithful preachers of the Word, who ably set forth the Biblical concept that faith, saving faith, involved trust, commitment, involving the whole man to the whole Christ as Prophet, Priest, and King, as He is freely offered to us in the Gospel. The unBiblical pattern that today's preachers adopt needs to be weeded out and purged by the clear teaching of the whole Gospel to the whole man. Upon the testimony of Christ we may safely depend, "Who is the faithful witness, and the first begotten of the dead, and the prince of the kings of the earth. Unto Him that loved us, and washed us from our sins in His Own blood, and hath made us kings and priests unto God and His Father; to Him be glory and dominion for ever and ever, Amen", (Rev. 1 v.5-6).

In order to reform what is amiss in today's Church, it is important as a first step that obstinate preachers, blind leaders of the blind (Matt. 15 v.4; Luke 6 v.39), who "outwardly appear righteous unto men, but within ye are full of hypocrisy and iniquity" (Matt. 23 v.28), should be admonished, disciplined, and the impenitent removed from office. "Examine yourselves, whether ye be in the faith; prove your own selves", (2 Cor.13 v.5). It is the duty of all who call themselves Christians, especially Christian preachers, to examine themselves concerning their spiritual state. "Know ye not your own selves, how that Jesus Christ is in you, except ye be reprobates?" (2 Cor.13 v.5).

Sinful presumption is a deadly sin and will damn a preacher however polished and skilled he may think himself to be in modern philosophy and higher education. But the distinguishing traits of a true servant of

God will come forth in an experimental way that will bear the marks of genuine Christian faith as opposed to false belief. The substitution of pragmatism and humanism for truth and righteousness is a major problem in the onslaught of the modern age. "Thou believest that there is one God; thou doest well: the devils also believe, and tremble. But wilt thou know, O vain man, that faith without works is dead"? (James 2 v.19-20).

Christian leaders in God's house must not fail to exercise proper duty and discipline, weighty responsibility though that be, to tell false preachers that if they are not hearing the Saviour calling, and if they are not following the Master as true disciples of Jesus Christ and walking in obedience to His Word, they have no grounds to claim that they are His servants. It is rank hypocrisy to claim to have communion with God, pretending to be ministers of the Gospel, and all the while not pilgrims of Christ and ignorant of the way heavenward. "Why call ye Me, Lord, Lord, and do not the things which I say?" (Luke 6 v.46).

Early New Testament Church Theology

The theology of the early New Testament Church represents the whole of the Scriptures as being covered by two covenants. When God created Adam, He entered into a COVENANT OF LIFE with him, upon condition of his perfect obedience. The penalty of disobedience was death. "And the Lord God commanded the man, saying, Of every tree of the garden thou mayest freely eat: But of the tree of the knowledge of good and evil, thou shalt not eat of it: for in the day that thou eatest thereof thou shalt surely die", (Gen.2 v.16-17). By Adam's sin, the whole human race is lost, "for the wages of sin is death", (Rom. 6 v.23).

It is of God's mercy and power alone that there is a way of escape for sinful men in the COVENANT OF GRACE which was made from all eternity, and put into operation at the Fall of man to bring salvation and deliverance from sin and its penalty. The first promise of the Gospel is given by God in Gen. 3 v.15: "And I will put enmity between thee and the women, and between thy seed and her seed; it shall bruise thy head, and thou shalt bruise his heel". This was to result in the bruising of Jesus Christ by the crushing and defeat of Satan and his power. We know how the bruising of the Lord Jesus Christ took place. It happened at the Cross, and it included the hatred of the religious leaders, the mocking of the crowds, the beatings, and eventually the cruel hanging on a wooden Cross with its great suffering and agony. It was a bruising of vengeance, but not of defeat, for on the third day Christ rose again triumphantly from the tomb: "Who hath abolished death, and hath brought life and immortality to light through the Gospel", (2 Tim. 1 v.10).

We are commissioned "to preach Christ crucified", (1 Cor. 1 v.23). The crucial point here is that it is the crucified Christ alone Who draws human beings. "And I, if I be lifted up from the earth, will draw all men unto Me", (John 12 v.32). This is an encouragement for us to lift up Christ in our preaching, and it is always a shame when any preacher allows anything else to take the primary place in his preaching. Jesus is the blessed Son of God Who became flesh in His incarnation by assuming human nature. "And the Word (that is Christ) was made flesh, and dwelt among us, and we beheld His glory, the glory as of the only begotten of the Father, full of grace and truth", (John 1 v.14). He lived a sinless life of perfect obedience in this world, and died for His elect, to purchase our redemption "that He might bring us to God", (1 Peter 3 v.18).

As the Scriptures declare, it is the Christ of Calvary Who draws all men unto the Father, the Christ Whose blood was shed and Whose body was broken, (1 Cor. 11 v.24). It is the Christ Who gave Himself as a ransom (1 Tim. 2 v.6), in the place of sinners so that He might bear in Himself the proper and just wrath of God for His people. He "was delivered for our offences", was buried, "and was raised again for our justification", (Rom. 4 v.25). Contemporary preachers fail to preach such a Gospel message, ever wallowing with great indulgence in their liberalism, socialism and modernism which do not draw. Only the crucified Christ draws men and women, boys and girls, to the realisation that "Man's chief end is to glorify God, and to enjoy Him for ever", (W.S.C. No1). "All that the Father giveth Me shall come to Me; and him that cometh to Me I will in no wise cast out", (John 6 v.37). In His great love, mercy, and grace, the atonement is God's answer to human sin, and by grasping something of the depth of our depravity and guilt, we shall readily appreciate God's provision in the blood of His Son, Jesus Christ, the Saviour we need. It is the responsibility and blessedness of every true preacher to hold tenaciously to the declaration that the Lord Jesus Christ is "the way, the truth, and the life: no man cometh unto the Father, but by Me", (John 14 v.6).

What a glorious Gospel we have to proclaim!! Christ died to redeem us from sin, and give us eternal life, for "as many as are led by the Spirit of God, they are the sons of God", (Rom. 8 v.14). We become partakers of so great salvation by the effectual working of God's Spirit in our hearts, uniting us to Christ by faith. Faith in Christ means trust in Christ, bringing about union with Him (1 Cor. 12 v.3), and always comes savingly to the sinner through the Word of God (1Cor. 1 v.23-24). "And when the Gentiles heard this, they were glad, and glorified the Word of the Lord: and as many as were ordained to eternal life believed", (Acts 13 v.48).

The Central Issues of the Gospel

Contemporary preachers tell us that in the Bible there are deficiencies of theology and low morality, and that it contains sub-Christian teaching. In reply to the detractors of the Word and false leaders of our day, we would answer in the words of Jesus, "the Scripture cannot be broken", (John 10 v.35). Modern preachers would have us disregard the great central issues of the Gospel for the sake of unity at the expense of truth, thus compromising the teaching of Scripture. When challenged, may God give us grace to stand up

and declare Biblical truth as faithful "servants of Jesus Christ -----
separated unto the Gospel of God", (Rom. 1 v.1). Because of our love
for God, love for the Gospel, and love for the Church, it is better to be
divided by truth than united in error and false doctrine. As Martin
Luther declared, we need a conscience that is bound to the Word of
God. We must be committed to the sufficiency and authority of
Scripture. Let us, therefore, pray that it may please the Lord yet again
to reform and revive the Church, and raise up true preachers and
pastors to expound the Word and shepherd the flock. "Preach the
Word; be instant in season, out of season; reprove, rebuke, exhort with
all longsuffering and doctrine", (2 Tim. 2 v.2).

The Scripture does not say that Christ will draw men and women,
boys and girls, to a visible Church, or to a particular denomination, or
movement. It is possible that He may bless these endeavours, raise up
leaders and preachers for them, but the promise is only that He will
draw them to Himself. "And I, if I be lifted up from the earth, will
draw all men unto Me", (John 12 v.32). As servants of Christ, called
by God, and committed to His Word, we are to lead others to Him, not
drive them, but love them for Christ's sake and draw them through the
power of the Gospel. We must ever learn as we seek to preach the
Word that it is Christ Who draws, and Who liberates from the
bondage of sin and an evil conscience. We must lift Him up and
present Him to the people as the Saviour of the world. "And as Moses
lifted up the serpent in the wilderness, even so must the Son of man be
lifted up: That whosoever believeth in Him should not perish, but
have eternal life", (John 3 v.14-15).

"Preach the Word" (2 Tim. 4 v.2), "preach Christ crucified"
(1 Cor. 1 v.23), preach the Christ Who died for sinners (Rom. 5 v.6,8)
"the Just for the unjust, that He might bring us to God",
(1 Peter 3 v.18). In our preaching we must press forth the central
issues of the Gospel as set out by the Apostle John in his Epistles.
He also wrote the Gospel of John, and the book of the Revelation
which have blessed the hearts of God's people throughout the
centuries. In his writings we find him presenting the evidence that

Jesus Christ is God. He expresses in a profound way the doctrines of the sovereignty and grace of God, which greatly encourages every true preacher in the service of Jesus of Nazareth, the Son of God, our Lord and Saviour.

"In the beginning was the Word"; in the Greek New Testament; the "Word" here is "Logos", "and the Word was God ----- And the Word was made flesh, and dwelt among us, and we beheld His glory, the glory as of the only begotten of the Father, full of grace and truth", (John 1 v.1,14). The incarnation of Christ is a great and mighty truth which is of fundamental importance to the preaching of the Gospel. Great indeed is the mystery of the Divine plan that Christ the Lord, "the King of glory" (Psalm 24 v.7-10), Who became man, could also love us enough to go to the Cross and die for us personally. Such was the love of the Son of God that He became the Son of man, to die for the sins of men, to save the sons of men, and to make them the sons of God. He is "the bread of life" (John 6 v.48) that satisfies all our hunger, and the "living water" (John 7 v.38) that quenches our deepest thirst. "I am the bread of life", said Jesus, "he that cometh to Me shall never hunger; and he that believeth on Me shall never thirst", (John 6 v.35).

In all of John's writings we have a powerful source of instruction that has benefited and comforted God's people down through the ages to the present time. But in his Epistles, John urgently addresses his readers, who like those to whom the Apostle Peter wrote, were facing the heresy and corrupt teaching of false preachers. He wrote to refute the false beliefs and to explain the marks of those who truly know and believe the truth of God. "These things have I written unto you that believe on the name of the Son of God; that ye may know that ye have eternal life, and that ye may believe on the name of the Son of God", (1 John 5 v.13).

In these three Epistles, John, the beloved disciple, was profoundly concerned about his people, and keeps exhorting and addressing his readers as his "little children", (1 John 2 v.1,12,13,28; 3 v.7,18; 4 v.4;

5 v.21). We, too, need to show that same compassion for souls and warn our hearers:

(1)   that sin does indeed interfere with our fellowship with God (1 John 1 v.5-6);

(2)   that sin resides in our nature (1 John 1 v.8-10); and

(3)   that the Scripture assures us of God's readiness to forgive and pardon sin (1 John 1 v.7).

"My little children, these things write I unto you, that ye sin not. And if any man sin, we have an Advocate with the Father, Jesus Christ the righteous: And He is the propitiation for our sins: and not for ours only, but also for the sins of the whole world. And hereby we do know that we know Him, if we keep His commandments", (1 John 2 v.1-3).

The Apostle emphases that the marks of true faith in Jesus Christ will be evident:

(1)   by our belief (1 John 2,v.18-27; 4 v.1-6,13-21);

(2)   by our obedience (1 John 2 v.3-6,28-29; 3 v.1-10; 4 v.21; 5 v.1-5);

(3)   by our love (1 John 2 v.7-11; 3 v.11-18; 4 v.7-12);

and the summary of these characteristics ----- faith, love, obedience ----- is presented in the opening verses of Chapter 5. The power of God is victoriously operative only in true believers, who persevere in Christian love and truth: "and this is the victory that overcometh the world, even our faith", (1 John 5 v.4).

The Apostle John, the servant of the Lord (Rev. 1 v.1) greatly highlights the theme of "walking in truth", (2 John v.4; 3 John v.3-4). It is not surprising that contemporary 'Christian' beliefs and behaviour of most 'Church' people and preachers is not much different from those of the world. God demands of us a complete surrender of ourselves to Himself and a radical obedience of His Word. "They that worship Him must worship Him in spirit and in truth", (John 4 v.24). We must never be ashamed of Christ and of His Gospel (Luke 9 v.26), and ever heed His call: "If any man will come after Me, let him deny himself, and take up his cross daily, and follow Me", (Luke 9 v.23).

If the light of the Gospel is not shining clearly, it is because of our disobedience to the truth. My God deliver us from coldness of heart and a mere satisfaction with the formula of orthodoxy. Only by the unction and anointing of the Holy Spirit upon our preaching shall we manifest that power, passion and performance when conviction strikes and the consciences of our hearers are wounded, so that they will truly enquire how to be in the faith, and walk in the faith, according to the standard of the Word of God.

Preaching all the Counsel of God

A return to Biblical exposition and application of Scripture truth is the dire need of the hour. Our Churches are swamped with all kinds of innovations, and it is imperative, therefore, that we deal honestly, truthfully, and faithfully in our preaching of the whole "counsel of God", (Acts 20 v.27). We must pray fervently, walk worthily, watch diligently, and obey "from the heart that form of doctrine which was delivered you", (Rom. 6 v.17).

In regard to the Church we have no right to be so broad and inclusive in our fellowship as to receive people and preachers who deny the Deity of Christ as He is presented in the Gospel. Such men weaken the testimony of the Church. As for the necessity of loyalty to truth, the Bible calls for separation from all who fail to fulfil the Scriptural responsibilities of fellowship in light, love, and truth. "Be ye not unequally yoked together with unbelievers: for what fellowship hath righteousness with unrighteousness? And what communion hath light with darkness? ----- Wherefore come out from among them, and be ye separate, saith the Lord, and touch not the unclean thing; and I will receive you, and will be a Father unto you, and ye shall be My sons and daughters, saith the Lord Almighty", (2 Cor. 6 v.14-18).

In the communication of Divine truth from our Church pulpits, Bible Colleges, and Theological Seminaries, it is of prime importance that certain characteristics are distinctive and evident both in the preacher and in the preaching. By the power of the Holy Ghost we must speak with the authority of Scripture in such urgency and earnestness that will command, not only the attention, but also arouse sinners out of their slumber because of the imminent danger of hell fire. They must hear the God-centred Gospel through the faithful labours of men, who, like Luther, Calvin, Knox, and others, gave their lives unstintingly to uphold, maintain, and defend Biblical truth; men, who, like Paul, when faced with error and false doctrine, give "place by subjection, no, not for an hour; that the truth of the Gospel might continue with you", (Gal. 2 v.5).

Ministers who pride themselves in fine elocution lessons and public recitals with polished accents and fine pronunciations will find little success in awakening men of their need of salvation or stir their souls into action. Most people today are out of touch with the Christian Gospel message. We must work and pray for Churches that are consistent for truth and godliness, that are intolerant of sin, false teachers and sceptical preachers within their ranks, and that walk humbly in the fear of God. "What doth the Lord require of thee, but to do justly, and to love mercy, and to walk humbly with thy God"? (Micah 6 v.8). A holy walk with God is the best evidence of genuine religion. We are to be prayerful, watchful, and obedient unto the Lord by conforming ourselves to His will according to His Word. Through the outpouring of the sovereign Spirit of God in reformation and revival, may we "adorn the doctrine of God our Saviour in all things ----- Teaching us that, denying ungodliness and worldly lusts, we should live soberly, righteously, and godly, in this present world", (Titus 2 v.10-12).

Genuine faith, love, and concern for the spread of Biblical truth must be maintained if we are to communicate the message of the Gospel effectively to needy men and women, boys and girls. As instruments in the hand of Almighty God, may He be pleased to use us as His true servants to do that which is "our duty to do", (Luke 17 v.10), to arrest the hearts and minds of sinners to the truth of God's Holy Word with conviction of the saving power of Christ in salvation. As we preach the infallible and inspired Word, and gain the attention of our listeners to the truth of Christ, God alone by His Holy Spirit can give the increase by planting the seed of the Gospel in the individual heart. "I have planted", says Paul, "Apollos watered; but God gave the increase. So then neither is he that planteth any thing, neither he that watereth; but God that giveth the increase", (1 Cor. 3v.6-7).

In our ministry of preaching and teaching, we must ever cry to God for grace and strength to do His will as we expound and apply the Word of Truth effectively and directly at all times. As we plead the mercy of God with sinners to draw them unto Himself, and urge the saints unto a life of obedience in Him, we must cause men to consider their ways and walk of life. The sinner must see his doomed state before a Holy God, and be convinced of how to find peace with his Creator. "Come now, and let us reason together, saith the Lord: though your sins be as scarlet, they shall be as white as snow; though they be red like crimson, they shall be as wool", (Isaiah 1 v.18).

As for many Christians today, they most need renewal and a fresh awareness of God's grace, presence and power. We must always come before Him in perpetual repentance and faith, feeding upon His Holy Word, if we are to be useful servants of the Lord Jesus Christ. Jude, "the servant of Jesus Christ" (v.1), addresses the "beloved" (v.3, 17,20), the believers, the saints, exhorting them that they "should earnestly contend for the faith which was once delivered unto the saints" (v.3). So also, in our day, being exposed to the dangers of false teaching and the rising tide of apostasy, it is necessary to warn and instruct the people of God that they be preserved in the crisis. The crisis in contemporary preaching is becoming more acute, and the Scriptures speak of compromise and "ungodly men" (Jude v.4), who have crept in among the saints, turned "the grace of God into lasciviousness" (v.3) and deny their Master and Lord. Having warned of these false preachers, Jude turns to exhortations and instructions (v.20-25) for the true saints and servants of God to learn more and more of what it is to characterise Christian teaching in their daily lives: "Building up yourselves on your most holy faith, praying in the Holy Ghost, Keep yourselves in the love of God, looking for the mercy of our Lord Jesus Christ unto eternal life", (Jude v.20-21).

True preachers have a duty towards themselves, to others, and to God Himself. Any occupation or truck with compromise, failure and sin, whether in apostates or in saints, can be soul-destroying and soul-withering, for it is both discouraging and depressing. Constant meditation on the Word of God and conscientious application of Scriptural truth to our behaviour and conduct will prove its effectiveness to edify. "As ye have therefore received Christ Jesus the Lord, so walk ye in Him: Rooted and built up in Him, and stabilised in the faith, as ye have been taught, abounding therein with thanksgiving", (Col. 2 v.7).

Holding on to Sound Doctrine and Godly Practise

We need to pray that God will preserve and protect us from haughty, independent and presumptuous preachers who would cause us to stumble and fall away from the faith. May our prayer be that of the Psalmist: "I have trusted also in the Lord; therefore I shall not slide", (Psalm 26 v.1). Let us ever be on guard against erring brethren, seducers, false teachers and sceptical preachers, and pray that we shall endeavour by God's grace to hold tenaciously to sound doctrine and godly practice with fervent passion and persevering constancy in truth and holiness: "that the Word of God be not blasphemed", (Titus 2 v.5).

The Church at large today needs deliverance from contemporary preachers who adopt worldly arts and modern culture as their standard. May God enable us to receive, believe, obey and adhere to the authority of Holy Scripture, not upon the testimony of any mere man or Church, but wholly upon God, the Author of the Bible. "The Sword of the Spirit, which is the Word of God" (Eph. 6 v.17), the Bible, offers limitless resources and blessings to us. "Thy Word is truth", said Jesus, (John 17 v.17). The people today of our so-called modern world, look everywhere except to the Bible for answers to life. The source of all truth about God and man, life and death, time and eternity, men and women, right and wrong, heaven and hell, damnation and salvation, is God's own Word. "Blessed are they that hear the Word of God, and keep it", (Luke 11 v.28).

As we are entrusted by God and empowered by Holy Spirit to proclaim His Truth, may we do so in such a fashion as men will know and realise that we are preaching "weighty and powerful" (2 Cor. 2 v.10) things to them personally from the Scriptures. When weighed in the balances of God for our service, may we not be "found wanting", (Dan. 5 v.27). May the substance of what we preach be anchored solely on the authority of God's Word. May our presentation and manner in which we communicate Biblical truth be well-pleasing to the Lord.

The Word of God is so powerful and mighty, it transforms men from the realm of falsehood to that of truth, from the realm of darkness to that of light, and from the realm of sin and death to that of righteousness and life. Our only task really is to submit, wholeheartedly and unreservedly, to God's teaching in Holy Scripture by studying and proclaiming the Word of truth to all mankind with all sincerity and commitment, to the everlasting praise, honour, and glory of His great and holy name: "For the Word of God, and for the testimony of Jesus Christ", (Rev.1 v.9).

Let us then look to the Lord that He may grant us such grace, mercy, and power, that where any of the weaknesses, failures and deficiencies remarked upon in this book apply to us by way of reproof, rebuke, caution, correction, and exhortation, that we shall conform by the transforming grace of God to be more obedient preachers, more worthy servants that are enabled by the Spirit of God to "rightly divide the Word of truth" (2 Tim.2 v.15), and to communicate the Gospel of peace to a very needy world. (Gal. 2 v.2; Eph. 6 v.15).

The Westminster Divines rightly point out in the Shorter Catechism, "The Word of God, which is contained in the Scriptures of the Old and New Testaments, is the only rule to direct us how we may glorify and enjoy Him", (No. 2). It is essential for the Word of God to be known, loved, obeyed, and practised, if we are to win the battle against Satan. The more we know and understand Scripture, the more we will be able to understand the strongholds of Satan, "stand against the wiles of the devil" (Eph. 6 v.11), and lead people into the Kingdom of God. The effective preacher, teacher, must be ready as God leads, to "Preach the Word; be instant in season, out of season; reprove, rebuke, exhort with all longsuffering and doctrine", (2 Tim. 4 v.2).

A Deeper Knowledge of God

The crisis in contemporary preaching is merely symptomatic of the one thing above all else we most urgently need ----- a deeper knowledge of God, a more thorough understanding of His Word, and a more out-and-out preaching and teaching of Holy Scripture. There is a real danger today and a growing tendency to forget what the Reformers and Covenanters actually achieved in their time, and also a further tendency to presume that we have advanced so far these five centuries since the Reformation, that we can afford to forget them and their triumphs. The victory which these Heroes of the Faith gained was so complete, decisive and far-reaching, that we are in danger not only of failing to estimate it at its true worth, but also of surrendering the truth of God's Word to accommodate the 'modern-learned' man.

It should be remembered, however, that the liberties we enjoy today ----- political, civil, and religious ----- sprang from the Great Reformation of the sixteenth century movement. May the Spirit of the Lord stir up our hearts to a new devotion of the God of all grace, mercy, and love, so that by His power we may be enabled to hold forth the Banner of Scripture Truth, maintain and defend the tenets of the Christian Faith, and unashamedly seek to witness and pray for the advancement of Christ's Kingdom wherever Providence has placed us in this world.

Although feebly written, this book has a clear message, yet penetrating and profound, for our day, and by God's help may these words not fail to reach the heart of thoughtful preachers. We thank God for the preaching of the great men of the past, Moses, Daniel, John the Baptist, Augustine, Luther, Calvin, Knox, Rutherford, Edwards, Whitefield, and others, who subdued kingdoms, wrought righteousness, stopped the mouth of lions. May the power of Gospel truth show itself again in our day to build up the Church, to convince the gainsayers, and to gather precious lost souls within the fold of Christ, to the glory of God.

The preacher whose heart is right toward God according to His Word, must be "apt to teach" (1 Tim 3 v.2; 2 Tim 2 v.24), able to think, to arrange his thoughts, and to express them as a 'man of the Book', the true Book, the Bible; and whether his name finds a permanent place in the records of the Church below, or not, he will receive the Divine approval, "Well done, thou good and faithful servant", (Matt. 25 v.21).

"Preach the Word", (2 Tim. 4 v.2). It is imperative that all our preaching is based on clear Biblical warrant. As we preach the whole counsel of truth, we must ensure that all things necessary for God's glory, man's salvation, faith, and life, is expressly set down in

Scripture, or, clearly implied in His Word. The words of Andrew Bonar are very true, "It is one thing to bring truth from the Bible and another thing to bring it from God Himself, through the Bible." If we are to be true "ambassadors for Christ" (2 Cor. 5 v.20), it is only as we are "mighty in the Scriptures" that we can speak and teach "diligently the things of the Lord", and expound unto others "the way of the Lord more perfectly", (Acts 18 v.24-26).

The True Gospel of Christ

In Mark's Gospel we read how "Jesus came into Galilee, preaching the Gospel of the Kingdom of God", (Mark 1 v.14). The original New Testament Greek word for Gospel is:

(1)   EUAGGELION, which quite literally means "Good News". In Greek, the original language of the New Testament, its root meaning is, "to tell forth, to publish, to proclaim, to evangelise". It means "to declare" without compromise to all the world the Good News of salvation. It means to proclaim God's great plan of redemption from sin:

  (i)   that the enmity between God and man has been removed;

  (ii)   that Christ has paid the penalty for our sin;

  (iii)   that He has met God's requirement in full obedience on our behalf and by taking the punishment in our stead which we deserve;

  (iv)   that Divine justice has been fully and completely satisfied for the saving of His people eternally, "Herein is love, not that we loved God, but that He loved us, and sent His Son to be the precipitation for our sins", (John 4 v.10).

(2)   Another New Testament Greek word that describes the message of the Gospel is KERIGMA, meaning "the proclamation". This New Testament Greek word involves "the proclamation" of the whole life and work of the Lord Jesus Christ. To present Christ means to proclaim His eternal Deity; His Incarnation and Virgin Birth; His perfect and sinless humanity; His ministry upon earth; His substitutionary atonement and sacrificial death on the Cross as the one propitiatory and expiatory sacrifice for sin forever; His triumphant resurrection; His glorious ascension; His mediatorial reign; His continuing presence amongst His people in the Person of the Holy Spirit; His continual intercession at the Throne of God as the believer's Great High Priest and Advocate; His Crown Rights as King and Head of His Church and Lordship over all nations; His pre-eminence in all things; His visible and personal Return for His bride the Church in glory, and future judgment. All of these Biblical truths make up the KERIGMA, the proclamation as revealed in Holy Scripture, the precious "oracles of God", (1 Peter 4 v.11). The true preacher must unashamedly, emphatically, and faithfully proclaim all "the doctrine of God our Saviour in all things" (Titus 2 v.10) to mankind. The evils of materialism, humanism, naturalism, ecumenism, liberalism, Romanism, Islamism, and many other 'isms', are among the present-day tools that Satan uses to destroy the life and witness of the Church at this time. We are exhorted in the Book of Proverbs, "to buy the truth, and sell it not", "and meddle not with them that are given to change", (Prov. 23 v.23; 24 v.21).

(3)   Another New Testament Greek word for preaching is DIDACHE, and its translation means "the teaching". The great need in the Church today is for men approved and called of God, and equipped by God, "to expound" the

teaching of the doctrines of the "Everlasting Covenant, ordered in all things, and sure" (2 Sam. 23 v.5); so that all who are "born again" (John 3 v.3), might "grow in grace, and in the knowledge of our Lord and Saviour Jesus Christ" (2 Peter 3 v.18), and bear much fruit that will abide and remain, to the glory of God. "Teaching" in New Testament times meant, what it ought still to mean today. It means "to explain" the truths of the Everlasting Gospel; "to instruct" in the doctrines of grace; and "to expound" and "apply" the teaching of the Word of God to every day life and living. Scripture gives us a classic example of a teacher, Paul, teaching a teacher, Timothy, who, in turn, teaches other teachers, who then teach still other teachers. This is a continuing process in the promulgation of the Gospel from generation to generation. Paul, and the other Apostles, proclaimed the Gospel they had received from Christ to other faithful men, elders, deacons, and many other preachers, among whom was Timothy. It was now Timothy's turn to entrust the Gospel, and all other Divinely revealed truths, to others. "The things that thou hast heard of me among many witnesses, the same commit thou to faithful men, who shall be able to teach others also", (Tim. 2 v.2).

(4)   Before leaving this particular aspect of preaching, there is one other New Testament Greek word worthy of attention, PARAKLESIS, which is mostly translated to mean "exhortation". This is a most vital aspect of preaching. It carries with it the deep rooted idea of "beseeching, entreating, begging, exhorting, and at times consoling". Here we have the persuasive mood of preaching as portrayed in the New Testament:

(i)   "persuasion" to be drawn to the Saviour and be saved by His Grace. "For by grace are ye saved through faith; and that not of yourselves: it is the

123

gift of God: Not of works, lest any man should boast. For we are His workmanship", the Bible declares, "created in Christ Jesus unto good works", (and if those good works are not forthcoming, you are none of His), "which God hath before ordained that we should walk in them", (Eph. 2 v.8-10);

(ii)   "persuasion" to act upon the teaching of Holy Scripture and to live by it in the power of the Holy Spirit, so that God's believing children might demonstrate and "adorn the doctrine of God our Saviour in all things ----- Teaching us that, denying ungodliness and worldly lusts, we should live soberly, righteously, and godly, in this present world; Looking for that blessed hope, and the glorious appearing of the great God and our Saviour Jesus Christ", (Titus 2 v.10-13).

The Sincere Milk of the Word

Many contemporary preachers often pride themselves in the idea that they are great religious leaders when in fact they are not at all efficient in the handling of the Word of God. In the Epistle to the Hebrews the Holy Spirit explicitly says such men really are unqualified to teach. They do not understand the truths of the sovereign grace of God, and vast numbers of them do not know, or accept, what the Bible says. "For when for the time ye ought to be teachers, ye have need that one teach you again which be the first principles of the oracles of God; and are become such as have need of milk, and not of strong meat. For every one that useth milk is unskilful in the Word of righteousness: for he is a babe. But strong meat belongeth to them that are of full age, even those who by reason of use have their senses exercised to discern both good and evil", (Heb. 5 v.12-14). They may be 'advanced' students of Scripture for decades, and yet all the while they do not know Jesus Christ. They may 'preach' and 'teach', but it is not the pure Word of God that they teach.

Today's Christian Leaders need to articulate the great Biblical doctrines afresh rather than just adopt the theology of our culture. We must proclaim the truth of the Gospel of God in all its fullness forthrightly. We must not adopt the world's theology. We must not accept the theology of a worldly Church. Those who do, are not only disobedient disciples, but also are unfit servants, unfaithful preachers. If they continue not to accept and remain uncommitted to the whole truth of God's Word, their Churches will not prosper and will not be blessed.

In the Great Commission the word "all" occurs four times:

(i)   Jesus possesses "all" power, all authority;

(ii)   He sends us to teach "all" nations;

(iii)   We are to teach people "all" things He has commanded; and

(iv)   As we do so, we are to know that Jesus will be with us "always", "all" the days.

"All power", says Jesus, "is given unto Me in heaven and in earth. Go ye therefore, and teach all nations, baptising them in the name of the Father, and of the Son, and of the Holy Ghost: Teaching them to observe all things whatsoever I have commanded you: and, lo, I am with you alway, even unto the end of the world", (Matt. 28 v.18-20).

We are strictly commanded to preach and to teach people "to observe all things", which means that today's Church needs to recapture the entire counsel of God. In our very superficial age this seems to many to be but foolishness. Liberal preachers are trying to undercut the

Church's traditionally high view of the Bible, saying that it is not trustworthy, authoritative, or sufficient for dealing with today's challenges. The true proclamation, explanation, and application of Scriptural truths must always constitute the heart, soul and life of all genuine preaching. The Scriptures are the instrument by which men and women are born again, and they are also the "meat upon which to nurture that life. Such must Christians' desires be for "the sincere milk of the Word, that ye may grow thereby", (1Peter. 2 v.2). Strong desires and affections to the Word of God are a sure evidence of a person who is born again, and thus continues to grow and improve in wisdom and grace in the Christian life.

Preaching to the Crowd and to the Individual

True preachers of the Word must have a systematic theology, and they must preach sermons that are exegetically sound and thoroughly drenched in the Scriptures. C. H. Spurgeon has said, "Verbiage is too often the fig-leaf which does duty as a covering for theological ignorance". Preaching, when it is truly God-honouring, is distinctive and Biblical. Jay Adams says that what makes preaching distinctive "is the all-pervading presence of a saving and sanctifying Christ. Jesus Christ must be the heart of every sermon you preach. That is just as true of edificational preaching as it is of evangelistic preaching". The inspired and inerrant Word of God is the instrument of regeneration and sanctification, and only the preaching that is based solely on Scripture will be owned and blessed by God to build up His saints and convert sinners.

The faithful minister, pastor, or lay preacher, is commanded to preach, to herald forth, to proclaim publicly the Word of God, for it is only His Word that the Lord calls and commissions His preachers to proclaim. "Preach the Word; be instant in season, out of season; reprove, rebuke, exhort with all longsuffering and doctrine ----- But watch thou in all things, endure afflictions, do the work of an evangelist, make full proof of thy ministry", (2 Tim. 4 v.2 and 5).

(i)   Some of us are to preach to the crowd, like Philip the deacon of whom we read in Acts, Chapter 8. The preachers of the persecuted Church of the New Testament at Jerusalem "were all scattered abroad throughout the regions of Judaea and Samaria, except the apostles", (Acts 8 v.1). They "went every where preaching the Word" (Acts 8 v.4), and Philip we are told" went down to the city of Samaria, and preached Christ unto them", (Acts 8 v.5).

(ii)   Some of us are to preach to the individual, for we read again in Acts, Chapter 8 of the Ethiopian eunuch as he was returning from Jerusalem, reading Isaiah the prophet, that the Spirit of God spoke to Philip to draw near and join his chariot, and he "began at the same Scripture, and preached unto him Jesus", (Acts 8 v.35).

(iii)   And some of us are to preach to the crowd and to the individual. The Apostle Paul was truly a plain Christian evangelical preacher. He declares, "I kept back nothing that was profitable unto you, but have shewed you, and have taught you publickly, and from house to house, Testifying both to the Jews, and also to the Greeks, repentance toward God, and faith toward our Lord Jesus Christ", (Acts 20 v.20-21).

The word "preach" simply means "to tell thoroughly", whether it is to one person, to a group of persons, or to a large crowd of persons. The Lord Jesus Christ often had an audience with only one person. In John, Chapter 4, we have an excellent illustration of this, as He encounters the woman of Samaria. Christianity presents a two-fold revelation, first there is the revelation of God primarily in Jesus Christ, and second there is the revelation of ourselves. In this story of the Samaritan woman, Jesus revealed to her not only His Divinity and power to save, but also her need to face the truth by recognising her sin and depravity. "All have sinned, and come short of the glory of God", (Rom. 3 v.23). "There is therefore now no condemnation to them which are in Christ Jesus, who walk not after the flesh, but after the Spirit", (Rom. 8 v.1).

There are three great "musts" in John's Gospel, worthy of notice:

    (i)   "Ye must be born again", (John 3 v.7);

    (ii)   "Even so must the Son of man be lifted up", (John 3 v.14);

    (iii) "They that worship Him must worship Him in spirit and in truth", (John 4 v.24).

The necessity of these three great doctrines ----- the new birth, the death of Christ, and true worship ----- are the most essential elements of coming before God, for we can only approach unto Him through Christ, as He said to His disciples, "I am the way, the truth, and the life: no man cometh unto the Father, but by Me", (John 14 v.6).

There is no other way to come to God, only through Christ, the way He has established, not in any way of human devising. "But the hour cometh, and now is, when the true worshippers shall worship the Father in spirit and in truth: for the Father seeketh such to worship Him. God is a Spirit: and they that worship Him must worship Him in spirit and in truth", (John 4 v.23-24).

Some Other Aspects of Preaching

As preachers it is of the highest importance that we are Biblically clear in:

(1)   THE MESSAGE OF OUR PREACHING: "We preach Christ crucified" (Cor.1 v.23), "Christ in you, the hope of glory" (Col. 1 v.27). Christ is the substance of all preaching that is Divinely authentic, authoritative, and saving. It is when we preach Christ, that God is honoured, the Holy Spirit is active, the Word

is empowered, believers are edified, and lost sinners are saved and born again. To preach Christ is to set forth the Lord Jesus Christ in all the Beauty and Dignity of His glorious Person and in the all-sufficiency of His matchless work and grace, as a Living, Loving, and all-sufficient Saviour and Lord.

In Holy Scripture, Christ is variously described by many wonderful titles, "For it pleased the Father that in Him should all fulness dwell", (Col. 1 v.19). He is the eternally Divine Christ (Col. 2 v.9); the creating and sustaining Christ (Col. 1 v.16-17); the redeeming and forgiving Christ (Eph.1 v.7); the risen and exalted Christ (1 Cor. 15 v.20); the authoritative Pre-eminent Christ (Col. 1 v.18); the indwelling Christ (Col. 1 v.27); and the returning Christ "ordained of God to be the Judge of quick and dead", (Acts. 10 v.42). "Christ is all, and in all" (Col. 3 v.11), He is God, Creator, Saviour, and Head of the Church ----- "that in all things He might have the pre-eminence", (Col. 1 v.18).

(2) THE METHOD OF OUR PREACHING: "Whom we preach, warning every man, and teaching every man in all wisdom", (Col. 1 v.28).

(i) "Warning": means presenting all the facts and claims of Christ, proclaiming the message of the Gospel in all its fulness, and calling upon sinners to get right with God. "Now then we are ambassadors for Christ, as though God did beseech you by us: we pray you in Christ's stead, be ye reconciled to God", (2 Cor. 5 v.20).

(ii) "Teaching": means giving our people systematic instruction in the teaching of Scripture and the doctrines of grace, that they may "grow in grace, and in the knowledge of our Lord and Saviour Jesus Christ" (2 Peter 3 v.18) so as to develop and mature in the Christian faith and life, and become "strong in the Lord, and in the power of His might", (Eph. 6 v.10). There is an urgent need today for an effective teaching ministry to build up converts on their "most holy faith", (Jude v.20).

The method we are to adopt in preaching Christ is:

(i)   To present Him to sinners as their all-sufficient Saviour. "This is a faithful saying, and worthy of all acceptation, that Christ Jesus came into the world to save sinners", (1 Tim. 1 v.15); and

(ii)   To present Him to the saints as their all-sufficient Sanctifier and Lord. "As ye have therefore received Christ Jesus the Lord, so walk ye in Him: Rooted and built up in Him, and stablished in the faith, as ye have been taught, abounding therein with thanksgiving", (Col. 2 v.6-7). We must faithfully proclaim the whole "counsel of God", (Acts 20 v.27).

(3)   THE MOTIVE OF OUR PREACHING: the objective should be "that we may present every man perfect in Christ Jesus", (Col. 1 v.28). God has appointed a great Judgement Day which none shall escape: "for we shall all stand before the judgement seat of Christ" (Rom. 14 v.10; 2 Cor. 5 v. 10), at which "every one of us shall give account of himself to God", (Rom. 14 v.12). "It is appointed unto men once to die, but after this the Judgment", (Heb 9 v.27). We must therefore preach in the light of eternity:

(i)   To sinners, remembering that unless they are saved by grace through Christ alone as their Lord and Saviour, they "shall be cast into outer darkness" (Matt. 8 v.12; 22 v.13; 25 v.30) for evermore, where the lost shall be damned and turned into hell for all eternity (Rev. 20 v.15), and the everlasting Divine pronouncement will be the awful sentence, "Depart from Me, ye workers of iniquity" (Luke 13 v.27), "ye cursed, into everlasting fire, prepared for the devil and his angels", (Matt. 25 v.41).

(ii)   To the saints, remembering that they will appear at the Judgement Seat of Christ to give an account of their life of service for the Master. On that day, my Christian friends and fellow preachers, we will not be asked what kind of cars we drove, or the square footage of our houses, or details of the designer labels in our wardrobes, or the particular neighbourhoods in which we lived. Rather the call of God to all of us right here and now, is to glorify God, not self. Let us stop playing at Christianity, stop pretending Church; let us have done with hypocrisy, humbug, the mask, the veneer: "Be not deceived; God is not mocked: for whatsoever a man soweth, that shall he also reap", (Gal. 6 v.7).

Preaching is serious business, an awesome responsibility: "present every man perfect", (Col. 1 v.28). This means that the goal of the ministry is the maturity of the saints. Our aim as preachers is not merely to win people to Christ, but to bring them to spiritual maturity, to be more and more like Christ, by feeding upon the pure exposition of God's Word. True saving faith contains repentance and obedience, it is a redirection of the human will, a purposeful decision to forsake all unrighteousness and pursue righteousness instead. (Acts 11 v.18; 2 Tim. 2 v.25).

The faith that saves involves more than mere intellectual assent and emotional conviction. It also includes the resolution of the will to obey the commands and laws of God's Word. "All Scripture is given by inspiration of God, and is profitable for doctrine, for doctrine, reproof, for correction, for instruction in righteousness: That the man of God may be perfect, thoroughly furnished unto all good works", (2 Tim. 3 v.16-17). Obedience is the hallmark of the true believer, and as Martin Luther expresses the Biblical link between saving faith and good works thus, "Good works do not make a man good, but a good man does good works".

The faith, hope, and love that God grants to His people are inseparably linked, permanent, and will endure. God gives us, feeble though we are, the wonderful privilege and weighty responsibility of being His servants in proclaiming the Gospel of His grace and truth. May we be faithful messengers to share the Good News of Christ with sinners, and encourage believers in the Christian pathway as pilgrims to the Celestial City, giving thanks and praying always for them, as Paul did for the Colossians: "Since we heard of your FAITH in Christ Jesus, and of the LOVE which ye have to all the saints, For the HOPE which is laid up for you in heaven, whereof ye heard before in the Word of the truth of the Gospel; Which is come unto you, as it is in all the world and bringeth forth fruit, as it doth also in you, since the day ye heard of it, and knew the grace of God in truth ----- For this cause we also, since the day we heard it, do not cease to pray for you, and to desire that ye might be filled with the knowledge of His will in all wisdom and spiritual understanding; That ye might walk worthy of the Lord unto all pleasing, being fruitful in every good work., and increasing in the knowledge of God; Strengthened with all might, according to His glorious power, unto all patience and longsuffering with joyfulness", (Col. 1 v.4-6,9-11).

(4) THE MANNER OF OUR PREACHING: "in all wisdom ----- whereunto I also labour, striving -----", (Col. 1 v.28-29). A true preacher is one whose spirit, mind, and body, are wholly given to the task of preaching. If we are to be effective preachers:

(i) We must have informed minds, know our Bible, firmly grounded in the written Word, and be strongly established and rooted in Christ, the Incarnate Word of God. (John 1 v.1, 14). We must know Christ in all the Scripture. "And beginning at Moses and all the prophets, He expounded unto them in all the Scriptures the things concerning Himself", (Luke 24 v.27). We are tasked to "rightly dividing the Word of truth" (2 Tim. 2 v.15), to "cutting straight" the Holy Scriptures, not to invent a new 'gospel' or "bring in damnable heresies" (2 Peter 2 v.1) to the destruction of the Church.

(ii)   We must yield our bodies, for it is hard work to prepare properly for preaching. The word "labour" (Col. 1 v.29), means "a wearing out", and when the preaching is done, virtue has gone out of the preacher. (Mark 5 v.30).

(iii)   We must have spirits that are aflame: "striving according to His working" (Col. 1 v.29), which means "agonising" for the spiritual well-being of the souls of men, that sinners might be saved; and that saints might "live soberly, righteously, and godly, in this present world; Looking for that blessed hope, and the glorious appearing of the great God and our Saviour Jesus Christ", (Titus 2 v.12-13).

The Apostle Paul showed a very high pang of zeal and affection, great love and concern, and continual sorrow and anguish, for his country men that he "could wish that myself were accursed from Christ for my brethren, my kinsmen according to the flesh" (Rom. 9 v.3), that they might believe. Israel's rejection of the Messiah weighed so heavily upon Paul's heart that he was continually lamenting, yearning, weeping, striving, agonising, and longing for the salvation of his Jewish people. Does the love of Christ constrain us (2 Cor. 5 v.14) with such passion, anguish and genuine concern that portrays the burden of a compassionate preacher's heart within us for the eternal welfare of our fellow-man? When

Jesus "saw the multitudes, He was moved with compassion on them, because they fainted, and were scattered abroad, as sheep having no shepherd" (Matt. 9 v.36).

In our day too we must see men and women throughout our nation, "dead in trespasses and sins" (Eph. 2 v.1), needing to be saved, having no shepherd, yet we do not yearn over them as we ought. Many within our land need to hear the message of the Gospel: "The harvest truly is plenteous, but the labourers are few; Pray ye therefore the Lord of the harvest, that He will send forth labourers into his harvest", (Matt. 9 v.37-38). There appears to be so little weeping, so little prayer, so little compassion, so little concern amongst us for the spiritual welfare of the souls of men.

As we look at humanity today, do not the evils of modern times move us to pray for reformation and revival within the Church at large, that the people may again return to the God of the Bible. "Wilt Thou revive us again: that Thy people may rejoice in Thee?"(Psalm 85 v.6).

It was when Bunyan's Pilgrim felt the weight of the burden he carried that he realised how great was his need of deliverance. The Lord Jesus Christ invited those who labour to come to Him for rest (Matt. 11 v.28), but to others, He said, "And ye will not come to Me, that ye might have life", (John 5 v.40). It is the great task of the preacher to show to men their sinful state as it is before a holy God, and to persuade them that they are in need of Christ because of their sin. Paul's preaching was "in demonstration of the Spirit and of power: That your faith should not stand in the wisdom of men, but in the power of God", (1Cor. 2 v.4-5). The Apostle further states, "For we preach not ourselves, but Christ Jesus the Lord; and ourselves your servants for Jesus' sake", (2 Cor. 4 v.5). The greatest needs men have are pardon for past sins, and power for future obedience, and all this is found in the Lord Jesus Christ. "But of Him are ye in Jesus Christ, Who of God is made unto us wisdom, and righteousness, and sanctification, and redemption: That, according as it is written, He that glorifieth, let him glory in the Lord", (1Cor. 1 v.30-31).

(5) THE MIGHT OF OUR PREACHING: "which worketh in me mightily", (Col. 1 v.29). We cannot preach in our own strength. It is "not by might, nor by power, but by My Spirit, saith the Lord of hosts", (Zech. 4 v.6). "Our sufficiency is of God; Who also hath made us able ministers of the New Testament; not of the letter, but of the spirit . . . . Now the Lord is that Spirit: and where the Spirit of the Lord is, there is liberty", (2 Cor. 3 v.5-6,17). We have a great role model in the Apostle Paul as a minister, pastor, preacher, teacher, elder, and although we can never hope to equal his leadership, yet we may well seek grace to follow his example. The more we labour in the work of the Lord, the greater the measures of help and strength we may expect from God. In His eternal purpose, Paul states that he "was made a minister, according to the gift of the grace of God given unto me by the effectual working of His power. Unto me, who am less than the least of all saints, is this grace given, that I should preach among the Gentiles the unsearchable riches of Christ", (Eph. 3 v.7-8).

As we labour and toil in the Master's vineyard, may we prove the power of the grace of God working in us, and through us, in all our ministries wherever Providence allows. May God the Holy Spirit make us true preachers of the Word according to His commandment, to the honour, praise, and glory of His name.

"A good minister of Jesus Christ" (1 Tim. 4 v.6) is one who "is sanctified by the Word of God and prayer", (1 Tim. 4 v.5). All who are summoned to serve Christ are called to excellence in their usefulness to His Cause. The faithful servant of the Lord will be bold, yet gentle and gracious, in the performance of his duty. By the help of the Holy Spirit he will uphold the truth of God, and confront sin, unbelief, error, and disobedience without hesitation or vacillating or capitulating to the whims and wishes of men. Every sermon should be marked by:

(i)   A strong commitment to the authority and all-sufficiency of God's Word;

(ii)   A proper exegesis and interpretation of Holy Scripture;

(iii) A genuine passion and concern to uphold and enforce Biblical truth by church discipline; and

(iv)   A heartfelt desire to please God and boldly proclaim "all the counsel of God" (Acts 20 v.27), without fear or favour.

The Centrality of the Bible in Ministry and Worship

If contemporary preaching continues on the course it has followed over the last four to five decades, the continued erosion of the fundamental beliefs and practices of the Church will be catastrophic and utterly calamitous. The past half-century has seen a major shift and deterioration in Biblical standards, a serious drift away from the doctrines of grace, and an increasing departure from the absolute authority and all-sufficiency of the Word of God as the only infallible rule in every matter of faith and conduct.

The present crisis in contemporary preaching looms high with grave dangers for the future of an already decaying and faltering Church, and with dire consequences to the point that even now, it has little or no effective voice, and become no longer a power for good in the world. We greatly need a mighty revival of powerful preaching of the Word of God to purge the Church of its weaknesses, failures and corruption. May God grant us a great awakening that will restore twenty-first century Christianity back to the teaching of the early New

Testament Church, and rediscover the Great Reformation doctrines and Covenanting heritage from which it has strayed and fallen so much. The secular preaching of our day has the devilish and deadly effect of undermining and nullifying the most basic beliefs and foundational truths of the Christian faith.

It is most obvious that historic evangelical Protestantism throughout our nation is in serious trouble. There is the disturbing attitude and ongoing trend prevailing, even among so-called 'evangelical' preachers of our day, who no longer maintain a genuine concern to uphold truth and the authoritative role of Scripture in the life and practice of the Church at large. Current anti-Biblical movements and influences continue to infiltrate the Church by the adaptation of worldly standards, worldly theology, and worldly practices. The opening of the flood-gates of modern secular preaching is not only very damaging to the Church, but lethal. In calling the Church, and all preachers, back to the Word of God, we need preaching that will serve to strengthen its witness and restore the centrality of the Bible in ministry and worship. We need to "give ourselves continually to prayer and to the ministry of the Word (Acts 6 v.4), and it is imperative, therefore, that we uphold, maintain, and defend the Biblical doctrine of the inerrancy and sufficiency of Scripture (2 Tim. 3 v.14-17), and the finality of the Gospel of Christ as "the power of God unto salvation to everyone that believeth", (Rom. 1 v.16).

It is necessary, then, that we re-affirm, as did the Reformers and Covenanters in their day, that Scripture ----- Sola Scriptura ----- is the only source of truth, which means that we must not preach, teach, command, exhort, or practice anything contrary to the Written Word of God. The Westminster Confession of Faith, Chapter One, Section VI, very clearly and succinctly states: "The whole counsel of God, concerning all things necessary for His own glory, man's salvation, faith, and life, is either expressly set down in Scripture, or by good and necessary consequence may be deduced from Scripture: unto which nothing at any time is to be added, whether by claims of new revelations of the Spirit, or traditions of men. Nevertheless, we acknowledge the inward illumination of the Spirit of God to be necessary for the saving understanding of such things as are revealed in the Word, and that there are some circumstances concerning the worship of God, and government of the Church, common to human actions and societies, which are to be ordered by the light of nature and Christian prudence, according to the general rules of the Word, which are always to be observed".

With unwavering steadfastness in the faith, it is our duty at all times, by the grace and help of God, to bear unwearying witness to the inspiration and inerrancy by the Holy Spirit and the consequent infallibility of the Bible. On God's Word alone we must build our testimony and fully submit to the truth and authority of Scripture for strength and power to "earnestly contend for the faith which was once delivered unto the saints", (Jude v.3).

The Scripture-Alone Principle

It is to the Scriptures alone we must go to understand the Gospel, how we must preach, and how we must worship the one living and true God acceptably. "Thou shalt worship the Lord thy God, and Him only shalt thou serve", (Matt. 4 v.10). Contemporary worship is in great crisis precisely because it has abandoned the absolute authority of the Bible as the very Word of God. "What thing soever I command you, observe to do it: thou shalt not add thereto, nor diminish from it", (Deut. 12 v.32). The rejection of the Scripture-Alone principle also means that all the other related truths of the Gospel, by faith alone, in Christ alone, through grace alone, are adversely affected. Preaching that is not focused solely on the Person and Work of Christ alone as revealed in Scripture, is dishonouring to the Lord and a hindrance to blessing in the Church. Today much of the emphasis is switched to what is going on inside a person and on what the sinner 'does' that determines his salvation. "For by grace are ye saved through faith;

and that not of yourselves: it is the gift of God; Not of works, lest any man should boast", (Eph. 2 v.8-9).

Contemporary preaching has drifted so far from authoritative Biblical truth that the message of "Christ, and Him crucified" (1Cor. 2 v.2) is down-played and become man-centred to the detriment and diminution of the whole Church. No one has the right to interpret Scripture in isolation from the Scripture itself, and we need to guard against the abuses and confusion of modern culture replacing the Scriptures as our sole rule of faith and practice. By Divine grace we need to return to true Biblical religion of the Gospel of God with full confidence in the all-sufficiency and sovereignty of His Word, power, and grace. "For Christ sent me ----- to preach the Gospel: not with wisdom of words, lest the Cross of Christ should be made of none affect. For the preaching of the Cross is to them that perish foolishness; but unto us which are saved it is the power of God", (1 Cor.1 v.17-18).

Christianity does not rest on the testimony of any mere man. It rests on the claim of its Founder, Who is the Messiah, God incarnate, the Saviour of the world, upon which foundation the apostles and prophets built, "Jesus Christ Himself being the chief corner-stone; In Whom all the building fitly framed together groweth into a holy temple in the Lord" (Eph. 2 v.20-22).

The contemporary worship service is now so far removed from the Biblical pattern and become a place of shambles, a muddle, a place where people wish to be entertained, have their ears tickled (2 Tim. 4 v.3-4), and indulge in a 'feel good' factor about our modern culture, and all the while the famine of hearing the Word of the Lord appears to be taking hold yet more and more. As contemporary preachers continue in such a rut, it is inevitable that the result will be the increasing downward spiral of declension, barrenness, and apostasy of the Church. Present-day Church modernism with its unBiblical forms of worship, human innovations, and secular influences have the damaging effect of pushing out the Scriptures yet further to the sidelines, and discarding of doctrinal distinctives altogether, in an all-out assault and rejection of the Gospel. "There is a way which seemeth right unto a man, but the end thereof are the ways of death", (Prov. 14 v.12).

The remedy for such a dire situation is the Bible itself. We should regard Scripture with the highest degree of confidence, and endeavour to bring its authority, wisdom, guidance, and influence, to bear upon humanity for the good of the Church and of the world. Jude in his epistle urges the preacher to "earnestly contend for the faith which was once delivered unto the saints", (Jude v.3). We pray that God may transform us by the renewing of our minds, so that we need "not be ashamed, rightly dividing the Word of Truth", (2 Tim. 2 v.15).

As we recover the true message of the Gospel as revealed in Scripture in our preaching, God creates new life and gives the gift of faith to those who are "dead in trespasses and sins", (Eph. 2 v.1). A regenerate sinner becomes a living soul, being born again of God: "He hath quickened us together with Christ, by grace are ye saved", (Eph. 2 v.5). It is in Him we live: "because I live, ye shall live also", (John 14 v.19). As the Lord said to Moses, "I will have mercy on whom I will have mercy, and I will have compassion on whom I will have compassion", (Rom. 9 v.15; see also Exod. 2 v.19).

Pure Biblical Preaching

The present crisis in contemporary preaching is plainly due to the absence of doctrinal teaching and setting aside the authority of the Bible. Pure Biblical preaching is greatly lacking in our pulpits, and modern preachers seem to take upon themselves to know better than God how 'Church' should be done in the twenty-first century! They distort, undermine, and misapply the message of redemption and fail to show the perfect teaching the Bible presents of the Father sacrificing His Son, the Son willingly offering Himself, and the Holy Spirit applying the several benefits that flow from the atonement to

God's elect. The true message of the Gospel clearly proclaims that the mediatorial work and suffering of Christ not only obtained for God's people redemption from the penal consequences of their sins, but has also secured their personal sanctification. The reality of Christ's substitutionary sacrifice, His death on the Cross, His burial, His resurrection, His ascension and intercession, should fill our hearts with wonder, adoration, and thanksgiving. "We have an advocate with the Father, Jesus Christ the righteous", (1 John 2 v.1). Like the Psalmist of old there is much to inspire our worship to "bless the Lord" (Psalm 103 v.1) and call upon our souls and all that is within us to praise and magnify His holy name. "O magnify the Lord with me, and let us exalt His name together", (Psalm 34 v.3).

The unceasing burden of every preacher's heart ought to be the restoration of true Biblical ministry to its rightful place in the Church, and a proper relationship established between sound doctrine and sincere heavenly zeal in evangelism. In comparing the preaching and labours of the Prophets, the Apostles, the Reformers, the Covenanters, the Puritans, and other esteemed men who were mightily used of God in the proclamation of truth, such as Bunyan, Edwards, Whitefield, Carey, and Spurgeon, with much of the present-day preaching, we soon see that there is a great difference in respect to the message and methods. Anyone who will make an honest comparison will notice a vast difference in the message in many areas, but particularly in respect to the character of God, the condition of unregenerate men, the Biblical doctrines of election and regeneration, the Spirit's effectual calling of sinners to Christ, the Person and Work of Christ as it relates to redemption accomplished and applied, the relationship of the law to Gospel proclamation, the perseverance of the saints, and the eternal security of believers. The true servant of Christ, because he is one under the authority of God's Word, will always be seeking to reform or conform his life, practice, and preaching more closely according to the teaching of Holy Scripture.

Our primary task is to "preach the Word" (2 Tim. 4 v.2). But if we are to seriously teach and rightly "divide" (2 Tim. 2 v.15) the truth of

Scripture, our effectiveness and wisdom in preaching will be marked by humility, a teachable spirit, and due diligence to show ourselves "approved unto God", workmen "that needeth not to be ashamed", (2 Tim. 2 v.15).

CONCLUSION

The crisis in contemporary preaching, and the unhealthy state, declension and decadence of large swathes of Western Christianity, are due to the abandonment of the authority of God's Word, and the increasing secularisation of the worship service. We earnestly pray for a return to the apostolic priority of Acts 6v.4: "But we will give ourselves continually to prayer, and to the ministry of the Word". May God raise up and anoint an army of preachers in our day who will preach His Word with clarity, accuracy, compassion, and power. May God grant us a fresh reformation of the Church and a great revival with a mighty awakening by His Holy Spirit through the powerful preaching of the Gospel of truth, that is bathed in prayer and rooted in Holy Scripture, as a means to Church growth and blessing in our generation.

To God be the glory.

"And they continued stedfastly in the apostles' doctrine and fellowship, and in breaking of bread, and in prayers", (Acts. 2 v.42).

"And the Lord added to the Church daily such as should be saved", (Acts. 2 v.47).

"Preach the Word", (2 Tim. 4 v.2).

BIBLIOGRAPHY

J. E. Adams   Preaching with Purpose
                     Zondervan, Grand Rapids, 1982

                     Preaching According to the Holy Spirit
                     Timeless Text, Woodruff, 2000

A. G. Azurdia   Spirit Empowered Preaching
                     Christian Focus, Ross-shire, 1998

R. Baxter   The Reformed Pastor
                     Pickering, Basingstoke, 1982

W. G. Blaikie   The Preachers of Scotland
                     Banner of Truth, Edinburgh, 2001

J. M. Boice   The Glory of God's Grace
                     Kregel, Grand Rapids, 1993

                     Whatever Happened to the Gospel of Grace?
                     Paternoster, Carlisle, 2002

J. M. Boice (Ed.)   The Foundation of Biblical Authority
                     Pickering, Glasgow, 1979

A. Bonar   Memoir and Remains of R. M. McCheyne
                     Banner of Truth, London, 1966

H. Bonar   Night of Weeping
                     James Nisbet & Co., London, 1850

                     The Everlasting Righteousness
                     Banner of Truth, Edinburgh, 1993

B. Borgman   My Heart for Thy Cause
                     Christian Focus, Ross-shire, 2002

C. Bridges   The Christian Ministry
                     Banner of Truth, London, 1959

H. T. Bryson   Epository Preaching
                     Broadman, Nashville, 1995

143

| J. Calvin | Institutes of the Christian Religion
Eerdmans, Grand Rapids, 1989 |

J. Carrick — The Imperative of Preaching
Banner of Truth, Edinburgh, 2002

R. A. Carson — A Call to Spiritual Reformation
I.V.P., Nottingham, 1999

W. J. Chantry — Today's Gospel: Authentic or Synthetic?
Banner of Truth, London, 1970

B. Chapell — Christ-Centered Preaching
Baker, Grand Rapids, 1994

A. C. Cheyne — Studies in Scottish Church History
T. & T. Clark, Edinburgh, 1999

H. Cooke — Sermons: A Living Church
Religious Tract and Book Depot, Belfast, 1888

W. Cunningham — The Reformers and the Theology of the Reformation
Banner of Truth, Edinburgh, 1967

J. R. deWitt — What is the Reformed Faith?
Banner of Truth, Edinburgh, 1981

D. Eby — Power Preaching for Church Growth
Mentor, Ross-shire, 1996

J. Edwards — Works
Banner of Truth, Edinburgh, 1974

E. Erskine — Works
Free Presbyterian, Glasgow, 2001

Evangelical Ministry — Preaching the Living Word
Assembly — Christian Focus, Ross-shire, 1999

R. A. Finlayson — A Just God and a Saviour
Knox, Edinburgh, 2002

S. Greidanus — The Modern Preacher and the Ancient Text
I.V.P., Leicester, 1988

G. Gurganus	Perspectives on Evangelism Ambassador, Belfast, 1997
W.M.H.	The Revival of Religion Banner of Truth, Edinburgh, 1984
G. Henderson	Lectures to Young Preachers Barbour, Edinburgh, 1961
P. Hicks	Evangelicals and Truth I.V.P., Leicester, 1998
A. A. Hoekema	Saved by Grace Paternoster, Carlisle, 1989
C. F. Hogg	Gospel Facts and Doctrines Pickering, London, 1951
J. Howe	The Scots Worthies Banner of Truth, Edinburgh, 1995
J. Hughes	Epository Preaching Christian Focus, Ross-shire, 2001
Johnston, Hunter & Co., Edinburgh	The Westminster Confession of Faith The Larger and Shorter Catechisms The Sum of Saving Knowledge
J. Ker	Lectures on the History of Preaching Hodder and Stoughton, London, 1880
D. Kistler (Ed.)	Sola Scriptura Soli Deo Gloria, Morgan, 1995
R. Lischer	The Company of Preachers Eerdmans, Grand Rapids, 2002
D. M. Lloyd-Jones	Preaching and Preachers Hodder and Stoughton, London, 1971
H. Lockyer	The Art and Craft of Preaching Baker, Grand Rapids, 1975

S. T. Logan (Ed.)	The Preacher and Preaching in the Twentieth Century Evangelical Press, Welwyn, 1986
M. Luther	Works Baker, Grand Rapids, 2000
J. MacArthur	Expository Preaching Word, California, 1992
R. M. McCheyne	Sermons of McCheyne Banner of Truth, London, 1961 The Believer's Joy Free Presbyterian Publications, Glasgow, 1987
A. E. McGrath	A Passion for Truth I.V.P., Leicester, 1996
C. P. McIlwaine	Preaching Christ: The Heart of Gospel Ministry Banner of Truth, Edinburgh, 2003
J. G. Machen	What is Faith? Hodder and Stoughton, London, 1925 God Transcendent Banner of Truth, Edinburgh, 1982
I. Macpherson	The Burden of the Lord Epworth, London, 1955 The Faith once Delivered Word (UK), Milton Keynes, 1988
T. Manton	A Body of Divinity Banner of Truth, London, 1958
A. N. Martin	What's Wrong with Preaching Today? Banner of Truth, Edinburgh, 1967
B. Mawhinney	Preaching with Freshness Kregel, Grand Rapids, 1997
F. B. Meyer	Jottings and Hints for Lay Preachers Morrison and Gibb, Edinburgh, 1903

R. A. Mohler	Preaching: The Centrality of Scripture Banner of Truth, Edinburgh, 2002
E. M. Moore	Our Covenant Heritage Christian Focus, Ross-shire, 2000
G. C. Morgan	Imperative of the Christian Faith H. E. Walter Ltd., Worthing, 1964
L. Morris	The Apostolic Preaching of the Cross Tyndale, London, 1955
R. Nicole	Our Sovereign Saviour Christian Focus, Ross-shire, 2002
D. C. Norrington	To Preach or not to Preach? Paternoster, Carlisle, 1996
J. Owen	Works Banner of Truth, Edinburgh, 1965
J. Piper	The Supremacy of God in Preaching Kingsway, Eastbourne, 1990
H. W. Robinson	Expository Preaching I.V.P., Leicester, 1980
S. Rutherford	Letters Banner of Truth, Edinburgh, 1984
C. L. Ryan	Connecting Ministry with Holy Scripture Majesty Print, Birmingham, 2001 The Ministry and Ministers Majesty Print, Birmingham, 2003 Understanding the Ministerial Call Majesty Print, Birmingham, 2003
J. C. Ryle	Old Paths Clarke, Cambridge, 1977
W. E. Sangster	The Approach to Preaching Epworth, London, 1951
M. A. Seifrid	Christ, our Righteousness I.V.P., Leicester, 2000

A. Smellie   Men of the Covenant
         Banner of Truth, Edinburgh, 1960

J. C. Smith   Robert Murry McCheyne: A Good Minister of Jesus Christ
         Ambassador, Belfast, 1998

C. H. Spurgeon   Lectures to my Students
         Marshall M.&S., Basingstoke, 1954

John Stott   Evangelical Truth
         I.V.P., Leicester, 1999

J. R. W. Stott   Basic Christianity
         I.V.P., Leicester, 1958

J. Tracy   The Great Awakening
         Banner of Truth, Edinburgh, 1976

H. Uprichard   A Son is Promised
         Evangelical Press, Darlington, 1994

T. Wells   The Moral Basis of Faith
         Banner of Truth, Edinburgh, 1986

W. W. Weirsbe   Preaching and Teaching with Imagination
         Baker, Grand Rapids, 1994

G. Whitefield   Sermons
         William Tegg, London, 1867

         Journals
         Banner of Truth, London, 1960

J. E. Wilson   The Authentic Gospel
         Banner of Truth, Edinburgh, 1990

O. Winslow   Personal Declension and Revival of Religion in the Soul
         Banner of Truth, Edinburgh, 1960

R. B. Zuck   Vital Theological Issues
         Kregel, Grand Rapids, 1994

         Vital Biblical Issues
         Kregal, Grand Rapids, 1994

EXTRACTS FROM THE GREAT CONFESSIONS
OF THE REFORMATION

The Augsburg Confession, Lutheran Churches, Germany 1530

ARTICLE V
OF THE MINISTRY OF THE CHURCH

For the obtaining of this faith, the ministry of teaching the Gospel and administering the Sacraments was instituted.

For by the Word and Sacraments, as by instruments, the Holy Spirit is given: Who worketh faith, where and when it pleaseth God, in those that hear the Gospel, to wit, that God, not for our merit's sake, but for Christ's sake, doth justify those who believe that they for Christ's sake are received into favor.

The French Confession, 1559

XXV

Now as we enjoy Christ only through the Gospel, we believe that the order of the Church, established by His authority, ought to be sacred and inviolable, and that, therefore, the Church can not exist without pastors for instruction, whom we should respect and reverently listen to, when they are properly called and exercise their office faithfully. Not that God is bound to such aid and subordinate means, but because it pleaseth Him to govern us by such constraints. In this we detest all visionaries who would like, so far as lies in their power, to destroy the ministry and preaching of the Word and sacraments.

XXVI

We believe that no-one ought to seclude himself and be contented to be alone; but that all jointly should keep and maintain the union of the Church, and submit to the public preaching, and to the yoke of Jesus Christ, wherever God shall have established a true order of the Church, even if the magistrates and their edicts are contrary to it. For if they do not take part in it, or if they separate themselves from it, they do contrary to the Word of God.

XXVII

Nevertheless we believe that it is important to discern with care and prudence which is the true Church, for this title has been much abused. We say, then, according to the Word of God, that it is the company of the faithful who agree to follow His Word, and the pure religion which it teaches; who advance in it all their lives, growing and becoming more confirmed in the fear of God according as they feel the want of growing and pressing onward. Even although they strive continually, they can have no hope save in the remission of their sins. Nevertheless we do not deny that among the faithful there may be hypocrites and reprobates, but their wickedness can not destroy the title of the Church.

XXVIII

In this belief we declare that, properly speaking, there can be no Church where the Word of God is not received, nor profession made of subjection to it, nor use of the sacraments.

The Scots Confession, Scotland 1560

CHAPTER XVIII
THE NOTES BY WHICH THE TRUE SHALL BE DETERMINED FROM THE FALSE, AND WHO SHALL BE JUDGE OF DOCTRINE

The notes of the true Kirk, therefore, we believe, confess, and avow to be: first, the true preaching of the Word of God, in which God has revealed Himself to us, as the writings of the prophets and apostles declare; secondly, the right administration of the sacraments of Christ Jesus, with which must be associated the Word and promise of God to seal and confirm them in our hearts; and lastly, ecclesiastical discipline uprightly ministered, as God's Word prescribes, whereby vice is repressed and virtue nourished.

The Belgic Confession, The Low Countries, 1561

ARTICLE XXIX
THE MARKS OF THE TRUE CHURCH, AND WHERE IN IT DIFFERS FROM THE FALSE CHURCH

We believe that we ought diligently and circumspectly to discern from the Word of God which is the true Church, since all sects which are in the world assume to themselves the name of the Church . . .

The marks by which the true Church is known are these: If the pure doctrine of the gospel is preached therein; if it maintains the pure administration of the sacraments as instituted by Christ; if Church discipline is exercised in punishing of sin; in short, if all things are managed according to the pure Word of God, all things contrary thereto rejected, and Jesus Christ acknowledged as the only Head of the Church. Hereby the true Church may certainly be known, from which no man has a right to separate himself.

The 39 Articles of the Church of England London, 1562

Article 1   Of Faith in the Holy Trinity

There is but one living and true God, everlasting, without body, parts, or passions; of infinite power, wisdom, and goodness; the maker and preserver of all things, both visible and invisible. And in unity of this Godhead, there be three persons, of one substance, power, and eternity; the Father, the Son and the Holy Ghost.

Article 2   Of the Word, or Son of God, which was made very Man

The Son, which is the Word of the Father, begotten from everlasting of the Father, the very and eternal God, of one substance with the Father, took man's nature in the womb of the blessed Virgin, of her substance; so that two whole and perfect natures, that is to say, the Godhead and manhood, were joined together in one person, never to be divided; whereof is one Christ, very God, and very man: Who truly suffered, was crucified, dead and buried, to reconcile His Father to us, and to be a sacrifice, not only for original guilt, but also for actual sins of men.

Article 3   Of the going down of Christ into Hell

As Christ died for us, and was buried; so also is it to be believed, that He went down into hell.

Article 4   Of the Resurrection of Christ

Christ did truly rise again from death, and took again His body, with flesh, bones, and all things appertaining to the perfection of man's nature, wherewith He ascended into heaven, and there sitteth, until He return to judge all men at the last day.

Article 5   Of the Holy Ghost

The Holy Ghost, proceeding from the Father and Son, is of one substance, majesty, and glory with the Father and the Son, very and eternal God.

Article 6   Of the Sufficiency of the Holy Scriptures for Salvation

Holy Scripture containeth all things necessary to salvation: so that whatsoever is not read therein, nor may be proved thereby, is not to be required of any man, that it should be believed as an article of the faith, or be thought requisite or necessary to salvation. In the name of the Holy Scripture we do understand those Canonical books of the Old and New Testament, of whose authority was never any doubt in the Church.

The Heidelberg Catechism, Germany 1563

65 Q *You confess that by faith alone you share in Christ and all His blessings: where does that faith come from?*

A The Holy Spirit produces it in our hearts by the preaching of the Holy Gospel and confirms it through our use of the holy sacraments.

83 Q *What are the keys to the kingdom?*

A The preaching of the Holy Gospel and Christian discipline towards repentance. Both preaching and discipline open the kingdom of heaven to believers and close it to unbelievers.

84 Q *How does preaching the Gospel open and close the kingdom of heaven?*

A According to the command of Christ: The kingdom of heaven is opened by proclaiming and publicly declaring to each and every believer that, as often as he accepts the Gospel promise in true faith, God, because of what Christ has done, truly forgives all his sins.

The kingdom of heaven is closed, however, by proclaiming and publicly declaring to believers and hypocrites that, as long as they do not repent, the anger of God and eternal condemnation rest on them.

God's judgement, both in this life and in the life to come, is based on this Gospel testimony.

The Second Helvetic Confession, Switzerland 1564

CHAPTER 1

OF THE HOLY SCRIPTURE BEING THE TRUE WORD OF GOD

The preaching of the Word of God is the Word of God. Wherefore when this Word of God is now preached in the Church by preachers lawfully called, we believe that the very Word of God is proclaimed, and received by the faithful; and that neither any other Word of God is to be invented nor is to be expected from heaven: and that now the Word itself which is preached is to be regarded, not the minister that preaches; for even if he be evil and a sinner, nevertheless the Word of God remains still true and good.

Neither do we think that therefore the outward preaching is to be thought as fruitless because the instruction in true religion depends on the inward illumination of the Spirit, or because it is written, 'And no longer shall each man teach his neighbour . . ., for they shall all know Me' (Jeremiah 31:34), and 'Neither he who plants nor he who waters is anything but only God

Who gives the growth' (I Corinthians 3:7). For although 'no one can come to Christ unless he be drawn by the Father' (John 6:44), and unless the Holy Spirit inwardly illumines him, yet we know that it is surely the will of God that his Word should be preached outwardly also. God could indeed, by His Holy Spirit, or by the ministry of an angel, without the ministry of St. Peter, have taught Cornelius in the Acts; but, nevertheless, He refers him to Peter, of whom the angel speaking says, 'He shall tell you what you ought to do.'

Inward illumination does not eliminate external preaching. For He that illuminates inwardly by giving men the Holy spirit, the same One, by way of commandment, said unto His disciples, 'Go into all the world, and preach the Gospel to the whole creation' (Mark 16:14). And the same Paul, after a beautiful development of his thought, in Romans 10:17 at length comes to the conclusion, 'So faith comes from hearing, and hearing from the Word of God by the preaching of Christ.'

At the same time we recognize that God can illuminate whom and when He will, even without the external ministry, for that is in His power; but we speak of the usual way of instructing men, delivered unto us from God, both by commandment and examples.

CHAPTER XVI
OF FAITH AND GOOD WORKS, AND OF THEIR REWARD, AND OF MAN'S MERIT

Faith is the gift of God. But his faith is a pure gift of God which God alone of His grace gives to His elect according to His measure when, to whom and to the degree He wills. And He does this by the Holy Spirit by means of the preaching of the Gospel and steadfast prayer.

The 19 Articles of Religion of the Church of Ireland Dublin, 1615

In these Articles are comprehended, almost word for word, the nine Articles agreed on at Lambeth, the 20th November 1595

6   *Of Christ, the Mediator of the Second Covenant*

(29)   The Son, which is the Word of the Father, begotten from everlasting of the Father, the true and eternal God, of one substance with the

Father, took man's nature in the womb of the blessed Virgin, of her substance: so that two whole and perfect natures (that is to say, the Godhead and Manhood) were inseparably joined in one person, making one Christ, very God and very man.

(30)   Christ, in the truth of our nature, was made like unto us in all things, sin only expected, from which He was clearly void, both in His life and in His nature. He came as a lamb without spot, to take away the sins of the world by the sacrifice of Himself once made; and sin (as John saith, John iii.5.) was not in Him. He fulfilled the law for us perfectly: for our sakes He endured most grievous torments immediately in His soul, and most painful sufferings in His body. He was crucified, and died, to reconcile His Father unto us, and to be a sacrifice, not only for original guilt, but also for all our actual transgressions. He was buried, and descended into hell; and the third day rose from the dead, and took again His body, with flesh, bones, and all things appertaining to the perfection of man's nature; wherewith He ascended into Heaven, and there sitteth at the right hand of His Father, until He returns to judge all men at the last day.

7   *Of the Communicating of the Grace of Christ*

(31)   They are to be condemned, that presume to say, that every man shall be saved by the law or sect which he professeth, so that he be diligent to frame his life according to that law, and the light of nature. For Holy Scripture doth set out unto us only the name of Jesus Christ whereby men must be saved.

(32)   None can come unto Christ unless it be given unto him, and unless the Father draw him. And all men are not so drawn by the Father, that they may come unto the Son; neither is there such a sufficient measure of grace vouchsafed unto every man, whereby he is enabled to come unto everlasting life.

(33)   All God's elect are in their time inseparably united unto Christ, by the effectual and vital influence of the Holy Ghost, derived from Him, as from the Head, unto every true member of His mystical body, And being thus made one with Christ, they are truly regenerated, and made partakers of Him and all His benefits.

The Canons of Dort, International Synod, Dordrecht, Netherlands, 1618-1619

FIRST HEAD OF DOCTRINE
DIVINE ELECTION AND REPROBATION

ARTICLE 3

And that men may be brought to believe, God mercifully sends the messengers of these most joyful tidings to whom He will and at what time He pleases; by whose ministry men are called to repentance and faith in Christ crucified. *How then shall they call on Him in Whom they have not believed? And how shall they believe in Him Whom they have not heard? And how shall they hear without a preacher? And how shall they preach except they be sent?* (Romans 10:14,15).

SECOND HEAD OF DOCTRINE
THE DEATH OF CHRIST, AND THE REDEMPTION OF MEN THEREBY

ARTICLE 5

Moreover, the promise of the Gospel is that whosoever believes in Christ crucified shall not perish, but have eternal life. This promise, together with the command to repent and believe, ought to be declared and published to all nations, and to all persons promiscuously and without distinction, to whom God out of His good pleasure sends the Gospel.

THIRD AND FOURTH HEADS OF DOCTRINE
THE CORRUPTION OF MAN, HIS CONVERSION TO GOD, AND THE MANNER THEREOF

ARTICLE 6

What, therefore, neither the light of nature nor the law could do, that God performs by the operation of the Holy Spirit through the Word or ministry of reconciliation; which is the glad tidings concerning the Messiah, by means whereof it has pleased God to save such as believe, as well under the Old as under the New Testament.

ARTICLE 11

But when God accomplishes His good pleasure in the elect, or works in them true conversion, He not only causes the Gospel to be externally preached to them, and powerfully illuminates their minds by His Holy Spirit, that they may rightly understand and discern the things of the Spirit of God; but by the efficacy of the same regenerating Spirit He pervades the inmost recesses of man; He opens the closed and softens the hardened heart, and circumcises that which was uncircumcised; infuses new qualities into the will, which, though heretofore dead, He quickens; from being evil, disobedient, and refactory, He renders it good, obedient, and pliable; actuates and strengthens it, that like a good tree, it may bring forth the fruits of good actions.

FIFTH HEAD OF DOCTRINE
THE PERSEVERANCE OF THE SAINTS

ARTICLE 14

And as it has pleased God, by the preaching of the Gospel, to begin this work of grace in us, so He preserves, continues, and perfects it by the hearing and reading of His Word by meditation thereon, and by the exhortations, threatenings, and promise thereof, and by the use of the sacraments.

The Westminster Confession of Faith, England, Scotland and Ireland, 1646

CHAPTER XIV
OF SAVING FAITH

The grace of faith, whereby the elect are enabled to believe to the saving of their souls, is the work of the Spirit of Christ in their hearts, and is ordinarily wrought by the ministry of the Word: by which also, and by the administration of the sacraments, and prayer, it is increased and strengthened.

By this faith, a Christian believeth to be true whatsoever is revealed in the Word, for the authority of God Himself speaking therein; and acteth differently upon that which each particular passage thereof containeth; yielding obedience to the commands, trembling at the threatenings, and embracing the promises of God for this life and that which is to come. But the principal acts of saving faith are, accepting, receiving, and resting upon Christ alone for justification, sanctification, and eternal life, by virtue of the covenant of grace.

This faith is different in degrees, weak or strong; may be often and many ways assailed and weakened, but gets the victory; growing up in many to the attainment of a full assurance through Christ, Who is both the author and finisher of our faith.

CHAPTER XXI
RELIGIOUS WORSHIP, AND THE SABBATH-DAY

The reading of the Scriptures with godly fear; the sound preaching, and conscionable hearing of the Word, in obedience unto God, with understanding, faith, and reverence; singing of Psalms with grace in the heart; as also the due administration and worthy receiving of the sacraments instituted by Christ; are all part of the ordinary religious worship of God.....

The Westminster Larger Catechism (1648)

67   Q   *What is effectual calling?*

A   Effectual calling is the work of God's almighty power and grace, whereby (out of His free and special love to His elect, and from nothing in them moving Him thereunto) He doth, in His accepted time, invite and draw them to Jesus Christ, by His Word and Spirit; savingly enlightening their minds, renewing and powerfully determining their wills, so as they (although in themselves dead in sin) are hereby made willing and able freely to answer His call, and to accept and embrace the grace offered and conveyed therein.

72 Q *What is justifying faith?*

A Justifying faith is a saving grace, wrought in the heart of a sinner by the Spirit and Word of God, whereby he, being convinced of his sin and misery, and of the disability in himself and all other creatures to recover him out of his lost condition, not only assenteth to the truth of the promise of the Gospel, but receiveth and resteth upon Christ and His righteousness, therein held forth, for pardon of sin, and for the accepting and accounting of his person righteous in the sight of God for salvation.

76 Q *What is repentance unto life?*

A Repentance unto life is a saving grace, wrought to the heart of a sinner by the Spirit and Word of God....

108 Q *What are the duties required in the second commandment?*

A The duties required in the second commandment are, the receiving, observing, and keeping pure and entire, all such religious worship and ordinances as God hath instituted in His Word; particularly prayer and thanksgiving in the name of Christ; the reading, preaching, and hearing of the Word; the administration and receiving of the sacraments; Church government and discipline; the ministry and maintenance thereof; religious fasting; swearing by the name of God, and vowing unto Him: as also the disapproving, detesting, opposing, all false worship; and, according to each one's place and calling, removing it, and all monuments of idolatry.

154 Q What are the outward means whereby Christ communicates to us the benefits of His mediation?

A The outward and ordinary means whereby Christ communicates to His church the benefits of His mediation, are all His ordinances; especially the Word, sacraments, and prayer; all which are made effectual to the elect for their salvation.

155 Q *How is the Word made effectual to salvation?*

A The Spirit of God maketh the reading, but especially the preaching of the Word, an effectual means of enlightening, convincing, and humbling sinners; of driving them out of themselves, and drawing them unto Christ; of conforming them to His image, and subduing them to His will; of strengthening them against temptations and corruptions; of building them up in grace, and establishing their hearts in holiness and comfort through faith unto salvation.

160 Q What is required of those that hear the Word preached?

A It is required of those that hear the Word preached, that they attend upon it with diligence, preparation, and prayer; examine what they hear by the Scriptures; receive the truth with faith, love, meekness, and readiness of mind, as the Word of God: meditated, and confer of it; hide it in their hearts, and bring forth the fruit of it in their lives.

The Westminster Shorter Catechism 1648

1 Q *What is the chief end of man?*

A Man's chief end is to glorify God, and to enjoy Him for ever.

2 Q *What rule hath God given to direct us how we may glorify and enjoy Him?*

A The Word of God, which is contained in the Scriptures of the Old and New Testaments, is the only rule to direct us how we may glorify and enjoy Him.

3 Q *What do the Scriptures principally teach?*

A The Scriptures principally teach what man is to believe concerning God, and what duty God requires of man.

39 Q *What is the duty which God requireth of man?*

A The duty which God requireth of man, is obedience to His revealed will.

86 Q *What is faith in Jesus Christ?*

A Faith in Jesus Christ is a saving grace, whereby we receive and rest upon Him alone for salvation, as He offered to us in the Gospel.

87 Q *What is repentance unto life?*

A Repentance unto life is a saving grace, whereby a sinner, out of a true sense of his sin, and apprehension of the mercy of God in Christ, doth, with grief and hatred of his sin, turn from it unto God, with full purpose of, and endeavour after, new obedience.

The Savoy Declaration of Faith London, 1658

VII

OF GOD'S COVENANT WITH MAN

I The distance between God and the creature is go great, that although reasonable creatures do owe obedience unto Him as their Creator, yet they could never have attained the reward of life, but by some voluntary condescension on God's part, which He has been pleased to express by way of covenant.

II The first covenant made with man was a covenant of works, wherein life was promised to Adam; and in him to his posterity, upon condition of perfect and personal obedience.

III Man, by his fall, having made himself incapable of life by that covenant, the Lord was pleased to make a second, commonly called the covenant of grace; wherein He freely offers unto sinners life and salvation by Jesus Christ; requiring of them faith in Him, that they may be saved, and promising to give unto all those that are ordained unto eternal life His Holy Spirit, to make them willing, and able to believe.

IV   This covenant of grace is frequently set forth in Scripture by the name of a testament, in reference to the death of Jesus Christ the Testator, and to the everlasting inheritance, with all things belonging to it, therein bequeathed.

V   Although this covenant has been differently and variously administered in respect of ordinances and institutions in the time of the law, and since the coming of Christ in the flesh; yet for the substance and efficacy of it, to all its spiritual and saving ends, it is one and the same; upon the account of which various dispensations, it is called the Old Testament and New Testament.

VIII
OF CHRIST THE MEDIATOR

1   It pleased God, in His eternal purpose, to choose and ordain the Lord Jesus, His only begotten Son, according to a covenant made between them both, to be the Mediator between God and man, the Prophet, Priest, and King, the Head and Saviour of His Church, the heir of all things, and Judge of the world: unto Whom He did from all eternity give a people, to be His seed, and to be by Him in time redeemed, called, justified, sanctified, and glorified.

XXII
OF RELIGIOUS WORSHIP AND THE SABBATH-DAY

1   The light of nature shows that there is a God, Who has lordship and sovereignty over all, is good, and does good unto all, and is therefore to be feared, loved, praised, called upon, trusted in, and served, with all the heart, and with all the soul, and with all the might. But the acceptable way of worshipping the true God is instituted by Himself, and so limited by His own revealed will, that He may not be worshipped according to the imaginations and devices of men, or the suggestions of Satan, under any visible representation, or any other way not prescribed in the Holy Scripture.

II   Religious worship is to be given to God, the Father, Son, and Holy Ghost; and to Him alone; not to angels, saints, or any other creature:

and, since the fall, not without a Mediator; nor in the mediation of any other but of Christ alone.

III   Prayer, with thanksgiving, being one special part of religious worship, is by God required of all men: and, that it may be accepted, it is to be made in the name of the Son, by the help of His Spirit, according to His will, with understanding, reverence, humility, fervency, faith, love and perseverance; and, if vocal, in a known tongue.

IV   Prayer is to be made for things lawful; and for all sorts of men living, or that shall live hereafter: but not for the dead, nor for those of whom it may be known that they have sinned the sin unto death.

V   The reading of the Scriptures, preaching, and hearing the Word of God, singing of Psalms, as also the administration of Baptism and the Lord's Supper, are all parts of religious worship of God, to be performed in obedience unto God, with understanding, faith, reverence, and godly fear; solemn humiliations, with fastings, and thanksgivings upon special occasions, are in their several times and seasons, to be used in a holy and religious manner.

VI   Neither prayer, nor any other part of religious worship, is now, under the Gospel, either tied unto, or made more acceptable by any place in which it is performed, or towards which it is directed: but God is to be worshipped everywhere, in spirit and truth; as, in private families daily, and in secret, each one by himself; so, more solemnly in the public assemblies, which are not carelessly or wilfully to be neglected, or forsaken, when God, by His Word or providence, calls thereunto.

VII   As it is the law of nature, that, in general, a due proportion of time be set apart for the worship of God; so, in His Word, by a positive, moral, and perpetual commandment binding all men in all ages, He has particularly appointed one day in seven, for a Sabbath, to be kept holy unto Him: which, from the beginning of the world to the resurrection of Christ, was the last day of the week: and, from the resurrection of Christ, was changed into the first day of the week, which, in Scripture, is called the Lord's Day, and is to be continued to the end of the world, as the Christian Sabbath.

VIII This Sabbath is then kept holy unto the Lord, when men, after a due preparing of their hearts, and ordering of their common affairs beforehand, do not only observe a holy rest, all the day, from their own works, words, and thoughts about their worldly employments and recreations, but also are taken up, the whole time, in the public and private exercises of His worship, and in the duties of necessity and mercy.

The Baptist Confession of Faith London, 1689

This is a recension of the Westminster Confession with very few alterations, except for some changes in two parts re-Church Government and Sacraments.

OF THE HOLY SCRIPTURES

1   The Holy Scripture is the only sufficient, certain and infallible rule of all saving knowledge, faith and obedience, although the light of nature and the works of creation and providence do so far manifest the goodness, wisdom and power of God, as to leave men inexcusable; yet are they not sufficient to give that knowledge of God and His will which is necessary unto salvation. Therefore it pleased the Lord at sundry times and in divers manners to reveal Himself, and to declare that His will unto His Church; and afterward for the better preserving and propagating of the truth, and for the more sure establishment and comfort of the Church against the corruption of the flesh, and the malice of Satan, and of the world, to commit the same wholly unto writing; which maketh the Holy Scriptures to be most necessary, those former ways of God's revealing His will unto His people being now ceased.

2   Under the name of Holy Scripture, or the Word of God written, are now contained all the books of the Old and New Testaments, which are the thirty-nine books of the Old Testament and the twenty-seven books of the New, all of which are given by the inspiration of God, to be the rule of faith and life.

3   The books commonly called Apocrypha, not being of Divine inspiration, are no part of the canon or rule of the Scripture, and, therefore, are of no authority to the Church of God, nor to be any otherwise approved or made use of than other human writings.

4   The authority of the Holy Scripture, for which it ought to be believed, dependeth not upon the testimony of any man or Church, but wholly upon God (Who is truth itself), the Author thereof; therefore it is to be received because it is the Word of God.

5   We may be moved and induced by the testimony of the Church of God to an high and reverent esteem of the Holy Scriptures; and the heavenliness of the matter, the efficacy of the doctrine, and the majesty of the style, the consent of all the parts, the scope of the whole (which is to give all glory to God), the full discovery it makes of the only way of man's salvation, and many other incomparable excellencies and entire perfections thereof, are arguments whereby it doth abundantly evidence itself to be the Word of God; yet notwithstanding, our full persuasion and assurance of the infallible truth, and Divine authority thereof, is from the inward work of the Holy Spirit bearing witness by and with the Word in our hearts.

6   The whole counsel of God concerning all things necessary for His own glory, man's salvation, faith and life, is either expressly set down or necessarily contained in the Holy Scripture: unto which nothing at any time is to be added, whether by new revelation of the Spirit, or traditions of men.

Nevertheless, we acknowledge the inward illumination of the Spirit of God to be necessary for the saving understanding of such things as are revealed in the Word, and that there are some circumstances concerning the worship of God, and government of the Church, common to human actions and societies, which are to be ordered by the light of nature and Christian prudence, according to the general rules of the Word, which are always to be observed.

7   All things in Scripture are not alike plain in themselves, nor alike clear unto all; yet those things which are necessary to be known, believed and observed for salvation, are so clearly propounded and opened in some place of Scripture or other, that not only the learned, but the unlearned, in a due use of ordinary means, may attain to a sufficient understanding of them.

8   The Old Testament in Hebrew (which was the native language of the people of God of old), and the New Testament in Greek (which at the time of the writing of it was most generally known to the nations), being immediately inspired by God, and by His singular care and providence kept pure in all ages, are therefore authentic; so as in all controversies of religion, the Church is finally to appeal to them. But because these original tongues are not known to all the people of God, who have a right unto, and interest in the Scriptures, and are commanded in the fear of God to read and search them, therefore they are to be translated into the vulgar [i.e. common] language of every nation unto which they come, that the Word of God dwelling plentifully in all, they may worship Him in an acceptable manner, and through patience and comfort of the Scriptures may have hope.

9   The infallible rule of interpretation of Scripture is the Scripture itself; and therefore when there is a question about the true and full sense of any Scripture (which is not manifold, but one), it must be searched by other places that speak more clearly.

10   The supreme judge, by which all controversies of religion are to be determined, and all decrees of councils, opinions of ancient writers, doctrines of men, and private spirits are to be examined, and in whose sentence we are to rest, can be no other but the Holy Scripture delivered by the Spirit, into which Scripture so delivered, our faith is finally resolved.

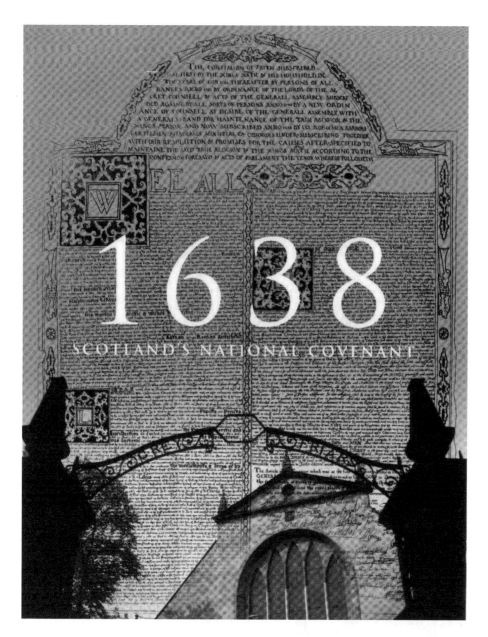

Scotland's National Covenant was read aloud and signed at Greyfriars Kirk in Edinburgh. Rev. John Livingstone of Killinchy, Co. Down, took it overnight to London. Copies of this Covenant were soon circulating and being signed in Ulster.

THE CONFESSION OF FAITH OF THE KIRK OF SCOTLAND: OR THE NATIONAL COVENANT, WITH A DESIGNATION OF SUCH ACTS OF PARLIAMENT AS ARE EXPEDIENT FOR JUSTIFYING THE UNION AFTER MENTIONED

The Signing of the National Covenant at Greyfriars Churchyard, Edinburgh

Greyfriars Kirk, Edinburgh
On 28 February 1638, Scotland's National Covenant was read aloud and signed by the Scottish nobility at Greyfriars Kirk. Over the following weeks, almost the entire population had signed it, and copies were known to be circulated in Ulster. Greyfriars was also the site of a Covenanter prison from 1679-1688. Today the Kirk has a visitor centre, an original 1638 Covenant, a collection of Covenanter banners, and a large monument.

JOSHUA 24:25.- *So Joshua made a covenant with the people that day, and set them a statue and an ordinance in Shechem.*
2 KINGS 11:17. - *And Jehoiada made a covenant between the Lord and the king and the people, that they should be the Lord's people; between the king also and the people.*
ISAIAH 44:5. - *One shall say, I am the Lord's; and another shall call himself by the name of Jacob; and another shall subscribe with his hand unto the Lord, and surname himself by the name of Israel.*

ASSEMBLY AT EDINBURGH, August 30, 1639. Sess. 23.
ACT *ordaining, by Ecclesiastical Authority, the Subscription of the* CONFESSION OF FAITH AND COVENANT, *with the* ASSEMBLY'S *Declaration.*

THE General Assembly considering the great happiness which may flow from a full and perfect union of this kirk and kingdom, by joining of all in one and the same Covenant with God, with the King's Majesty, and amongst ourselves; having, by our great oath, declared the uprightness and loyalty of our intentions in all our proceedings; and having withal supplicated his Majesty's high Commissioner, and the Lords of his Majesty's honourable Privy Council, to enjoin, by act of council, all the lieges in time coming to subscribe the Confession of Faith and Covenant; which, as a testimony of our fidelity to God, and loyalty to our King, we have subscribed: And seeing his Majesty's high Commissioner, and the Lords of his Majesty's honourable Privy Council, have granted the desire of our supplication, ordaining, by civil authority, all his Majesty's lieges, in time coming, to subscribe the foresaid Covenant: that our union may be the more full and perfect, we, by our act and constitution ecclesiastical, do approve the foresaid Covenant in all the heads and clauses thereof; and ordain of new, under all ecclesiastical censure, That all the masters of universities, colleges, and schools, all scholars at the passing of their degrees, all persons suspected of Papistry, or any other error; and finally, all the members of this kirk and kingdom, subscribe the same, with these words prefixed to their subscription, "The Article of this Covenant, which was at the first subscription referred to the determination of the General Assembly, being determined; and thereby the five articles of Perth, the government of the kirk by bishops, the civil places and power of kirkmen, upon the reasons and grounds contained in the acts of the General Assembly, declared to be unlawful within this kirk; we subscribe according to the determination foresaid." And ordain the Covenant, with this declaration, to be insert in the registers of the Assemblies of this kirk, general, provincial, and presbyterial, ad perpetuam rei memoriam. And in all humility supplicate his Majesty's high Commissioner, and the honourable estates of Parliament, by their authority, to ratify and enjoin the same, under all civil pains; which will tend to the glory of God, preservation of religion, the King's Majesty's honour, and perfect peace of this kirk and kingdom.

Charles I. Parl. 2. Act 5.

ACT *anent the Ratification of the* COVENANT, *and of the Assembly's Supplication, Act of Council, and Act of Assembly concerning the Covenant.*
At Edinburgh, June 11, 1640.

THE Estates of Parliament, presently convened by his Majesty's special authority, considering the supplication of the General Assembly at Edinburgh, the 12th of August 1639, to his Majesty's high Commissioner, and the Lords of his Majesty's honourable Privy Council; and the act of council of the 30th of August 1639, containing the answer of the said supplication; and the act of the said General Assembly, ordaining, by their ecclesiastical constitution, the subscription of the Confession of Faith and Covenant mentioned in their supplication: and withal, having supplicated his Majesty to ratify and enjoin the same by his royal authority, under all civil pains, as tending to the glory of God, the preservation of religion, the King's Majesty's honour, and the perfect peace of this kirk and kingdom; do ratify and approve the said supplication, act of council, and act of Assembly; and, conform thereto, ordain and command the said Confession and Covenant to be subscribed by all his Majesty's subjects of what rank and quality soever, under all civil pains' and ordain the said supplication, act of Council, and act of the Assembly, with the whole Confession and Covenant itself, to be insert and registrate in the acts and books of Parliament; and also ordain the same to be presented at the entry of every parliament, and, before they proceed to any other act, that the same be publickly read, and sworn by the whole members of parliament claiming voice therein; otherwise the refusers to subscribe and swear the same shall have no place nor voice in parliament: And sicklike, ordain all judges, magistrates, or other officers, of whatsoever place, rank, or quality, and ministers at their entry, to swear and subscribe the same Covenant, whereof the tenor follows.

THE NATIONAL COVENANT; OR, THE CONFESSION OF FAITH

Subscribed at first by the King's Majesty, and his Household, in the year 1580; thereafter by persons of all ranks in the year 1581, by ordinance of the Lords of secret council, and acts of the General Assembly; subscribed again by all sorts of persons in the year 1590, by a new ordinance of council, at the desire of the General Assembly: with a general bond for the maintaining of the true Christian religion, and the King's person; and, together with a resolution and promise, for the causes after expressed, to maintain the true religion, and the King's Majesty, according to the foresaid Confession and acts of Parliament, subscribed by Barons, Nobles, Gentlemen, Burgesses, Ministers, and Commons, in the year 1638: approven by the General Assembly 1638 and 1639; and subscribed again by persons of all ranks and qualities in the year 1639, by an ordinance of council, upon the supplication of the General Assembly, and act of the General Assembly, ratified by an act of Parliament 1640: and subscribed by King *Charles II.* at *Spey, June* 23, 1650, and *Scoon, January* 1. 1651.

We all and every one of us under-written, protest, That, after long and due examination of our own consciences in matters of true and false religion, we are now thoroughly resolved in the truth by the Word and Spirit of God: and therefore we believe with our hearts, confess with our mouths, subscribe with our hands, and constantly affirm, before God and the whole world, that this only is the true Christian faith and religion, pleasing God, and bringing salvation to man, which now is, by the mercy of God, revealed to the world by the preaching of the blessed Evangel; and is received, believed, and defended by many and sundry notable kirks and realms, but chiefly by the kirk of Scotland, the King's Majesty, and three estates of this realm, as God's eternal truth, and only ground of our salvation; as more particularly is expressed in the Confession of our Faith, established and publickly confirmed by sundry acts of Parliaments, and now of a long time hath been openly professed by the King's Majesty, and whole body of this realm both in burgh and land. To the which Confession and Form of

Religion we willingly agree in our conscience in all points, as unto God's undoubted truth and verity, grounded only upon his written Word. And therefore we abhor and detest all contrary religion and doctrine; but chiefly all kind of Papistry in general and particular heads, even as they are now damned and confuted by the Word of God and Kirk of Scotland. But, in special, we detest and refuse the usurped authority of that Roman Antichrist upon the Scriptures of God, upon the kirk, the civil magistrate, and consciences of men; all his tyrannous laws made upon indifferent things against our Christian liberty; his erroneous doctrine against the sufficiency of the written Word, the perfection of the law, the office of Christ, and his blessed Evangel; his corrupted doctrine concerning original sin, our natural inability and rebellion to God's law, our justification by faith only, our imperfect sanctification and obedience to the law; the nature, number, and use of the holy sacraments; his five bastard sacraments, with all his rites, ceremonies, and false doctrine, added to the ministration of the true sacraments without the Word of God; his cruel judgment against infants departing without the sacrament; his absolute necessity of baptism; his blasphemous opinion of transubstantiation, or real presence of Christ's body in the elements, and receiving of the same by the wicked, or bodies of men; his dispensations with solemn oaths, perjuries, and degrees of marriage forbidden in the Word; his cruelty against the innocent divorced; his devilish mass; his blasphemous priesthood; his profane sacrifice for sins of the dead and the quick; his canonization of men; calling upon angels or saints departed, worshipping of imagery, relicks, and crosses; dedicating of kirks, altars, days; vows to creatures; his purgatory, prayers for the dead; praying or speaking in a strange language, with his processions, and blasphemous litany, and multitude of advocates or mediators; his manifold orders, auricular confession; his desperate and uncertain repentance; his general and doubtsome faith; his satisfaction of men for their sins; his justification by works, opus operatum, works of supererogation, merits, pardons, peregrinations, and stations; his holy water, baptizing of bells, conjuring of spirits, crossing, sayning, anointing, conjuring, hallowing of God's good creatures, with the superstitious opinion joined therewith; his worldly monarchy, and wicked hierarchy; his three solemn vows, with all his shavelings of sundry sorts; his erroneous and bloody decrees made at Trent, with all the subscribers or approvers of that cruel and bloody band, conjured against the kirk of God. And finally, we detest all his vain allegories, rites, signs, and traditions brought in the kirk, without or against

172

the Word of God, and doctrine of this true Reformed Kirk; to the which we join ourselves willingly, in doctrine, faith, religion, discipline, and use of the holy sacraments, as lively members of the same in Christ our Head: promising and swearing, by the great name of the LORD our GOD, that we shall continue in the obedience of the doctrine and discipline of this kirk [The Confession which was subscribed at Halyrud-house the 25th of February 1587-8, by the King, Lennox Huntly, the Chancellor, and about 95 other persons, hath here added, "Agreeing to the Word." Sir John Maxwell of Pollock hath the original parchment.], and shall defend the same, according to our vocation and power, all the days of our lives; under the pains contained in the law, and danger both of body and soul in the day of God's fearful judgment.

And seeing that many are stirred up by Satan, and that Roman Antichrist, to promise, swear, subscribe, and for a time use the holy sacraments in the kirk deceitfully, against their own conscience; minding hereby, first, under the external cloak of religion, to corrupt and subvert secretly God's true religion within the kirk; and afterward, when time may serve, to become open enemies and persecutors of the same, under vain hope of the Pope's dispensation, devised against the Word of God, to his greater confusion, and their double condemnation in the day of the Lord Jesus: we therefore, willing to take away all suspicion of hypocrisy, and of such double dealing with God, and His kirk, protest, and call the Searcher of all hearts for witness, that our minds and hearts do fully agree with this our Confession, promise, oath, and subscription: so that we are not moved with any worldly respect, but are persuaded only in our conscience, through the knowledge and love of God's true religion imprinted in our hearts by the Holy Spirit, as we shall answer to Him in the day when the secrets of all hearts shall be disclosed.

And because we perceive, that the quietness and stability of our religion and kirk doth depend upon the safety and good behaviour of the King's Majesty, as upon a comfortable instrument of God's mercy granted to this country, for the maintaining of His kirk, and ministration of justice amongst us; we protest and promise with our hearts, under the same oath, hand-writ, and pains, that we shall defend his person and authority with our goods, bodies, and lives, in the defence of Christ, His Evangel, liberties of our country, ministration of justice, and punishment of iniquity, against all enemies within this realm or without, as we desire our God to be a strong and merciful defender to us in the day of our death, and coming of our Lord Jesus Christ; to whom, with the Father, and the Holy Spirit, be all honour and glory eternally. Amen.

Likeas many Acts of Parliament, not only in general do abrogate, annul, and rescind all laws, statutes, acts, constitutions, canons civil or municipal, with all other ordinances, and practique penalties whatsoever, made in prejudice of the true religion, and professors thereof; or of the true kirk, discipline, jurisdiction, and freedom thereof; or in favours of idolatry and superstition, or of the Papistical kirk: As Act 3, Act 31, Parl. 1; Act 23, Parl. 11; Act 114, Parl. 12 of King James VI., That Papistry and superstition may be utterly suppressed, according to the intention of the Acts of Parliament, repeated in the fifth Act, Parl. 20, King James VI. And to that end they ordain all Papists and Priests to be punished with manifold civil and ecclesiastical pains, as adversaries to God's true religion, preached, and by law established, within this realm, Act 24, Parl. 11, King James VI.; as common enemies to all Christian government, Act 18, Parl. 16, King James VI.; as rebellers and gainstanders of our Sovereign Lord's authority, Act 47, Parl.3, King James VI.; and as idolaters, Act 104, Parl.17, King James VI. But also in particular, by and attour the Confession of Faith, do abolish and condemn the Pope's authority and jurisdiction out of this land, and ordains the maintainers thereof to be punished, Act 2, Parl.1; Act 51, Parl.3; Act 106, Parl. 7; Act 114, Parl. 12, King James VI.: do condemn the Pope's erroneous doctrine, or any other erroneous doctrine repugnant to any of the articles of the true and Christian religion, publickly preached and by law established in this realm; and ordains the spreaders and makers of books or libels, or letters or writs of that nature, to be punished, Act 46, Parl. 3; Act 106, Parl. 7; Act 24, Parl. 11, King James VI.: do condemn all baptism conform to the Pope's kirk, and the idolatry of the mass; and ordains all sayers, willful hearers, and concealers of the mass, the maintainers and resetters of the priests, Jesuits, trafficking Papists, to be punished without any exception or restriction, Act 5, Parl. 1; Act 120, Parl. 12; Act 164, Parl. 13; Act 193, Parl. 14; Act 1, Parl. 19; Act 5, Parl. 20, King James VI.: do condemn all erroneous books and writs containing erroneous doctrine against the religion presently professed, or containing superstitious rites and ceremonies Papistical, whereby the people are greatly abused; and ordains the home-bringers of them to be punished, Act

25, Parl. 11, King James VI.: do condemn the monuments and dregs of bygone idolatry, as going to crosses, observing the festival days of saints, and such other superstitious and Papistical rites, to the dishonour of God, contempt of true religion, and fostering of great error among the people; and ordains the users of them to be punished for the second fault, as idolaters, Act 104, Parl.7, King James VI.

Likeas many Acts of Parliament are conceived for maintenance of God's true and Christian religion, and the purity thereof, in doctrine and sacraments of the true Church of God, the liberty and freedom thereof, in her national, synodal assemblies, presbyteries, sessions, policy, discipline, and jurisdiction thereof; as that purity of religion, and liberty of the Church was used, professed, exercised, preached, and confessed, according to the reformation of religion in this realm: As for instance, the 99th Act, Parl.7; Act 25, Parl. 11; Act 114, Parl. 12; Act 160, Parl. 13 of King James VI. ratified by the 4th Act of King Charles. So that the 6th Act, Parl. 1, and 68th Act, Parl. 6 of King James VI. in the year of God 1579, declare the ministers of the blessed Evangel, whom God of His mercy had raised up, or hereafter should raise, agreeing with them that then lived, in doctrine and administration of the sacraments; and the people that professed Christ, as He was then offered in the Evangel, and doth communicate with the holy sacraments (as in the Reformed Kirks of this realm they were presently adminstrate) according to the Confession of Faith, to be the true and holy kirk of Christ Jesus within this realm. And decerns and declares all and sundry, who either gainsay the Word of the Evangel received and approved as the heads of the Confession of Faith, professed in Parliament in the year of God 1560, specified also in the first Parliament of King James VI., and ratified in this present Parliament, more particularly do express; or that refuse the administration of the holy sacraments, as they were then ministrated; to be no members of the said kirk within this realm, and true religion presently professed, so long as they keep themselves so divided from the society of Christ's body. And the subsequent Act 69, Parl. 6 of King James VI. declares, that there is no other face of kirk, nor other face of religion, than was presently at that time, by the favour of God, established within this realm: "Which therefore is ever styled God's true religion, Christ's true religion, the true and Christian religion, and a perfect religion;" which, by manifold Acts of Parliament, all within this realm are bound to profess, to subscribe the articles thereof, the Confession of Faith, to recant all doctrine and errors repugnant to any of the said articles, Act 4 and 9, Parl. 1; Acts 45,46,47, Parl. 3; Act 71, Parl. 6; Act 106, Parl. 7; Act 24, Parl. 11; Act 123, Parl. 12; Act 194 and 197, Parl. 14 of King James VI. And all magistrates, sheriffs, &c. on the one part, are ordained to search, apprehend, and punish all contraveners: For instance, Act 5, Parl. 1; Act 104, Parl. 7; Act 25, Parl. 11, King James VI.; and that notwithstanding of the King's Majesty's licences on the contrary, which are discharged, and declared to be of no force, in so far as they tend in any wise to the prejudice and hinder of the execution of the Acts of Parliament against Papists and adversaries of true religion, Act 106, Parl. 7, King James VI. On the other part, in the 47th Act, Parl. 3, King James VI. it is declared and ordained, Seeing the cause of God's true religion and his Highness's authority are so joined, as the hurt of the one is common to both; that none shall be reputed as loyal and faithful subjects to our sovereign Lord, or his authority, but be punishable as rebellers and gainstanders of the same, who shall not give their confession, and make their profession of the said true religion: and that they who, after defection, shall give the confession of their faith of new, they shall promise to continue therein in time coming, to maintain our sovereign Lord's authority, and at the uttermost of their power to fortify, assist, and maintain the true preachers and professors of Christ's religion, against whatsoever enemies and gainstanders of the same; and namely, against all such, of whatsoever nation, estate, or degree they be of, that have joined or bound themselves, or have assisted, or assist, to set forward and execute the cruel decrees of the council of Trent, contrary to the true preachers and professors of the Word of God; which is repeated, word by word, in the articles of pacification at Perth, the 23d of February 1572, approved by Parliament the last of April 1573, ratified in Parliament 1587, and related Act 123, Parl. 12 of King James VI.; with this addition, "That they are bound to resist all treasonable uproars and hostilities raised against the true religion, the King's Majesty, and the true professors."

Likeas, all lieges are bound to maintain the King's Majesty's royal person and authority, the authority of Parliaments, without the which neither any laws or lawful judicatories can be established, Act 130 and 131, Parl. 8, King James VI., and the subjects' liberties, who ought only to live and be governed by the King's laws, the common laws of this realm allenarly, Act 48, Parl.3, King James I.; Act 79, Parl. 6, King James IV.; repeated in the Act 131, Parl. 8, King James VI., which if they be innovated and prejudged, "the commission anent the union of the two kingdoms of Scotland and England, which is the sole act of the 17th Parl. of King James VI. declares," such confusion would ensue as this realm could be no more a free monarchy: because, by the fundamental laws, ancient privileges, offices, and liberties of this kingdom, not only the princely authority of his Majesty's royal descent hath been these many ages maintained, but also the people's security of their lands, livings, rights, offices, liberties, and dignities preserved. And therefore, for the preservation of the said true religion, laws, and liberties of this kingdom, it is statute by the 8th Act, Parl. 1, repeated in the 99th Act, Parl. 7, ratified in the 23d Act, Parl. 11, and 114th Act, Parl. 12, of King James VI., and 4th Act, Parl. 1, of King Charles I. "That all Kings and Princes at their coronation, and reception of their princely authority, shall make their faithful promise by their solemn oath, in the presence of the eternal God, that, enduring the whole time of their lives, they shall serve the same eternal God, to the uttermost of their power, according as he hath required in His most holy Word, contained in the Old and New Testament; and according to the same Word, shall maintain the true religion of Christ Jesus, the preaching of His holy Word, the due and right ministration of the sacraments now received and preached within this realm, (according to the Confession of Faith immediately preceding,) and shall abolish and gainstand all false religion contrary to the same; and shall rule the people committed to their charge, according to the will and command of God revealed in His foresaid Word, and according to the laudable laws and constitutions received in this realm, nowise repugnant to the said will of the eternal God; and shall procure, to the uttermost of their power, to the kirk of God, and whole Christian people, true and perfect peace in all time coming: and that they shall be careful to root out of their empire all hereticks and enemies to the true worship of God, who shall be convicted by the true kirk of God of the foresaid crimes." Which was also observed by his Majesty, at his coronation in Edinburgh 1633, as may be seen in the order of the coronation. In obedience to the commandment of God, conform to the practice of the godly in former times, and according to the laudable example of our worthy and religious progenitors, and of many yet living amongst us, which was warranted also by act of council, commanding a general band to be made and subscribed by his Majesty's subjects of all ranks; for two causes: one was, For defending the true religion, as it was then reformed, and is expressed in the Confession of Faith above written, and a former large Confession established by sundry acts of lawful General Assemblies and of Parliaments, unto which it hath relation, set down in publick Catechisms; and which hath been for many years, with a blessing from heaven, preached and professed in this kirk and kingdom, as God's undoubted truth, grounded only upon His written Word. The other cause was, For maintaining the King's Majesty, his person and estate; the true worship of God and the King's authority being so straitly joined, as that they had the same friends and common enemies, and did stand and fall together. And finally, being convinced in our minds, and confessing with our mouths, that the present and succeeding generations in this land are bound to keep the foresaid national oath and subscription inviolable.

We Noblemen, Barons, Gentlemen, Burgesses, Ministers, and Commons under-subscribing, considering divers times before, and especially at this time, the danger of the true Reformed Religion, of the King's honour, and of the publick peace of the kingdom, by the manifold innovations and evils, generally contained, and particularly mentioned in our late supplications, complaints, and protestations; do hereby profess, and before God, His angels, and the world, solemnly declare, That with our whole heart we agree, and resolve all the days of our life constantly to adhere unto and to defend the foresaid true religion, and (forbearing the practice of all innovations already introduced in the matters of the worship of God, or approbation of the corruptions of the publick government of the kirk, or civil places and power of kirkmen, till they be tried and allowed in free Assemblies and in Parliament) to labour, by all means lawful, to recover the purity and liberty of the Gospel, as it was established and professed before the foresaid novations. And because, after due examination, we plainly perceive, and undoubtedly believe, that the innovations and evils contained in our supplications, complaints, and protestations, have no warrant of the Word of God, are contrary to the articles of the foresaid Confession, to the intention and meaning of the blessed Reformers of religion in this land, to the above-written acts of Parliament; and do sensibly tend to the re-establishing of the Popish religion and tyranny, and to the subversion and ruin of the true Reformed Religion, and of our liberties, laws, and estates; we also declare, That the foresaid Confessions are to be interpreted, and ought to be understood of the foresaid novations and evils, no less than if every one of them had been expressed in the foresaid Confessions; and that we are obliged to detest and abhor them, amongst other particular heads of

Papistry abjured therein. And therefore, from the knowledge and conscience of our duty to God, to our King and country, without any worldly respect or inducement, so far as human infirmity will suffer, wishing a further measure of the grace of God for this effect; we promise and swear, by the GREAT NAME OF THE LORD OUR GOD, to continue in the profession and obedience of the foresaid religion; and that we shall defend the same, and resist all these contrary errors and corruptions, according to our vocation, and to the uttermost of that power that God hath put in our hands, all the days of our life.

And in like manner, with the same heart, we declare before God and men, That we have no intention nor desire to attempt anything that may turn to the dishonour of God, or to the diminution of the King's greatness and authority; but, on the contrary, we promise and swear, That we shall, to the uttermost of our power, with our means and lives, stand to the defence of our dread sovereign the King's Majesty, his person and authority, in the defence and preservation of the foresaid true religion, liberties, and laws of the kingdom; as also to the mutual defence and assistance every one of us of another, in the same cause of maintaining the true religion, and his Majesty's authority, with our best counsel, our bodies, means, and whole power, against all sorts of persons whatsoever; so that whatsoever shall be done to the least of us for that cause, shall be taken as done to us all in general, and to every one of us in particular. And that we shall neither directly nor indirectly suffer ourselves to be divided or withdrawn, by whatsoever suggestion, combination, allurement, or terror, from this blessed and loyal conjunction; nor shall cast in any let or impediment that may stay or hinder any such resolution as by common consent shall be found to conduce for so good ends; but, on the contrary, shall by all lawful means labour to further and promote the same: and if any such dangerous and divisive motion be made to us by word or writ, we, and every one of us, shall either suppress it, or, if need be, shall incontinent make the same known, that it may be timeously obviated. Neither do we fear the foul aspersions of rebellion, combination, or what else our adversaries, from their craft and malice, would put upon us; seeing what we do is so well warranted, and ariseth from an unfeigned desire to maintain the true worship of God, the majesty of our King, and the peace of the kingdom, for the common happiness of ourselves and our posterity. And because we cannot look for a blessing from God upon our proceedings, except with our profession and subscription we join such a life and conversation as beseemeth Christians who have renewed their covenant with God; we therefore faithfully promise for ourselves, our followers, and all others under us, both in publick, and in our particular families, and personal carriage, to endeavour to keep ourselves within the bounds of Christian liberty, and to be good examples to others of all godliness, soberness, and righteousness, and of every duty we owe to God and man.

And, that this our union and conjunction may be observed without violation, we call the LIVING GOD, THE SEARCHER OF OUR HEARTS, to witness, who knoweth this to be our sincere desire and unfeigned resolution, as we shall answer to JESUS CHRIST in the great day, and under the pain of God's everlasting wrath, and of infamy and loss of all honour and respect in this world: most humbly beseeching the LORD to strengthen us by his HOLY SPIRIT for this end, and to bless our desires and proceedings with a happy success; that religion and righteousness may flourish in the land, to the glory of GOD, the honour of our King, and peace and comfort of us all. In witness whereof, we have subscribed with our hands all the premises.

The article of this covenant, which was at the first subscription referred to the determination of the General Assembly, being now determined; and thereby the five articles of Perth, the government of the Kirk by bishops, and the civil places and power of kirkmen, upon the reasons and grounds contained in the Acts of the General Assembly, declared to be unlawful within this Kirk, we subscribe according to the determination aforesaid.

Covenanter Battles

Pentland Rising / Rullion Green
28 November 1666
A group of 900 Covenanters (led by former Governor of Belfast, James Wallace) were attacked here by 2000 of King Charles II's troops, led by Thomas Dalzell. Fifty Covenanters were killed, including the two Ulster ministers who were named on the monument. The monument is in Pentland Hills Regional Park, at Flotterstone near Penicuik (10 miles from Edinburgh).

Battle of Drumclog
1 June 1679
On this Sunday morning, the Covenanters were holding a "conventicle" meeting when they were attacked by Royal troops led by "Bloody Claverhouse". The Covenanters fought back, and won a famous victory. Drumclog Memorial Kirk is on the A71 between Kilmarnock and Strathaven, with the monument signposted on the other side of the road.

Battle of Bothwell Bridge
22 June 1679
Three weeks after Drumclog, the Covenanters were again attacked, at Bothwell Bridge which crosses the River Clyde near Hamilton. 400 Covenanters were killed and 1200 were taken prisoner. Many of the Covenanters who escaped, like William Kelso, fled to Ulster for refuge. The monument is on the Hamilton side of the bridge, just off the M74 motorway – where the A7825 meets the B7071 (Bothwell Road).

Battle of Airds Moss
22 July 1680
Located in a wild moor between Cumnock and Muirkirk, north of the A70, is a monument to nine Covenanters who were killed here by Royal troops. Among the nine was Richard Cameron. His head and hands were then severed and sent to his father who was in prison in Edinburgh. The monument was updated in 2006, and can be clearly seen from the main road.

THE WESTMINSTER ASSEMBLY

By Dr John H. Leith (1972), who was Professor of Theology at Union Theological Seminary, Virginia, U.S.A.

THE ASSEMBLY

The Westminster Assembly was the product not simply of the internal theological life of the Church, but also of the economic, social, and political forces of the time. While it is impossible to ignore the religious factors that were involved in the upheavals of English history in the 1640's and 1650's, recent studies have made it apparent that the term *puritan Revolution* has to be qualified. Economic factors such as prices and land, political factors such as the increased power of Parliament or the converging of the interests of the gentry with the Puritan preachers, international factors such as the threat of continental powers played their parts, not only for English Protestants but also for English traders.

The political preparation that preceded the Westminster Assembly was deliberate, partly from choice and partly from the force of events. The origins of the Westminster Assembly reach far back into the Puritan movement and especially into the conflict between the Puritans and the Stuart Kings, James I and Charles I.

The immediate background includes Charles' attempt to force the Prayer Book on the Church of Scotland in 1637 as part of his effort to bring the Church of Scotland into conformity with the Episcopal Church of England. This led to the National Covenant in Greyfriar's churchyard in Edinburgh (1638), to the General Assembly of the Church of Scotland (1638) that protested the policies of Charles, and subsequently to the First Bishops' War when Charles attempted to put down the Scottish rebellion. Charles now had to call Parliament to raise funds, but Charles adjourned Parliament when it began listing its grievances. The controversy with the Scots continued and the Second Bishops' War broke out in 1640. Scottish troops marched into England. Charles was forced once again to call Parliament in November 1640. This Parliament continued in session until it was purged by Cromwell in 1648 and dispersed by him in 1653. Parliament was also in conflict with the King on religious as well as political and social grounds, and it regarded the invading Scottish army as an ally. This controversy erupted in a struggle that would continue until the King had been executed in 1649 and the Protectorate established in 1653.

The controversy between King and Parliament was rooted in the deep-seated religious, social, and political ferment in the whole of society. In the Root and Branch petition of 1640 a long list of theological and ecclesiastical grievances was presented to Parliament by his majesty's subjects in London and in several counties of the kingdom. Subsequently numerous petitions calling for reformation and for a synod to deal with the religious situation were presented. On December 1, 1641, the House of Commons presented the King with the Grand Remonstrance, which outlined many of the theological and ecclesiastical grievances and called for a synod. 'And the better to effect the intended reformation, we desire there may be a general synod of the most grave, pious, learned and judicious divines of this island; assisted with some from foreign parts, professing the same religion with us, who may consider all things necessary for the peace and good government of the Church, and represent the results of their consultations unto the Parliament, to be there allowed of and confirmed, and receive the stamp of authority, thereby to find passage and obedience throughout the kingdom'.

In April 1642, Parliament began the selection of members for the prospective Assembly. In May 1642, a bill was introduced in Parliament calling for an Assembly, but the King withheld his approval. In June 1643, both houses of Parliament, disregarding the refusal of the King, agreed upon an ordinance calling the Assembly into existence. The ordinance is specific as to the task of the Assembly and as to its limitations.

Whereas, amongst the infinite blessings of Almighty God upon this nation, none is or can be more dear unto us than the purity of our religion; and for that, as yet, many things remain in the Liturgy. Discipline, and Government of the Church, which do necessarily require a further and more perfect reformation than as yet hath been attained; and whereas it hath been declared and resolved by the Lords and Commons assembled in Parliament, that the present Church-government by archbishops, bishops, their chancellors, commissaries, deans, deans and chapters, archdeacons, and other ecclesiastical officers depending upon the hierarchy, is evil, and justly offensive and burdensome to the kingdom, a great impediment to reformation and growth of religion, and very prejudicial to the state and government of this kingdom; and that therefore they are resolved that the same shall be taken away, and that such a government shall be settled in the Church as may be most agreeable to God's holy Word, and most apt to procure and preserve the peace of the Church at home, and nearer agreement with the Church of Scotland, and other Reformed Churches abroad; and, for the better effecting hereof, and for the vindicating and clearing of the doctrine of the Church of England from all false calumnies and aspersions, it is thought fit and necessary to call an Assembly of learned, godly, and judicious Divines, who, together with some members of both the Houses of Parliament, are to consult and advise of such matters and things, touching the premises, as shall be proposed unto them by both or either of the Houses of Parliament, and to give their advice and counsel therein to both or either of the said Houses, when, and as often as they shall be thereunto required.

...the said persons, or so many of them as shall be so assembled or sit, shall have power and authority, and are hereby likewise enjoined, from time to time during this present Parliament, or until further order be taken by both the said Houses, to confer and treat among themselves of such matters and things, touching and concerning the Liturgy, Discipline, and Government of the Church of England, or the vindicating and clearing of the doctrine of the same from all false aspersions and misconstructions, as shall be proposed unto them by both or either of the said houses of Parliament, and no other; and to deliver their opinions and advices of, or touching the matters aforesaid, as shall be most agreeable to the Word of God, to both or either of the said Houses, from time to time, in such manner and sort as by both or either of the said houses of Parliament shall be required; and the same not to divulge, by printing, writing, or otherwise, without the consent of both or either House of Parliament.

...That this Ordinance, or any thing therein contained, shall not give unto the persons aforesaid, or any of them, nor shall they in this Assembly assume to exercise any jurisdiction, power, or authority ecclesiastical whatsoever, or any other power than is herein particularly expressed.

The Assembly convened on July 1, 1643, in the face of a prohibition and warning by Charles I, with a sermon by the Prolocutor (presiding officer), William Twisse. The first work of the Assembly was a revision of the Thirty-Nine Articles in order to remove any possibility of Arminian, Pelagian, or Roman interpretation.

Arminianism and Romanism were slogans that connoted quite as much as they denoted.

Arminianism gets its name from Arminius, the Dutch theologian who sought to modify the doctrine of predestination that was held by Reformed orthodoxy; but English Arminianism cannot be identified with the views of Arminius. It did emphasize human freedom and tended, as Tuckney charged, to make the love of God so free as to make it shallow. But Arminianism was also identified with a more relaxed attitude toward theology and also toward the discipline of the Christian life. It was likewise associated with episcopacy and the divine right of kings. Pelagianism was closely related to Arminianism in popular theology, though Arminius had been careful to define his doctrine in distinction from pelagianism, insisting that man could not turn to God without divine grace. Pelagius, in his controversy with Augustine in the fifth century, had exalted man's freedom and his capacity to respond to the love of God. He denied original sin, and he limited grace to revelation and man's created capacities.

Romanism specifically referred to those elements in the liturgy and government of the Church that the Puritans did not feel had been sufficiently reformed. It too had political implications. There were Roman Catholics with great influence in the government, and many hoped England would be a Catholic nation again. The role of Catholics in government was also a sensitive issue in foreign policy, especially when Holland, with which many English sympathised, was still in conflict with Catholic Spain. Furthermore, the Thirty Years War, which Protestants understood as an effort to exterminate the Protestant community, was still in process when the Assembly met. Arminianism and Romanism had specific theological references, but they also had a range of social and political implications that a secular culture such as ours finds difficulty understanding. The effort to eliminate any remnants of either from the confession of the Church was directed to a broad range of concerns and would orient the whole work of the Assembly. By October 12 the revision of the first fifteen Articles had been completed and work had begun on the sixteenth. The work was never completed, but the debates and discussions served as a useful foundation for the later work on the Confession and Catechisms.

A new situation that had long been anticipated, and hoped for by some, was the occasion of another assignment. Parliament, faring badly in the war with the King during the summer of 1643, needed the support of Scotland. On August 17 a Solemn League and Covenant was approved by the Scottish Parliament, and in September it was approved by the English Parliament. The object of the Solemn League and Covenant was the defence and 'preservation of the Reformed Religion in the Church of Scotland in doctrine, worship, discipline, and government...(and) the reformation of religion in the kingdoms of England and Ireland...according to the Word of God, and the examples of the best Reformed Churches, and (the bringing of) the Churches of God in the three kingdoms to the nearest conjunction of uniformity in religion, confession of faith, form of Church government, directory for worship and catechising...' On September 25, 1643, members of the Assembly and the Scottish commissioners subscribed the Solemn League and Covenant. From this point the Assembly took a new direction.

The Solemn League and Covenant meant that the Assembly would devote a major proportion of its time to Church government and worship. In these areas members of the Assembly had their deepest differences. In the end the Assembly drew up a Form of Presbyterial Government in which the Presbyterianism of Melville, Cartwright, and Travers was tempered both by the Congregationalists and by the Erastians who insisted that the church's power was limited to moral persuasion. It also replaced the *Book of Common Prayer* with a Directory for Worship, that, in place of fixed forms, contained directions for worship, some of which were compromises or were ambiguous. The real consensus of the Assembly was in the area of theology, and in the Confession and Catechisms it reached its highest technical achievement.

It is important to note that the Assembly was an appointment of Parliament, not an ecclesiastical synod. Its purpose was to advise Parliament, not to act in the name of the Church. Its charter allowed it no freedom of initiative and permitted advice only on such things as were proposed to the Assembly by Parliament. Members were not to divulge by printing or writing or otherwise their proceedings except with permission of Parliament. The Assembly was explicitly prohibited from assuming 'to exercise any jurisdiction, power, or authority ecclesiastical whatsoever'. The members were appointed by Parliament. The lay members attended as members of Parliament, not as Church officers, except for the Scottish lay commissioners. Robert Baillie, a Scottish commissioner, observed, '...this is no proper Assembly, but a meeting called by the Parliament to advise them in what things they are asked...'

The Assembly carried on its theological work, however, in splendid isolation from the political and social events of the time. There is no indication that the members were put under any political pressure on theological issues. This was due to the theological consensus that was shared by the theologians and their culture. It does not mean that the theology was indifferent to political and social crises.

The preaching of the members of the Assembly to Parliament and to the public always included political and social applications. Indeed, seldom has preaching been so directly applied to the events of the day. The members of the Assembly understood the happenings of their time in terms of their theology and the providence of God, and they believed that God would fulfil his purposes in England either through reform or through apocalyptic events.

CHRONOLOGY

The following dates help to keep events in order:

1603 Accession of James I.
1625 Accession of Charles I.
1637 Imposition of Prayer Book on Church of Scotland.
1639 First Bishops War requires King to call 'Short' Parliament (1640).
1640 Second Bishops War. Scottish army marches into England.
1640, Nov King compelled to call Long Parliament.
1640, Dec London Petition, calling for abolishment of episcopacy, root, and branches.

1641, Nov Parliament passes Grand Remonstrance.

1643, May 13 Ordinance calling for Assembly introduced in the Commons. Passes **June 12, 1643.**

1643, July 1 Assembly convened.

1643, Aug 17 Solemn League and Covenant approved by Scottish Parliament.

1643, Sept Solemn League and Covenant approved by English Parliament.

1643, Sep 25 Members of Assembly and Parliament and Scottish Commissioners subscribe to Solemn League and Covenant.

1643, July 8-Oct 12 Revision of first fifteen of Thirty-nine Articles.

1643-1644 Work began on Form of Government and Directory of Worship.

1644, Aug 20 Committee appointed on Confession of Faith.

1646, Nov 26 Confession of Faith finished and presented to Parliament on **December 4-7, 1646.**

1647, April 5 Minutes note that Confession finished with proof texts.

1647, April 26 Scripture proofs for Confession given to Parliament.

1647, Aug 27 Confession approved by Church of Scotland.

1647, Oct 15 Larger Catechism completed.

1647, Nov 25 Shorter Catechism presented to House of Commons.

1648, April 14 Catechisms presented in final forms.

1648 Purge of Parliament by Oliver Cromwell.

1649, Feb 22 Last numbered Plenary Session of the Assembly.

1649, Feb 22 - 1652, Mar 25 Members of the Assembly met occasionally to examine and license candidates for the ministry.

1653, Dec Oliver Cromwell proclaimed Lord Protector.

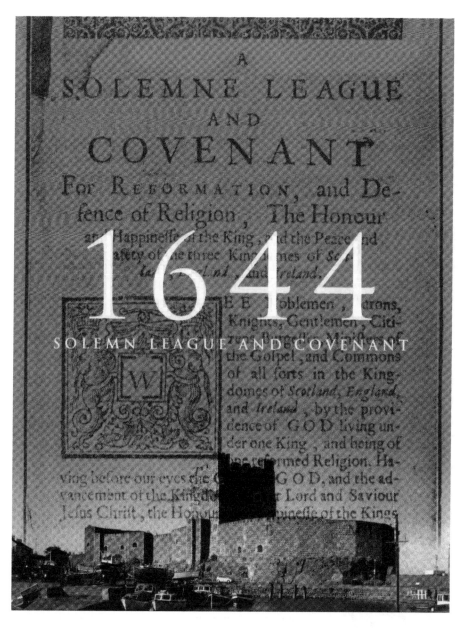

The 1643 Solemn League and Covenant was first administered in Ulster at Carrickfergus in April 1644. It was signed by around 30,000 people at 26 locations across Ulster, from Ballywalter in County Down to Ballyshannon in County Donegal.

Solemn League and Covenant in Ulster

Carrickfergus Castle

Carrickfergus is a special location – the Scottish Army arrived here in April 1642, forming the first Presbytery in Ireland on 10 June. On 4 April 1644 Carrickfergus was the site of the first administering of the Solemn League and Covenant in Ulster, with 1800 people taking the Covenant. The only man to refuse was a Scottish soldier, Major Tam Dalzell, who later became one of the Covenanters' most brutal persecutors.

The Carrickfergus Window

At Presbyterian Church House in Belfast, the beautiful "Carrickfergus Window" commemorates the establishment of the first Presbytery in Ireland by the Scots army on 10 June 1642. The window was installed in 1992 to mark the 350th anniversary of the event.

First Derry Presbyterian

In the vestibule of First Derry Presbyterian Church, on the world famous city Walls, a large marble memorial records the early years of the Scottish Presbyterian settlement in the city, including the signing of the Solemn League and Covenant in the Diamond in 1644.

Kellswater Reformed Presbyterian

In the late 1600s, the Covenanters of Kellswater met regularly on Ferniskey Hill, south of Kells where David Houston had preached, administered communion and baptised their children. In 1760 William Martin settled in Kellswater and a meeting house was built. The lecture hall beside the Church bears the following inscription: Memorial Hall erected by Henry H. Houston of Philadelphia, USA, in honour of his kinsman, the Rev. David Houston MA, who was buried by members of the Reformed Presbyterian Church in Connor Graveyard.

Hogsherd Memorial, Ballyrashane

In Spring 1661, 61 of Ulster's 68 Presbyterian ministers were removed from their Churches by orders of the recently crowned King Charles II. One of them, Rev. Robert Hogsherd of Ballyrashane, is remembered on a memorial plaque on front of the Ballyrashane Presbyterian Church building: *"ejected by a troop of dragoons in 1661 for his loyalty to Christ's Crown and Covenant, of whom the world was not worthy"*.

Josias Welsh grave, Templepatrick

Josias Welsh (1598-1634) was another of the early Presbyterian ministers to come to Ulster. He arrived at Templepatrick around 1622 and was a grandson of the Reformer John Knox. Josias' son John was born at Templepatrick and became a major Covenanter figure in Scotland in 1660s, at Irongray near Dumfries. Josias Welsh's grave is in the small graveyard at Castle Upton, Templepatrick.

James Johnston grave, Aghalurcher

James Johnston was another of the ministers ejected from their pulpits in Spring 1661. He had arrived to minister to the Presbyterians of Fermanagh around 1640, but he died just four years after his ejection, in 1665. He was buried at Aghalurcher Old Graveyard, Lisnaskea, where his carved gravestone can still be seen today.

Richard Cameron in Strabane

Richard Cameron, "Lion of the Covenant" was the leader of the Covenanters in the 1670s and early 1680s. In 1678 he was accused of having preached a "virulent sermon" in Strabane (specific location is unknown) in which he called the ministers who were co-operating with King Charles II "*idolators and persecutors*" and "*guilty of all the blood shed since Abel*".

The Execution of Daniel English

" . . . The execution of a Covenanter named Daniel English made a deeper impression than most of the hangings of that dreadful period, and the memory of it still lingers in local tradition. English was marched four long miles from the guard house at Ballymena to the gallows on the bridge of Connor, dressed in his graveclothes and attended by a great company of his co-religionists, who, as the procession wended its way among the hills, joined together in singing the 119th Psalm . . ." (from *Ulster and Ireland* by J. W. Good, 1919). Daniel English was executed in 1798, just opposite Kirk Hill (shown left) – where the Covenanter minister David Houston had been buried in 1696.

191

THE SOLEMN LEAGUE AND COVENANT

Taken and Subscribed several times by King Charles II, and by all ranks in the three kingdoms of Scotland, England and Ireland.

Jer. 50:5. – Come, and let us join ourselves to the Lord in a perpetual covenant that shall not be forgotten.

Prov. 25:5. – Take away the wicked from before the king, and his throne shall be established in righteousness.

2 Chron. 15:15. – And all Judah rejoiced at the oath: for they had sworn with all their heart, and sought Him with their whole desire; and He was found of them: and the Lord gave them rest round about.

Gal. 3:15. – Though it be but man's covenant, yet if it be confirmed, no man disannulleth, or addeth thereto.

Assembly at Edinburgh, August 17, 1643 - Sess. 14

The General Assembly's Approbation of the SOLEMN LEAGUE AND COVENANT.

The Assembly having recommended unto a Committee appointed by them to join with the Committee of the Honourable Convention of Estates, and the Commissioners of the Honourable Houses of the Parliament of England, for bringing the kingdoms to a more near conjunction and union, received from the foresaid Committees the Covenant after mentioned, as the result of their consultations: and having taken the same, as a matter of so publick concernment and so deep importance doth require, unto their gravest consideration, did, with all their hearts, and with the beginnings of the feelings of that joy, which they did find in so great measure upon the renovation of the National Covenant of this kirk and kingdom. All with one voice approve and embrace the same, as the most powerful mean, by the blessing of GOD, for settling and preserving the true Protestant religion with perfect peace in his Majesty's dominions, and propagating the same to other nations, and for establishing his Majesty's throne to all ages and generations. And therefore, with their best affections, recommend the same to the Honourable Convention of Estates, that, being examined and approved by them, it may be sent with all diligence to the kingdom of England, that, being received and approven there, the same may be, with publick humiliation, and all religious and answerable solemnity, sworn and subscribed by all true professors of the Reformed Religion, and all his Majesty's good subjects in both kingdoms.

Charles I. Parl. 3. Sess. 1. Act 5.

ACT *anent the Ratification of the calling of the Convention, Ratification of the League and Covenant, Articles of Treaty betwixt the Kingdoms of Scotland and England and remanent Acts of the Convention of estates, and Committee thereof.*

AT EDINBURGH, JULY 15, 1644

The Estates of Parliament, presently convened by virtue of the last act of the last Parliament, holden by his Majesty, and the three Estates, in *anno* 1641, considering, that the Lords of his Majesty's Privy Council, and Commissioners for conserving the articles of the treaty, having, according to their interests and trust committed to them by his Majesty and Estates of Parliament, used all means, by supplications, remonstrances, and sending of Commissioners, for securing the peace of this kingdom, and removing the unhappy distractions betwixt his Majesty and his subjects in England, in such a way as might serve most for his Majesty's honour, and good of both kingdoms; and their humble and dutiful endeavours for so good ends having proven ineffectual and their offer of mediation and intercession being refused by his Majesty; and thereby finding the weight and difficulty of affairs, and the charge lying on them to be greater than they could bear; did therefore, in the month of May 1643, meet together with the Commissioners for the common burdens, that, by joint advice, some resolution might be taken therein; and in respect of the danger imminent to the true Protestant Religion, his Majesty's honour, and peace of their kingdoms, by the multitude of Papists and their adherents in Arms in England and Ireland, and of many other publick and important affairs which could not admit delay, and did require the advice of the representative body of the kingdom; appointed and caused indict a meeting of the Convention of Estates (his Majesty having formally refused their humble desires for a Parliament) to be on the 22d of June following; which diet being frequently kept by the Noblemen, commissioners of shires and burghs, and they finding these dangers against this kirk and state still increasing, resolved, after serious deliberation and advice of the General Assembly, and joint concurrence of the Commissioners authorized by the Parliament of England, that one of the chiefest remedies for preventing of these and the like dangers, for preservation of religion, and both kingdoms from ruin and destruction, and for procuring of peace, That both kingdoms should, for these ends, enter into Covenant; which was accordingly drawn up, and cheerfully embraced and allowed. – And at last a treaty was agreed unto by both kingdoms, concerning the said Covenant, and assistance craved from this kingdom by the kingdom of England, in pursuance of the ends expressed therein: - And the Estates being still desirous to use all good means, that, without the effusion of more blood, there may be such a blessed pacification betwixt his Majesty and his subjects, as may tend to the good of religion, his Majesty's true honour and safety, and happiness of his people, did therefore give commission to John Earl of Loudoun, Lord Chancellor, Lord Maitland, Lord Warristoun, and Mr Robert Barclay, to repair to England, and endeavour the effectuating of these ends contained in the covenant of treaties, conform to their instructions. –

And the said Estates having taken the proceedings above written to their consideration, do find and declare, That the Lords of Council, and conservers of peace, did behave themselves as faithful counsellors, loyal subjects, and good patriots, in tendering their humble endeavours for removing the distractions betwixt his Majesty and his subjects, and in calling the commissioners for the common burdens, and, by joint advice, appointing the late meeting of Convention, wherein they have approven themselves answerable to the duty of their places, and that trust committed to them; and therefore ratifies and approves their whole proceedings therein, and declares the said Convention was lawfully called, and also full and free in itself, consisting of all members thereof, as any Convention hath been at any time bygone; and ratifies and approves the several acts made by them, or their committee, for enjoining the Covenant. – And also, the said estates of Parliament (but prejudice of the premises, and of the general ratification above mentioned) ratify, approve, and confirm the foresaid mutual League and Covenant, concerning the reformation and defence of religion, the honour and happiness of the King, and the peace and safety of the three kingdoms of Scotland, England, and Ireland; together with the acts of the Kirk and Estate authorizing the same League and Covenant; together also with the foresaid articles of treaty agreed upon betwixt the said Commissioners of the Convention of estates of Scotland and the Commissioners of both the Houses of Parliament of England, concerning the said Solemn League and Covenant. – And the said Estates ordain the same acts, with the League and Covenant above specified, acts authorizing the same, and the articles of treaty foresaid, to have the full force and strength of perfect laws and acts of Parliament, and to be observed by all his Majesty's lieges, conform to the tenors thereof respective. Of the which League and Covenant the tenor follows.

The Solemn League and Covenant, for reformation and defence of religion, the honour and happiness of the King, and the peace and safety of the three kingdoms of Scotland, England, and Ireland; agreed upon by commissioners from the Parliament and Assembly of Divines in England, with Commissioners of the Convention of Estates and General Assembly of the Church of Scotland; approved by the General Assembly of the Church of Scotland, and by both Houses of Parliament, and the Assembly of Divines in England, and taken and subscribed by them anno 1643; and thereafter, by the said authority, taken and subscribed by all ranks in Scotland and England the same year; and ratified by act of the Parliament of Scotland anno 1644. (And again renewed in Scotland, with an acknowledgement of sins and engagements to duties, by all ranks, anno 1648, and by Parliament, 1649; and taken and subscribed by King Charles II., at Spey, June 23, 1650; and at Scoon, January 1, 1651).

We, noblemen, barons, knights, gentlemen, citizens, burgesses, ministers of the Gospel, and commons of all sorts, in the kingdoms of Scotland, England, and Ireland, by the providence of GOD living under one king, and being of one Reformed Religion, having before our eyes the glory of God, and the advancement of the kingdom of our Lord and Saviour JESUS CHRIST, the honour and happiness of the king's majesty and his posterity, and the true public liberty, safety, and peace of the kingdom, wherein every one's private condition is included: and calling to mind the treacherous and bloody plots, conspiracies, attempts, and practices of the enemies of GOD, against the true religion and professors thereof in all places, especially in these three kingdoms, ever since the reformation of religion; and how much their rage, power, and presumption, are of late, and at this time, increased and exercised, whereof the deplorable state of the Church and kingdom of Ireland, the distressed state of the Church and kingdom of England, and the dangerous state of the Church and kingdom of Scotland, are present and public testimonies: we have now at last (after other means of supplication, remonstrance, protestation, and sufferings), for the preservation of ourselves and our religion from utter ruin and destruction, according to the commendable practice of these kingdoms in former times, and the example of GOD'S people in other nations, after mature deliberation, resolved and determined to enter into a Mutual and Solemn League and Covenant, wherein we all subscribe, and each one of us for himself, with our hands lifted up to the Most High GOD, do swear,-

1. That we shall sincerely, really, and constantly, through the grace of GOD, endeavour, in our several places and callings, the preservation of the Reformed Religion in the Church of Scotland, in doctrine, worship, discipline, and government, against our common enemies; the reformation of religion in the kingdoms of England and Ireland, in doctrine, worship, discipline, and government, according to the Word of GOD, and the example of the best Reformed Churches; and shall endeavour to bring the Churches of GOD in the three kingdoms to the nearest conjunction and uniformity in religion, Confession of Faith, Form of Church Government, Directory for Worship and Catechising; that we, and our posterity after us, may, as brethren, live in faith and love, and the Lord may delight to dwell in the midst of us.

2. That we shall, in like manner, without respect of persons, endeavour the extirpation of Popery, Prelacy (that is, Church government by archbishops, bishops, their chancellors and commissioners, deans, deans and chapters, archdeacons, and all other ecclesiastical officers depending on that hierarchy), superstition, heresy, schism, profaneness, and whatsoever shall be found contrary to sound doctrine and the power of Godliness; lest we partake in other men's sins, and thereby be in danger to receive of their plagues; and that the Lord may be one, and His name one, in the three kingdoms.

3.   We shall, with the same sincerity, reality, and constancy, in our several vocations, endeavour, with our estates and lives, mutually to preserve the rights and privileges of the Parliaments, and the liberties of the kingdoms; and to preserve and defend the King's majesty's person and authority, in the preservation and defence of the true religion and liberties of the kingdoms; that the world may bear witness with our consciences of our loyalty, and that we have no other thoughts or intentions to diminish his majesty's just power and greatness.

4.   We shall also, with all faithfulness, endeavour the discovery of all such as have been or shall be incendiaries, malignants, or evil instruments, be hindering the reformation of religion, dividing the king from his people, or one of the kingdoms from another, or making any faction or parties among the people, contrary to this League and Covenant; that they may be brought to public trial, and receive condign punishment, as the degree of their offences shall require or deserve, or the supreme judicatories of both kingdoms respectively, or others having power from them for that effect, shall judge convenient.

5.   And whereas the happiness of a blessed peace between these kingdoms, denied in former times to our progenitors, is, by the good providence of GOD, granted unto us, and hath been lately concluded and settled by both parliaments; we shall, each one of us, according to our place and interest, endeavour that they may remain conjoined in a firm peace and union to all posterity; and that justice may be done upon the wilful opposers thereof, in manner expressed in the precedent article.

6.   We shall also, according to our places and callings, in this common cause of religion, liberty, and peace of the kingdoms, assist and defend all those that enter into this League and Covenant, in the maintaining and pursuing thereof; and shall not suffer ourselves, directly or indirectly, by whatsoever combination, persuasion, or terror, to be divided or withdrawn from this blessed union and conjunction, whether to make defection to the contrary part, or to give ourselves to a detestable indifferency or neutrality in this cause, which so much

concerneth the glory of God, the good of the kingdom, and honour of the king; but shall, all the days of our lives, zealously and constantly continue therein against all opposition, and promote the same, according to our power, against all lets and impediments whatsoever; and what we are not able ourselves to suppress or overcome, we shall reveal and make known, that it may be timely prevented or removed: All which we shall do as in the sight of God.

And, because these kingdoms are guilty of many sins and provocations against GOD, and his Son JESUS CHRIST, as is too manifest by our present distresses and dangers, the fruits thereof; we profess and declare, before GOD and the world, our unfeigned desire to be humbled for our own sins, and for the sins of these kingdoms; especially that we have not, as we ought, valued the inestimable benefit of the Gospel; that we have not laboured for the purity and power thereof; and that we have not endeavoured to receive Christ in our hearts, not to walk worthy of Him in our lives; which are the causes of other sins and transgression so much abounding amongst us: and our true and unfeigned purpose, desire, and endeavour, for ourselves, and all others under our power and charge, both in public and private, in all duties we owe to GOD and man, to amend our lives, and each one to go before another in the example of a real reformation; that the Lord may turn away his wrath and heavy indignation, and establish these Churches and kingdoms in truth and peace. And this Covenant we make in the presence of ALMIGHTY GOD, the Searcher of all hearts, with a true intention to perform the same, as we shall answer at that great day, when the secrets of all hearts shall be disclosed; most humbly beseeching the LORD to strengthen us by his HOLY SPIRIT for this end, and to bless our desires and proceedings with such success, as may be deliverance and safety to His people, and encouragement to other Christian Churches, groaning under, or in danger of the yoke of antichristian tyranny, to join in the same or like association and covenant, to the glory of GOD, the enlargement of the kingdom of JESUS CHRIST, and the peace and tranquillity of Christian kingdoms, and commonwealths.

This document can also be found, along with other documents, in the volume entitled 'The Westminster Confession of Faith'.

Covenanter memorial at Auchengilloch, between Muirkirk and Strathaven

Anwoth

Anwoth, just off the A75 at Dumfries, was the Church of the famous writer and Covenanter Rev. Samuel Rutherford – a plaque there commemorates his time as minister of Anwoth. He was a close friend of the early Ulster-Scots ministers and wrote some of his world famous letters to them. In later years Michael Bruce was minister at Anwoth and was buried there.

Manorhamilton Castle, Co Leitrim

Manorhamilton Castle was built by Sir Frederick Hamilton around 1630. He was a major figure among the Scots settlers in the county, and signed the Covenant in Ulster (probably in Londonderry) in 1644. He returned to Scotland to join the Covenanters army and was killed in battle there in 1647.

DONALD CARGILL
Martyred for Christ's Crown and
Covenant, Edinburgh 1681

JOHN BROWN of Priesthill
Martyred for Christ's Crown
and Covenant, 1685

JAMES GUTHRIE
Martyred for Christ's Crown
and Covenant, June 1661

JOHN KNOX
1505 - 1572

JOHN WELSH
Minister of Ayr. Son in Law of John Knox

JAMES RENWICK
Martyred for Christ's Crown and Covenant,
Edinburgh Feb 17th 1688

THE SCOTS WORTHIES

WHO ARE THE COVENANTERS?

The Blue Banner for Christ's Crown and Covenant

Rev. Prof. Dr. R. H. Creane

Jeremiah 50 v.5

"They shall ask the way to Zion with their faces thitherward, saying, Come, and let us join ourselves to the Lord in a perpetual covenant that shall not be forgotten".

The Covenanters have a long and distinguished history of which most people today have little knowledge. Despite all the attempts to regard them as a rebellious set of narrow-minded bigots, it is true to say they were staunch men and women of faith with deeply held convictions and belief in sound Biblical truth. Their godly fame, worthy deeds, and magnificent Christian heroism must never be forgotten and should always be held in the highest admiration and honour by all people of the Evangelical Faith.

The Crown Rights of Jesus Christ

The historic Church of the Covenants with its electric influence and sublime Scriptural ideal of national devotion to Church, has long maintained a clear testimony for the Crown Rights of the Lord Jesus Christ as the King and Head of His Church and Governor of the nations. In recalling the momentous events surrounding the history of such a great movement, will help not only to shed light on our civil and religious heritage, but also restore a new love for the Covenanters of old. Their bravery and heroic efforts were decisive, showing great zeal and faithfulness of service in securing the fundamental principle of the autonomy of the Church, without which the Christian Church would cease to be either Christian or a Church. Such a noble cause demanded religious men whose dedicated lives under homage to Christ, were as Alexander Henderson states, "good examples to others, of all godliness, soberness, and righteousness, and of every duty we owe to Church and man".

The effective labours of the Covenanters in Gospel ministry and mission should encourage and inspire many in this generation to uphold, maintain, and defend both by word and deed the principles of our Covenanting forefathers, to carry forward in a solemn act of rededication their witness and ideals in this present evil world. (Gal. 1 v.4; Titus 2 v.12).

In the good providence of God, may it please the Lord to raise up yet again in our day, a committed army of true preachers and stalwarts who are resolute in the faith to contend for a pure Gospel, for a Scriptural form of worship, for national righteousness, for freedom to preach the Divine Word and maintain a distinctive testimony for the Truth of God as revealed in Holy Scripture. The Covenanters' faith could neither surrender nor equivocate. In theology they were Reformed Bible-believing Christians, whose devotion to Christ made them fear neither king nor bishop, agony nor death, and we owe them in great measure the civil and religious liberty we enjoy today.

Call to return to Covenant Obligations

Our nation has greatly fallen away from its covenant obligations which Britain should still recognise, so that Christ and His Word are given their rightful place in national life. We call upon Parliament to return to its covenanted allegiance to the Lord Jesus Christ as King and Lord in the Constitution and administration. In humble obedience and dependence upon Divine grace may all Church people unashamedly profess the true Biblical religion, and with fidelity and meekness "adorn the doctrine of Church our Saviour in all things", (Titus 2 v.10).

Covenanting has its roots in the Bible, as the following two Scriptures, among several others, affirm. "Jehoiada made a covenant between the Lord and the king and the people, that they should be the Lord's people; between the king also and the people", (2 Kings 11 v.17). "I will for their sakes remember the covenant of their ancestors", (Lev. 26 v.45). The only absolute authority recognised by true Protestantism is the authority of the Word of God, in Holy Writ, the Bible. It is not surprising then to find covenanting appearing in the annals of Scottish Church history.

John Knox and Religious Covenanting

Religious covenanting in Scotland covers a long period, beginning in 1556 under John Knox when certain believers did "band themselves" to maintain "the true preaching of the Evangel of Jesus Christ". This is known as 'The Dun Covenant'. The burning question at issue was 'The Headship and Lordship of the Lord Jesus Christ over all things in the Church and nation'.

There were several covenants drawn up by the Scottish people having regard to the maintenance of the Reformed Religion in Scotland. The covenant known as 'The Godly Band', the original of which is preserved in the Scottish National Museum, was subscribed in Edinburgh in 1557. In it the Covenanters for the first time described the Roman Church as the Synagogue of Satan. The mass of signatures appended to it came from among the rank and file members, together with the nobility and leading subscribers known as the Lords of the day. They petitioned the government for Christian liberty, for liberty of conscience, for freedom of religious worship, and for freedom to practice their faith according to the teaching of God's Word.

Being met with dissimulation, false pretension, and treachery, further covenants were signed and sworn, namely, 'The Perth Covenant' in 1559, 'The Sterling Covenant' in 1559, and 'The Leith Covenant' in 1560, among others. In these Bonds or Covenants, the Reformers bound themselves to mutual assistance in defence of their Biblical beliefs, religious rights, and the true liberty of Christ's Gospel.

In 1560 the French army was brought into Scotland to crush the Reformation. The appeal was made to arms, and the aid of Queen Elizabeth The First of England was called in to counteract the French troops invited by the Papal party. On the death of the Queen Mother, the French troops were withdrawn, and Parliament being left at liberty, ordered that the authority of the Pope be renounced, Popery abolished, and also ordered that the Reformed Church, holding to the Presbyterian form of Church Government, be the Established Church of Scotland. No other man could have guided the Church in Scotland as John Knox did in that stormy and critical period. The Kings of France and Spain had bound themselves to crush Protestantism in Europe. The danger was very real. But the year 1560 is long to be remembered in Scotland. With the help of England, the French were driven out, and a free Parliament was called. Also in that year 'The Scotch Confession of Faith', proposed by John Knox and his five friends, Spottiswood, Willock, Row, Douglas, and Winram, was adopted by the new parliament, and the 'First Book of Discipline' which contained the earliest Form of Church Government in Scotland, was warmly approved by the General Assembly of the Reformed Church of Scotland. These splendid statements of Reformed Doctrine and Church Discipline were received and approved with very great enthusiasm and remained in force as the symbol of Scottish religion until 1647 when they were replaced by the 'Westminster Confession of Faith'. During the next eighty years or so, even amid very testing circumstances and many trials, the faith of God's people was wonderfully sustained, and by Divine grace their hands were strengthened for the work of the Lord.

After the death of Knox, James and his advisers did their best to undermine Reformed Presbyterianism and establish Episcopacy. Tortuous policies and penalties were put in place, endeavouring to restore a prelatical Church to become a tool of the Royal Court. His aim was to secure at all costs the Throne of England on the death of Elizabeth. Andrew Melville, was first Principle of Glasgow University and then of St. Andrews, and arose as the great defender of the Reformed Faith and the Presbyterian Form of Church Government. In an interview with the king, Melville had the temerity to tell him to his face that there are two kings and two kingdoms in Scotland . . . . the kingdom of the Lord Jesus Christ where James was only a subject, and the civil kingdom where James was the sovereign. Through his duplicity and other means, James put an end to free assemblies, and the enforced restoration of Episcopacy brought the Reformed Church of Scotland into bondage to the Court until 1638.

The National Covenant

In 1638 the 'National Covenant' was subscribed by many thousands over all Scotland with great solemnity and enthusiasm. This was not only a repetition of the former covenants, but contained, moreover, a robust protest against the Papacy and Popery, a firm declaration against episcopacy and prelacy, and a steadfast refusal to offer worship to angels, saints, Mary or any other created being, or by any other way not prescribed in the Holy Scripture.

The Covenanters maintained that the only acceptable way of worshipping the true God is instituted by Himself according to His Word. In the bond attaching to the venerable 1638 document, they say, "We promise and swear by the name of the Lord our God to continue in the profession and obedience of the true religion; and that we shall defend the same, and resist all those contrary errors and corruptions, according to our vocation, and to the uttermost of that power that God hath put in our hands, all the days of our life".

The yoke of Erastian supremacy under James VI and Charles I was now broken. None but the Papists and some hard-line Royalists resisted, and, therefore, the Covenant in a very real sense was truly National. By the blessing of Almighty God many were awakened, converted and established in the truth of the Gospel.

The Solemn League and Covenant

The Solemn League and Covenant was an agreement or treaty entered into between England and Scotland in 1643 binding both kingdoms unitedly to mutual aid in the removal and extirpation of popery and prelacy, and for preservation of the true Reformed Faith, the maintenance of civil and religious liberty, and the advancement of the Cause of Christ in the realm. It was drafted and drawn up by Alexander Henderson, approved and passed unanimously by the Reformed Church of Scotland at her General Assembly on the 17th August 1643. Furthermore, it was ratified with cordial consent by the Convention of Estates, and wholeheartedly accepted and subscribed by the Westminster Assembly and also by the English Parliament on 25th September 1643. In Ireland, notwithstanding the bloody scenes and massacre of the 1641 rebellion, the Covenants were greatly welcomed by many Protestants in the South of the Country, and by large numbers in the Northern Counties. In 1645 it was again ratified by the Scottish General Assembly, together with the Directory for Worship framed by the Westminster Divines.

The avowed aim of the 'Solemn League and Covenant' was to promote the cause of religious reformation and revival, and prayerfully to preserve the closest uniformity in the profession and practice of the Christian Faith throughout England, Scotland, and Ireland, and to unite the three kingdoms in the call to uphold, maintain, and defend civil and religious liberty. In addition, the 'Metrical Psalter', on the recommendation of the English Lords and commons, was also considered by the Westminster Assembly and warmly approved for the Church's use in the public worship of God, and unanimously adopted by the General Assembly of the Reformed Church of Scotland. Although Charles I would not approve of the 'Solemn League and Covenant', Charles II engaged by oath to observe it, a promise which he broke upon the first opportunity. To its shame, the Scottish Parliament of 1661, in the interests of the King, established the royal supremacy, annulled the 'Solemn League and Covenant', and absolved its personnel employed by the government from its obligations. While the Gospel of salvation in all its fullness was faithfully proclaimed and a revival of true godliness became widespread, this blessed work and witness had continued until the restoration of Charles II in 1660 which had disastrous consequences. The cause of truth and righteousness, for which the Covenanters and Puritans hazarded so much, was now arrested and by the majority virtually abandoned.

Though Reformation principles were for a time nationally accepted and applied in both Church and State in the mid-seventeenth century, the present duty of the Church and nation is to acknowledge their sins and blatant defection from solemn Covenant engagements to honour God's Word, and they should take their stand on the high ground of the Covenanted Reformation to advance the Kingdom of Christ among men to the glory of God.

Reformed Presbyterians and Covenanting

The Covenants have always held a high place in the Reformed Church, but sadly Scotland and England have long since fallen away, and most Churches in the British Isles today do not make adherence to them obligatory on either clerical or lay members. However, certain Scottish and

Irish dissenters, though small in number, still profess attachment to the Covenants, and on particular occasions renew their subscription to them with much heart-searching and prayer to God in confession and thanksgiving.

The terms 'Dissenters' and 'Covenanters' are interchangeable, and are the names given primarily to that body of Reformed Presbyterians who objected to the Revolution Settlement in Church and State, and who desired to see in full force that kind of civil liberty and ecclesiastical polity of the Covenanted Reformation that prevailed in Scotland after the 1638 'National Covenant'. According to the 'Solemn League and Covenant', ratified by the Parliaments of England and Scotland, and also by the Westminster Assembly of Divines in 1643, Reformed Presbyterianism was to be maintained in the three kingdoms of England, Scotland, and Ireland . . . . and popery, prelacy, superstition, heresy, schism, and other evils were to be extirpated and rooted out.

The Covenanters in Scotland bravely contended for the faith, as is well known, and under much suffering, hardship, persecution, and martyrdom, especially during the Killing Times 1660-1688, they roundly defended the cause of the Reformed Faith and the Presbyterian Form of Church Government throughout the reigns of Charles II and James II.

Compromised Terms of the Revolution Settlement

In 1690 as a measure of pacification at the Revolution Settlement, Presbytery was granted and established in Scotland by an Act of Parliament under William III. This piece of legislation was of a much modified form and did not satisfy the strict and staunch Covenanters. Substantially the whole Church in Scotland was rendered a creature of the State, and prelacy was re-confirmed in England and Ireland. There was, however, a general toleration and acceptance of dissent by the Covenanters.

The Covenanter party, thus dissenting, and holding firmly to true civil and religious liberty, and upholding the principles of Biblical truth and righteousness without compromise, repudiated the government of William III and his successors, and still maintained the perpetually binding obligations of the Covenants. These Covenanters acted under strong convictions, being steadfast in the faith, and their only desire was to carry out the will of God in accordance with the teaching of Holy Scripture to His glory. It is in the standards of the historic Covenanters that we have to look for a true embodiment of the tenets held by the great body of English, Scotch, and Irish stalwarts of 1638 and 1643.

Many others gave in to the compromised terms of the Revolution Settlement of 1690, and even afterwards there were many more who defected and found cause to secede. But the true Covenanters never gave in, never compromised, never seceded, and were not willing by God's grace to surrender the truth of His Holy Word. In the years following, it was difficult for the Covenanters to assume and maintain a regular organised communion of ministers. The steadfastness of members was put to a severe trial by the defection of all their ministers, and for a time the people loyal to the cause of the Covenants, were as sheep without a shepherd.

Covenant Renovation and Renewal

At length, after their faith, patience and obedience had been tried for some sixteen years, they were joined by a number of ministers who were staunch and resolute to stand in the gap under the Blue Banner for Christ's Crown and Covenant. As a means of confirming the faith of the members, and of giving public testimony of their principles, it was resolved to renew the Covenants in 1712 and other subsequent dates. As their members grew in number, the Covenanters re-constituted Presbytery in 1743, under the name Reformed Presbytery. They continued to flourish mainly in the west of Scotland and in Northern Ireland.

As a distinctive part of the Church's history, Covenant Renewal took place on numerous occasions at various venues, and notably again in 1901 and 1911. At such events the people of God solemnly engaged before the Lord to uphold His Law, preach a Biblical Gospel, and adhere to Biblical truth, worship, and witness. Today, we pray and long to see a return to such noble practice being renovated and re-established to the glory of God, with due attention and care given to Paul's exhortation to mutual love, Christian purity, and holiness of life: "that ye walk worthy of the vocation wherewith ye are called, With all lowliness and meekness, with longsuffering, forbearing one another in love; Endeavouring to keep the unity of the Spirit in the bond of peace", (Eph. 4 v.1-3).

As we listen to and apply the Word of God to our lives, the experience of Jeremiah, a man that laid things much to heart (Jer. 23), will become ours. Only as we see the righteousness, holiness, and majesty of God, will we know true brokenness of heart and a real trembling before the Lord of Who He is, and how He has revealed Himself to sinful man in His Holy Word. The greatest need in the Church today, and alas, in the world at large, is that we as ministers and preachers speak the Word faithfully, "in demonstration of the Spirit and of power", (1 Cor. 2 v.4).

Holding strictly to the Covenants, and rejecting the compromised terms of the Revolution Settlement, the position of the Covenanters is rather peculiar, as they refuse in theory the political set up by not voting, and do not recognise any laws or institutions which are opposed to the Kingdom of Christ and His Word. The Reformed Presbyterians today, albeit scattered thinly in various parts of the globe, regard themselves as the heirs and modern representatives of the Covenanters.

"And the king went up into the house of the Lord, and all the men of Judah and all the inhabitants of Jerusalem with him, ... and made a covenant before the Lord, to walk after the Lord, and to keep His commandments and His testimonies and His statutes with all their heart and all their soul, to perform the words of this covenant that were written in this book. And all the people stood to the covenant", (2 Kings 23 v.2-3).

"Blessed is the nation whose God is the Lord", (Psalm 33 v.12).

"Vow, and pay unto the Lord your God", (Psalm 76 v.11).

"that in all things He might have the preeminence", (Col. 1 v.18).

209

John Knox preaching

There are many tombstones throughout Scotland of the Covenanters who were martyred for the faith during the Killing Times 1660-1688. This one is at The Auld Kirk, Ayr

(photographs reproduced courtesy of Mr & Mrs Kenny)

THE COVENANTERS IN ULSTER

"...The fire of persecution for non-conformity in Scotland soon extended to the North of Ireland. The king and his courtiers well knew that there were many valiant men in Ulster who would never bend before the blast, however furious it might blow..."

from "Sermons Delivered in Times of Persecution in Scotland" by Covenanter historian John Howie of Lochgoin, 1779

Every Presbyterian

in Scotland, Ireland and America owes their origin to the Covenanters.

The Covenanters' story is often presented as a Scotland-only history, yet it has a major Ulster dimension.

~

The first Scottish Presbyterians began to arrive in east Ulster from 1606 onwards, and their first minister, Rev Edward Brice, arrived at Ballycarry in County Antrim in 1613. More ministers arrived, and for the rest of the 1600s there was a regular flow of Presbyterian ministers and people between Scotland and Ulster.

Spiritual revivals of the early 1600s were followed by state persecution, and it was four of those early ministers - Robert Blair of Bangor, James Hamilton of Ballywalter, John McClelland of Newtownards and John Livingstone of Killinchy - who commissioned the famous emigrant ship *Eagle Wing*, which sailed from Groomsport in September 1636 in a quest to find religious freedom for the Ulster-Scots.

Eagle Wing didn't reach America, and the ministers came back to Ulster, and then returned to Scotland.

They had been searching for freedom overseas - now they found themselves at the forefront of the struggle for religious liberty at home.

The story of the Covenanters has an important Ulster chapter that most people don't know.

Through Scotland's National Covenant of 1638, and the Solemn League and Covenant of 1643 (which was administered across Ulster during 1644) the people protested against the King's interference in their church. These people, and those who followed, were known as Covenanters.

In the 1660s, hundreds of ministers in Scotland and Ulster were driven out of their churches by government troops, and were forced to meet secretly in fields and hillsides. Many were arrested, meetings were attacked, people were executed and banished overseas. An estimated 18,000 Covenanters were either killed or sent into exile for their beliefs.

Alexander Peden memorial at "Misty Burn", Glenwherry, County Antrim

During the *50 Years Struggle* from 1638-1688, 18,000 Covenanters were killed or sent into exile.

Thousands of Scottish Presbyterians fled across the North Channel to refuge and safety in Ulster. Many Ulster Presbyterians went to Scotland to join the fight for freedom. Presbyterian Covenanter ministers travelled back and forth between the two countries, preaching to the people and encouraging them in times of great persecution.

Scotland has over 300 Covenanter memorials, and while there are just a few in Ulster, there are many Ulster locations which are important in the story.

For example, in 1661, at the first of the public executions in Edinburgh it was James Hamilton of Ballywalter who prayed with the Marquis of Argyll before the axe fell on Argyll's neck.

At the Pentland Rising of November 1666, the Covenanters were led by Colonel James Wallace, the former Governor of Belfast. Two ministers were killed at Pentland - John Crookshanks of Raphoe and Andrew McCormick of Magherally (near Banbridge) - and are named on the monument there to this day.

Richard Cameron, *"The Lion of the Covenant"* and James Renwick (regarded as the last of the Covenanter martyrs, executed aged just 26) both spent time among the Presbyterians of Ulster.

In times of great persecution, Ulster was the Covenanters' refuge.

In times of resistance, Ulster was often the Covenanters' haven.

Every Presbyterian
should rediscover the story of the Covenanters.

Rev. Jonathan Edwards 1703–1758

CHAMPION OF EVANGELICAL RELIGION

The only son of the eleven children of Timothy and Esther Edwards

It was the preaching of Jonathan Edwards, together with that of George Whitefield, which led to the Great Awakening of 1735-1744

Edwards' Sermon Outline

on

"The Excellency of Christ", follows.

The Excellency of Christ

"Behold, the Lion of the tribe of Juda, the Root of
David, hath prevailed to open the book, and to loose
the seven seals thereof. And I beheld, and, lo, in the
midst of the throne and of the four beasts, and in the
midst of the elders, stood a Lamb as it had been slain,"
Revelation 5:5, 6

THE VISIONS and the revelations that the Apostle John had of future events
are here introduced with a vision of the book of God's decrees.

I.   THE EXCELLENCIES OF CHRIST REVEALED IN HIS NAMES.

    A.   The Names Given to Christ in the Text.

        1.   *The Lion.* He seems to be called this because of
        Jacob's blessing of the tribes (Genesis 49:9) and the
        standard of Judah which displayed a lion.

        2.   *The Lamb.* A lamb appears and opens the book, an
        exceeding diverse kind of creature from a lion.

    B.   The Significance of the Names Given to Christ in the Text.

        1.   *The Significance stated.* That which I would observe
        from the words of the text: there is an admirable
        joining of Divine excellencies in Christ.

        2.   *The significance briefly explained.* We see that Christ
        is in the text compared to both a lion and a lamb
        because the diverse excellencies of both wonderfully
        meet in Him.

II.   THE UNION OF THE DIVERSE EXCELLENCIES IN CHRIST

A.   There Is a Union of Such Excellencies in Christ
Which to Men Seem Diverse.

1.   *Infinite highness and infinite condescension.* Christ is higher than kings and angels. Yet none are so low or inferior, but Christ's condescension suffices to take notice of them.

2.   *Infinite justice and infinite grace.* Christ is the just Judge of the world and also the One who is infinitely gracious and merciful.

B.   There Is a Union of Such Excellencies in Christ
Which Seem to Men Incompatible in the Same Person.

1.   *Infinite glory and lowest humility.* Infinite glory and the virtue of humility meet in no other person but Christ. In Him these two diverse excellencies are united.

2.   *Infinite majesty and transcendent weakness.* Christ was a person of infinite majesty (Psalm 45:3). Yet He was the most marvellous instance of meekness (Matthew 21:4,5).

3.   *Deepest reverence to God and equality with God.* Christ, when He was upon earth, appeared full of holy reverence towards the Father and He was also equal with the Father.

4.   *Infinite worthiness of good and greatest patience under sufferings of evil.* He was perfectly innocent and deserved no suffering. He was worthy of infinite love. Yet He was perfectly patient under greatest sufferings.

5. *Spirit of obedience and dominion over heaven and earth.* Christ is Lord of all things as God-Man and Mediator. Yet in Him is found the greatest spirit of obedience to God.

6. *Absolute sovereignty and perfect resignation.* Christ, as God, is the absolute Sovereign of the world. He also was the most wonderful example of resignation (Matthew 26:39,42).

7. *Self-sufficiency and entire reliance upon God.* As Divine He is self-sufficient, standing in need of nothing. Yet He entirely trusted in God (Matthew 27:43; I Peter 2:23).

C. Such Diverse Excellencies Are Expressed in Christ Towards Men That Would Seem Impossible.

1. *Justice.* The strict justice of God, even His revenging justice, and that against the sins of men, never was so gloriously manifested as in Christ.

2. *Mercy.* How wonderfully is infinite mercy towards sinners displayed in Him. He is the Judge and also the Saviour (Romans 3:25,26).

3. *Truth.* The immutable truth of God was never so manifested as it is in Jesus Christ. In Him all of God's promises are yea and amen.

III. THE UNION OF THE EXCELLENCIES OF CHRIST APPEAR IN HIS ACTS.

A. It appears in Christ Taking Our Nature

1. *The incarnation reveals His condescension.* It appeared in that God became man and in the low circumstances of His birth.

2. *The incarnation reveals His Divine dignity.* He was conceived by the power of the Holy Spirit. His conception and birth was a holy thing (Luke 1:35).

B. It appears in the Acts of Christ's Earthly life.

1. *His infancy.* In the circumstances of His infancy His outward humiliation appeared, yet there was something then to show His Divine dignity.

2. *His public ministry.* At the same time that Christ appeared in meekness and humility to His disciples He also appeared with Divine authority and majesty in rebuking hypocrites.

C. It appears in Christ's Passion.

1. *Humiliation and glory.* Christ's humiliation was never so great as it was from the Garden to the Cross. When the fruit of it appeared then did the glory of it appear.

2. *Love to God and His enemies*; He never manifested His love to God and His love to God's enemies as He did in His death.

3. *Divine justice.* Christ never so eminently appeared for Divine justice and yet never suffered so much from Divine justice as at His death.

4. *Holiness and guilt.* His holiness appeared in His steadfast obedience to God unto death. Then, also, Christ was in the greatest degree treated as a wicked person.

5. *Unworthiness and worthiness.* He was therein dealt with as unworthy to live. Yet it was chiefly because of His passion that He was accounted worthy of His exaltation.

6. *Suffering from His Father.* He never suffered so much from His Father, for He then forsook Him. He never gave so great manifestation of love to God as then.

7. *Suffering from His enemies.* In Christ's last sufferings He was delivered up to the power of His enemies and by these He obtained victory over His enemies.

D. It Appears in His Acts and in the Present State of Exaltation.

1. *He is the exalted Lion.* In His exalted state Christ appears in a manifestation of those excellencies for which He is compared to a lion.

2. *He is the exalted Lamb.* Although Christ is now at God's right hand, He still excels in humility. He is a lamb still.

CONCLUSION

Let the consideration of this wonderful meeting of diverse excellencies in Christ induce you to accept Him as your Saviour. His fullness and all-sufficiency as a Saviour gloriously appear in that variety of excellencies that we have considered.

Rev. George Whitefield 1714-1770

SUPREME AMONG PREACHERS

"No preacher has ever retained his hold on his hearers so entirely as he did for thirty-four years".
Bishop J. C. Ryle 1816-1900
In 1880 became the first Bishop of Liverpool

* * * * * * * * *

"He followed Paul ----- his zeal a kindred flame, his apostolic charity the same".
William Cowper 1731-1880
A literary genius and leading poet of his day

* * * * * * * * *

"There is no end to the interest which attaches to such a man as George Whitefield. Often as I have read his life, I am conscious of distinct quickening whenever I turn to it. HE LIVED. Other men seem to be only half-alive; but Whitefield was all life, fire, wing, force. My own model, if I may have such a thing in due subordination to my Lord, is George Whitefield; but with unequal footsteps must I follow in his glorious track".
Rev. C. H. Spurgeon 1834-1892
The Prince of Preachers
Metropolitan Tabernacle, London

SERMON

by

George Whitefield

THE DUTY OF SEARCHING THE SCRIPTURES

"Search the Scriptures", John 5 v.39.

When the Sadducees came to our blessed Lord, and put to him the question, "Whose wife that woman should be in the next life, who had seven husbands in this?" he told them "they erred, not knowing the Scriptures." And if we would know whence all the errors, that have overspread the Church of Christ, first arose, we should find that in a great measure they flowed from the same fountain, ignorance of the Word of God.

Our blessed Lord, though He was the eternal God, yet, as man, He made the Scriptures His constant rule and guide. And, therefore, when He was asked by the lawyer, which was the great commandment of the law, He referred him to his Bible for an answer, "What readest thou?" And thus, when led by the Spirit to be tempted by the devil, He repelled all His assaults, with "It is written."

A sufficient confutation this, of their opinion, who say, "the Spirit only, and not the Spirit by the Word, is to be our rule of action." If so, our Saviour, Who had the Spirit without measure, needed not always to have referred to the written Word.

But how few copy after the example of Christ! How many are there who do not regard the word of God at all, but throw the sacred oracles aside, as an antiquated book, fit only for illiterate men!

223

Such do greatly err, not knowing what the Scriptures are, or for what they are designed.

I shall, therefore, *First*, **Shew, that it is every one's duty to search them.**

And, *Secondly*, **Lay down some directions for you, to search them with advantage.**

First place, I am to shew, that it is every person's duty to search the Scriptures.

By the Scriptures, I understand the law and the prophets, and those books which have in all ages been accounted canonical, and which make up that volume commonly called the Bible.

These are emphatically styled the *Scriptures*, and, in one place, the "Scriptures of truth," as though no other books deserved the name of true writings, or Scriptures, in comparison of them.

They are not of any private interpretation, authority, or invention, but holy men of old wrote them, as they were moved by the Holy Ghost.

The foundation of God's revealing Himself thus to mankind, was our fall in Adam, and the necessity of our new birth in Christ Jesus. And if we search the Scriptures as we ought, we shall find the sum and substance, the alpha and omega, the beginning and end of them, is to lead us to a knowledge of those two great truths.

All the threats, promises, and precepts, all the exhortations and doctrines, contained therein, all the rites, ceremonies, and sacrifices appointed under the Jewish law; nay, almost all the historical parts of Holy Scripture, suppose our being fallen in Adam, and either point out to us a Mediator to come, or speak of him as already come in the flesh.

Had man continued in a state of innocence, he would not have needed an outward revelation, because the law of God was so deeply written in the tables of his heart. But having eaten the forbidden fruit, he incurred the displeasure of God, and lost the Divine image, and, therefore, without an external revelation, could never tell how God would be reconciled unto him, or how he should be saved from the misery and darkness of his fallen nature.

That these truths are so, I need not refer you to any other book than your own hearts.

For unless we are fallen creatures, whence those abominable corruptions which daily arise in our hearts? We could not come thus corrupt out of the hands of our Maker, because He being goodness itself could make nothing but what is like Himself, holy, just and good. And that we want to be delivered from these disorders of our nature, is evident, because we find an unwillingness within ourselves to own we are thus depraved, and are always striving to appear to others of a quite different frame and temper of mind than what we are.

I appeal to the experience of the most learned disputer against Divine revelation, whether he does not find in himself that he is naturally proud, angry, revengeful, and full of other passions contrary to the purity, holiness, and long-suffering of God? And is not this a demonstration that some way or other he is fallen from God? And I appeal also, whether, at the same time that he finds these hurtful lusts in his heart, he does not strive to seem amiable, courteous, kind, and affable; and is not this a manifest proof that he is sensible he is miserable, and wants, he knows not how, to be redeemed or delivered from it?

Here then, God by His Word steps in, and opens to his view such a scene of Divine love, and infinite goodness, in the Holy Scriptures, that none but men of such corrupt and reprobate minds as our modern deists, would shut their eyes against it.

What does God in His written Word do more or less than shew thee, O man, how thou art fallen into that blindness, darkness, and misery, of which thou feelest and complainest? And, at the same time, He points out the way to what thou desirest, even how thou mayest be redeemed out of it by believing in, and copying after, the Son of His love.

As I told you before, so I tell you again, Upon these two truths rest all Divine revelation. It being given us for no other end, but to shew us our misery, and our happiness; our fall, and recovery; or, in one word, after what manner we died in Adam, and how in Christ we may again be made alive.

Hence then arises the necessity of searching the Scriptures: for since they are nothing else but the grand charter of our salvation, the revelation of a covenant made by God with men in Christ, and a light to guide us in the way of peace; it follows, that all are obliged to read and search them, because all are equally fallen from God, all equally stand in need of being informed how they must be restored to, and again united with Him.

How foolishly then do the disputing infidels of this generation act, who are continually either calling for signs from heaven, or seeking for outward evidence to prove the truth of Divine revelation! Whereas, what they so earnestly seek for is nigh unto, nay, within them. For let them but consult their own hearts, they cannot but feel what they want. Let them but consult the lively oracles of God, and they cannot but see a remedy revealed for all their wants, and that the written Word does as exactly answer the wants and desires of their hearts, as face answers to face in the water. Where then is the scribe, where is the wise, where is the solidity of the reasoning of the disputers of this world? Has not God revealed Himself unto them, as plain as their own hearts could wish? And yet they require a sign: but there shall no other sign be given them. For if they believe not a revelation which is every way so suited to their wants, neither will they be persuaded, though one should rise from the dead.

But this discourse is not designed so much for them that believe not, as for them who doth know and believe that the Scriptures contain a revelation which came from God, and that it is their duty, as being chief parties concerned, not only to read, but search them also.

I pass on, therefore, in the

Second place, to lay down some directions how you may search them with advantage.

First, Have always in view, the end for which the Scriptures were written, even to shew us the way of salvation, by Jesus Christ.

"Search the Scriptures," says our blessed Lord, "for they are they that testify of Me." Look, therefore, always for Christ in the Scripture. He is the treasure hid in the field, both of the Old and New Testament. In the Old, you will find Him under prophecies, types, sacrifices, and shadows; in the New, manifested in the flesh, to become a propitiation of our sins as a Priest, and as a Prophet to reveal the whole will of His heavenly Father.

Have Christ, then, always in view, when you are reading the Word of God, and this, like the star in the east, will guide you to the Messiah, will serve as a key to every thing that is obscure, and unlock to you the wisdom and riches of all the mysteries of the kingdom of God.

Secondly, Search the Scriptures with an humble child-like disposition.

For whosoever does not read them with this temper, shall in no wise enter into the knowledge of the things contained in them. For God hides the sense of them from those that are wise and prudent in their own eyes, and reveals them only to babes in Christ; who think they know nothing yet as they ought to know; who hunger and thirst after righteousness, and humbly desire to be fed with the sincere milk of the Word, that they may grow thereby.

Fancy yourselves, therefore, when you are searching the Scriptures, especially when you are reading the New Testament, to be with Mary sitting at the feet of the holy Jesus: and be as willing to learn what God shall teach you, as Samuel was, when he said, "Speak, Lord, for Thy servant heareth."

Oh that the unbelievers would pull down every high thought and imagination that exalts itself against the revealed will of God! O that they would, like new-born babes, desire to be fed with the pure milk of the Word! then we should have them no longer scoffing at Divine revelation, nor would they read the Bible any more with the same intent the Philistines brought out Samson, to make sport of it; but they would see the Divine image and superscription written upon every line. They would hear God speaking unto their souls by it, and, consequently, be built up in the knowledge and fear of Him, who is the Author thereof.

Thirdly, Search the Scriptures, with a sincere intention to put in practice what you read.

A desire to do the will of God is the only way to know it; if any man will do My will, says Jesus Christ, "he shall know of My doctrine, whether it be of God, or whether I speak of Myself." As He also speaks in another place to his disciples, "to you (who are willing to practise your duty) it is given to know the mysteries of the kingdom of God, but to those that are without, (who only want to raise cavils against My doctrine,) all these things are spoken in parables, that seeing they may see, and not perceive, and hearing they may hear, and not understand."

For it is but just in God to send those strong delusions, that they may believe a lie, and to conceal the knowledge of Himself from all such as do not seek Him with a single intention.

Jesus Christ is the same now, as formerly, to those who desire to know from His Word who He is, that they may believe on, and live by Him, and to him He will reveal Himself as clearly as He did to the woman of Samaria, when He said, "I that speak of thee, am He," or as He did to the man that was born blind, whom the Jews had cast out for His name's sake, "He that talketh with thee, is He." But to those who consult His Word with a desire neither to know Him, nor keep His commandments, but either merely for their entertainment, or to scoff at the simplicity of the manner in which He is revealed, to those, I say, He never will reveal Himself, though they should search the Scriptures to all eternity. As He never would tell those whether He was the Messiah or not, who put that question to Him either out of curiosity, or that they might have whereof to accuse Him.

Fourthly, In order to search the Scriptures still more effectually, make an application of every thing you read to your own hearts.

For whatever was written in the Book of God, was written for our learning. And what Christ said unto those aforetime, we must look upon as spoken to us also: for since the Holy Scriptures are nothing but a revelation from

God, how fallen man is to be restored by Jesus Christ; all the precepts, threats, and promises, belong to us and to our children, as well as to those to whom they were immediately made known.

Thus the apostle, when he tells us that he lived by the faith of the Son of God, adds, "who died, and gave himself for me." It is this application of Jesus Christ to our hearts, that makes His redemption effectual to each of us.

And it is this application of all the doctrinal and historical parts of Scripture, when we are reading them over, that must render them profitable to us, as they were designed for reproof, for correction, for instruction in righteousness, and to make every child of God perfect, thoroughly furnished to every good work. I dare appeal to the experience of every spiritual reader of Holy Writ, whether or not, if he consulted the Word of God in this manner, he was not at all times and at all seasons, as plainly directed how to act, as though he had consulted the Urim and Thummim which was upon the high priest's breast. For this is the way God now reveals Himself to man: not by making new revelations, but by applying general things that are revealed already to every sincere reader's heart.

And this, by the way, answers an objection made by those who say, "The Word of God is not a perfect rule of action, because it cannot direct us how to act or how to determine in particular cases, or what place to go to, when we are in doubt, and therefore the Spirit, and not the Word, is to be our rule of action."

But this I deny, and affirm, on the contrary, that God at all times, circumstances, and places, though ever so minute, ever so particular, will, if we diligently seek the assistance of His Holy Spirit, apply general things to our hearts, and thereby, to use the words of the Holy Jesus, will lead us into all truth, and give us the particular assistance we want: But this leads me to a

Fifth direction how to search the Scriptures with profit: Labour to attain that Spirit by which they were written.

For the natural man discerneth not the words of the Spirit of God, because they are spiritually discerned; the words that Christ hath spoken, they are spirit, and they are life, and can be no more understood as to the true sense and meaning of them, by the mere natural man, than a person who never had learned a language can understand another speaking in it. The Scriptures, therefore, have not unfitly been compared, by some, to the cloud which went before the Israelites, they are dark and hard to be understood by the natural man, as the cloud appeared dark to the Egyptians; but they are light, they are life to Christians indeed, as that same cloud which seemed dark to Pharaoh and his house, appeared bright and altogether glorious to the Israel of God.

It was the want of the assistance of this Spirit, that made Nicodemus, a teacher of Israel, and a ruler of the Jews, so utterly ignorant in the doctrine of regeneration: for being only a natural man, he could not tell how that thing could be: it was the want of this Spirit that made our Saviour's disciples, though He so frequently conversed with them, daily mistake the nature of the doctrines He delivered; and it is because the natural veil is not taken off from their hearts, that so many who now pretend to search the Scriptures, yet see no farther than into the bare letter of them, and continue entirely strangers to the spiritual meaning couched under every parable, and contained in almost all the precepts of the Book of God.

Indeed, how should it be otherwise, for God being a Spirit, He cannot communicate Himself any otherwise than in a spiritual manner to the hearts of men and consequently if we are strangers to His Spirit, we must continue strangers to His Word, because it is altogether like Himself, spiritual. Labour, therefore, earnestly for to attain this blessed Spirit; otherwise, your understandings will never be opened to understand the Scriptures aright: and remember, prayer is one of the most immediate means to get this Holy Spirit. Therefore,

Sixthly, Let me advise you, before you read the Scriptures, to pray, that Christ, according to His promise, would send His Spirit to guide you into all truth; intersperse short ejaculations whilst you are engaged in reading; pray over every word and verse, if possible; and when you close up the book, most earnestly beseech God, that the words which you have read, may be inwardly engrafted into your hearts, and bring forth in you the fruits of a good life.

Do this, and you will, with a holy violence, draw down God's Holy Spirit into your hearts; you will experience His gracious influence, and feel Him enlightening, quickening, and inflaming your souls by the Word of God; you will then not only read, but mark, learn, and inwardly digest what you read: and the Word of God will be meat indeed, and drink indeed, unto your souls: you then will be, as Apollos was, powerful in the Scriptures; be scribes ready instructed to the kingdom of God, and bring out of the good treasures of your heart, things both from the Old and New Testament, to entertain all those you converse with.

One direction more, which shall be the last: *Seventhly*, Read the Scripture constantly, or, to use our Saviour's expression in the text, "Search the Scriptures;" dig in them as for hid treasure; for here is a manifest allusion to those who dig in mines; and our Saviour would thereby teach us, that we must take as much pains in constantly reading His Word, if we would grow wise thereby, as those who dig for gold and silver. The Scriptures contain the deep things of God, and therefore, can never be sufficiently searched into by a careless, superficial, cursory way of reading them, but by an industrious, close, and humble application.

The Psalmist makes it the characteristic of a good man, that he "meditates on God's law day and night." And "this book of the law (says God to Joshua) shall not go out of thy mouth, but thou shalt meditate therein day and night;" for then thou shalt make thy way prosperous, and thou shalt have good success. Search, therefore, the Scriptures, not only devoutly, but daily, for in them are the words of eternal life; wait constantly at wisdom's gate, and she will then, and not till then, display and lay open to you her heavenly treasures. You that are rich, are without excuse if you do not; and you that are poor, ought to take heed and improve that little time you have: for by the Scriptures you are to be acquitted, and by the Scriptures you are to be condemned at the last day.

But perhaps you have no taste for this despised book; perhaps plays, romances, and books of polite entertainment, suit your taste better: if this be your case, give me leave to tell you your taste is vitiated, and unless corrected by the Spirit and Word of God, you shall never enter into His heavenly kingdom: for unless you delight in God here, how will you be made meet to dwell with Him hereafter? Is it a sin then, you will say, to read useless impertinent books? I answer, Yes: and that for the same reason as it is a sin to indulge useless conversation, because both immediately tend to grieve and quench that Spirit by which alone we can be sealed to the day of redemption. You may reply, How shall we know this? Why, put in practice the precept in the text; search the Scripture in the manner that has been recommended, and then you will be convinced of the danger, sinfulness, and unsatisfactoriness of reading any others than the Book of God, or such as are wrote in the same spirit. You will then say, When I was a child, and ignorant of the excellency of the Word of God, I read what the world call harmless books, as other children in knowledge, though old in years, have done, and shall do; but now I have tasted the good Word of Life, and am come to a more perfect knowledge of Christ Jesus my Lord, I put away these childish trifling things, and am determined to read no other books but what lead me to a knowledge of myself and of Christ Jesus.

Search, therefore, the Scriptures, my dear brethren; taste and see how good the Word of God is, and then you will never leave that heavenly manna, that angel's food, to feed on dry husks, that light bread, those trifling sinful compositions, in which men of false taste delight themselves: no, you will then disdain such poor entertainment, and blush that yourselves once were fond of it. The Word of God will then be sweeter to you than honey and the honey-comb, and dearer than gold and silver; your souls by reading it will be filled, as it were, with marrow and fatness, and your hearts insensibly moulded into the Spirit of its blessed Author. In short, you will be guided by God's wisdom here, and conducted by the light of his Divine Word into glory hereafter.

Urban Divinity Unit UK Limited

Affiliated to Canada Christian College and School of Graduate Theological Studies

Urban Divinity Ministries

11-13 Oughton Road, Highgate, Birmingham, B12 0DF
Telephone: 0121 440 3103

Introduction and Welcome

Board of Directors

Aims and Objectives

Doctrinal Basis

The Alone Principles

Effective Service

Associated Colleges

Introduction and Welcome

Urban Divinity Unit UK, Birmingham, is the collective name of the combined ministries of Urban Divinity Ministries and other affiliated Seminaries and Colleges. Originally established as an independent body, it is non-denominational, interdenominational and international, founded primarily to serve the needs of those who desire to continue their training and study while engaged in the ministry of preaching, teaching, evangelism, pastoral care, religious education, missionary work, and other spheres of service in the Lord's work worldwide.

Candidates who have received the call of God to serve Him in whatever capacity and field of service, are accepted and welcomed regardless of race, colour, or denominational allegiance from all over the world. "In the defence and confirmation of the Gospel, ye all are partakers of My grace", (Phil. 1 v.7). It is imperative, therefore, "to stand fast in the Lord" (Phil. 4 v.1), so that the labours of both teacher and student redound to the praise, honour, and glory of God.

Education that is distinctively Christian is based on the Bible, and the Christian philosophy of life cannot be embraced apart from the experience of the new birth which involves a real encounter with God through repentance from sin and faith in the Lord Jesus Christ. Christian education, therefore, in the true sense of the term, is structured on the Protestant Reformation viewpoint that the Bible is the infallible and inerrant Word of God. UDM Birmingham is not a secular group of colleges, but is unashamedly evangelical and conservative, and should not be confused with professional colleges of liberal arts. Our vision is "to make known the mystery of the Gospel" (Eph. 6 v.19) by promoting a high level of theological education, training and scholarship in the preparation of candidates for ministry and mission in the twenty-first century.

The superficiality of much of the modern teaching of Christianity with its doctrinal failures and errors lead only to impoverished service and a serious decline in true worship. This is due in no small measure to a misrepresentation and distorted view of the Bible and of the true character and nature of the Divine persons within the Triune Godhead. "The Word of the Lord endureth for ever. And this is the Word which by the Gospel is preached unto you", (1 Peter 1 v.25).

There is a great need in the Church today for men who are called to preach and are able to preach the everlasting Word. Jesus proclaimed, "Upon this Rock I will build My Church; and the gates of hell shall not prevail against it", (Matt. 16 v.18). God's spokesmen will be strong Biblical preachers and firm ambassadors in the line of the great leaders of the early New Testament Church, the Reformation age, the Covenanting period, the Puritan era, the Great Evangelical Awakening, and other Revival times, including the Martyrs and Heroes of the Faith who in every age have faithfully sought to hold "forth the Word of Life" (Phil. 2 v.16) in the most difficult and trying of circumstances. In order to fulfil such a need, UDM Birmingham was established and called into existence some two decades or more ago. "This is the Lord's doing, and it is marvellous in our eyes", (Psalm 118 v.23).

Students are encouraged to "live soberly, righteously, and godly, in this present world", (Titus 2 v.12). The Bible is the sole authority in all matters of doctrine and practice. All our courses and programmes major on the content, exegesis, application and communication of the Holy Scriptures. "Thy Word is true from the beginning: and every one of Thy righteous judgments endureth for ever", (Psalm 119 v.160).

We warmly welcome you to join us in an in-depth study of the Word of God. With UDM Birmingham you will discover "the unsearchable riches of Christ" (Eph. 3 v.8) that are to be found in the Bible.

President: Rev. Prof. Dr. C. L Ryan
Vice-President: Rev. Prof. Dr. R. H. Creane

Urban Divinity Unit UK Limited

Affiliated to Canada Christian College and School of Graduate Theological Studies

THE BOARD OF DIRECTORS

Clinton L. Ryan
Robert H. Creane
Patrick G. Powell
Joseph E. Badu
Joseph Roberts

Urban Divinity Ministries

MISSION STATEMENT

By the Word of God (2 Tim. 3 v.16-17) and guidance of the Holy Spirit (John 16 v.13), we are committed to training and equipping candidates called of the Lord (Acts 26 v.16), for a powerful and effective ministry (Acts 6 v.4; 1 Cor. 9 v.14) as servants of Christ (Eph. 6 v.6), the only Head and Lord of the Church (Col. 1 v.18), communicating the Gospel of God (Rom. 1 v.1; Gal. 6 v.6) around the world (Matt. 28 v.19-20) to men and women for their salvation (Acts 4 v.12; Rom. 1 v.16), and for the edifying of the Body of Christ (Eph. 4 v.12), preaching the Word (Acts 11 v.19), motivated by devotion and love to the Lord Jesus Christ (John 21 v.15-17; Col. 1 v.10), and compassion for souls (Matt. 9 v.36-38), to the glory of God (Rev. 7 v.12).

"Go ye therefore, and teach all nations, baptizing them in the name of the Father, and of the Son, and of the Holy Ghost: Teaching them to observe all things whatsoever I have commanded you: and, lo, I am with you alway, even unto the end of the world. Amen",
(Matt. 28 v.19-20)

236

Aims and Objectives

(1)   To uphold and promote the ministry of God's Word, to encourage men called to the Lord to preach His Gospel and to pastor churches, and to further the proclamation and defence of the doctrines of Free and Sovereign Grace, by offering residential and 'open distance' learning and programmes that are spiritually useful, intellectually stimulating and practically relevant.

(2)   To provide education and training for men and women called to serve God in other areas of Christian work at home and abroad, by offering specialised 'core' study courses and programmes tailored to their particular needs for future service in Christ's Church.

(3)   To promote relevant and rigorous Christian scholarship, to offer a solidly Biblical alternative to secular theology by helping in some measure to develop those gifts which only the Lord can give to make a man a preacher "to reprove the world of sin, and of righteousness, and of judgment", (John 16 v.8).

(4)   To organise in-service training for church ministers, pastors, missionaries and other Christian professionals, and to hold conferences and other services to re-affirm the old Biblical truths in these days of apostasy and declension.

(5)   To raise a testimony against the evils of rationalism, liberalism, higher criticism, and all other such matters of doctrine and practice that are contrary to sound Biblical teaching and at variance with Holy Scripture.

(6)   To serve the Church of Christ universal by providing effective theological education worldwide, to share divinity programmes inter-denominationally, and to extend its courses to private students aspiring to be professionals in religious education and other spheres of service believing there is no dichotomy between being deeply spiritual and unashamedly academic and work to encourage growth in both these vital areas of life.

(7)   To work with all who share these beliefs; to affirm and display the centrality of the Bible in worship, preaching, teaching, church life and mission; to defend the Truth; to voice the evangelical perspective on theology and ethics; and to declare "all the counsel of God", (Acts 20 v.27), without fear of favour.

"Set for the defence of the Gospel", (Phil. 1 v.17)

"Now the God of peace, that brought again from the dead our Lord Jesus, that great Shepherd of the sheep, through the blood of the everlasting covenant, make you perfect in every good work to do His will, working in you that which is well pleasing in His sight, through Jesus Christ; to Whom be glory for ever and ever", (Hebrews 13 v.20-21).

The Doctrinal Basis of Faith

Affiliation and candidature is open to all who ascribe to the following Articles of Faith and Practice.

(1)   The Divine plenary inspiration and supernatural inerrancy of Holy Scripture, the Old and New Testaments, originally given as the Word of God, and that its teaching and authority are absolute, supreme and final as the only infallible rule in every matter of faith and life.

(2)   The Trinity in unity of the Godhead --- one living and true God, eternally existing in Three Persons --- the Father, the Son and the Holy Spirit, the same in substance, equal in power and glory.

(3)   The Sovereignty of God in creation, providence and redemption, revealed in the Lordship of Jesus Christ, the only Mediator between God and men.

(4)   The God and Father of the Lord Jesus Christ, holy, righteous, full of grace, Who in His infinite love has sent forth His Son, that the world through Him might be saved.

(5)   The Personality and Deity of the Lord Jesus Christ, the only incarnate Son of God, begotten of the Holy Spirit, His virgin birth, His perfect and sinless humanity, truly God and truly man, in two distinct natures, and one Person for ever.

(6)   The Personality and Deity of the Holy Spirit, the source and power of all acceptable worship and service, the infallible interpreter of the infallible Word, and His essential work in conviction, regeneration and sanctification, Who indwells every true believer with grace and strength to live and witness as unto the Lord.

(7)   The creation of man in the image of God, his subsequent total depravity and utter ruin through the Fall, the fallen state and lost condition of the whole human race, the subjection of all men to God's wrath and condemnation, the necessity of the new birth of the sinner and his acceptance with God only on the ground of the imputed righteousness of the Lord Jesus Christ.

(8)   The substitutionary and redemptive nature of the atonement in the life and death of Christ as the one propitiatory and expiatory sacrifice for sin, His triumphant bodily resurrection, His glorious ascension, His mediatorial reign, His continual intercession at the Throne of God as the believer's Great High Priest and Advocate, and His visible and personal return for His Church in glory and future judgement.

(9)   Salvation from the penalty of sin only by the grace of God in repentance unto life and justification of the sinner through faith in Jesus Christ alone, Who is the sole King and Head of His Church which is composed of all those who truly believe in Him as Saviour and Lord, and not by any human merit or works whatsoever.

(10)   The personality of the Devil, his evil opposition to God and the Divine purposes, the corruption and enslavement of man by Satan, and his final doom.

(11)   The resurrection and eternal blessedness of the redeemed in heaven, and the conscious everlasting punishment of the impenitent in hell.

(12)   The spiritual unity and eternal security of all believers in the Lord Jesus Christ, and the responsibility of all saved souls to "live soberly, righteously and godly in this present world", (Titus 2 v.12).

(13)   The expository, evangelical preaching of the Word of God; the preservation and purity of doctrine, worship and life, avoiding schism and heresy; and the encouragement of the exercise of all true gifts for the edification of the saints to the glory of God.

"To the law and to the testimony: if they speak not according to this Word, it is because there is no light in them", (Isaiah 8 v.20).

"Now therefore ye are no more strangers and foreigners, but fellow citizens with the saints, and of the household of God; And are built upon the foundation of the apostles and prophets, Jesus Christ Himself being the chief corner stone", (Eph. 2 v.19-20).

The Alone Principles of Historic Christianity

Sola Scriptura	:	the Scriptures are the sole authority in all matters of doctrine and practice
Christo Solum	:	the certain salvation by Christ alone of all that the Father has given to Him, having put away sin by the sacrifice of Himself
Cruce Solum	:	the efficacy of the atoning work and death of Christ on the Cross alone for the remission of sins
Sola Gratia	:	the invincibility of God's grace alone in saving His people from their sins and drawing them unto Jesus Christ
Sola Fide	:	the justification of sinners through faith alone in the person and work of the Lord Jesus Christ
Soli Deo gloria	:	The ultimate purpose of creation, providence, and redemption, is the glory of God

"And He is the Head of the body, the church: Who is the beginning, the firstborn from the dead; that in all things He might have the pre-eminence", (Col. 1 v.18).

Effective Service

The seeds of Urban Divinity Ministries were planted in 1984 and soon thereafter established with the sole aim of promoting the ministry of God's infallible and inerrant Word around the world to the glory of His great and holy name.

We give thanks and praise to Almighty God for the many achievements by Divine grace over the years. "The Lord hath done great things for us; whereof we are glad", (Psalm 126 v.3). Under His Providential care, guidance and blessing, much noble work is being done for the extension and furtherance of Christ's Kingdom on earth. "Thou art worthy, O Lord, to receive glory and honour and power: for Thou hast created all things, and for Thy pleasure they are and were created". (Rev. 4 v.11).

In bearing witness for the Truth of God's Word, whether by staff or student, the Biblical exhortation to steadfastness is imperative by showing an unflinching maintenance to Apostolic Doctrine, which must be clearly apprehended, earnestly embraced, firmly held, and stoutly defended. "Therefore, brethren, stand fast, and hold the traditions which ye have been taught, whether by word, or our epistle", (2 Thess. 2 v.15).

The Word of God firmly declares that it is "Not by might, nor by power, but by My Spirit, saith the Lord of Hosts", (Zech. 4 v.6). As God's servants we are charged with the solemn task and awesome responsibility of preaching the righteous demands of a Holy God. "For we preach not ourselves, but Christ Jesus the Lord; and ourselves your servants for Jesus' sake", (2 Cor. 4 v.5).

By the grace of God, wherever our lot shall be cast in future days, let us endeavour by the help of the Holy Spirit to be steadfast in the faith, faithful in ministry, devoted in pastoral duties, with the unceasing burden of a preacher's heart to proclaim and uphold the truth of God's inspired Word by maintaining a proper relationship between sound doctrine and sincere heavenly zeal in evangelism. "Upon this Rock I will build My Church; and the gates of hell shall not prevail against it", (Matt. 16 v.18). So may the time come when "the earth shall be full of the knowledge of the Lord, as the waters cover the sea", (Isaiah 11 v.9).

Anyone wishing to join us in an in-depth study of the Word of God is very welcome to write for information, and you will find that 'open distance' learning programmes provide an incredibly flexible way to achieving your aims.

Urban Divinity Unit UK and Associated Colleges

Affiliated to Canada Christian College and School of Graduate Theological Studies

Highgate UDU Theological Seminary, Birmingham

Calvary Theological College, London

Urban Divinity Unit, St. Vincent

International Theological College, London

South Florida International College, U.S.A.

First Born Theological College, Birmingham

City Theological College, Leicester

The Grenadines Divinity Unit, West Indies

Reformed Bible Seminary UDU Scotland

Covenant School of Theology UDU Ireland

FOR THE GLORY OF GOD

AND

THE INCREASE OF HIS KINGDOM

THROUGH

THE PROCLAMATION OF THE DIVINE WORD

AND

DEFENCE OF THE DOCTRINES OF FREE AND

SOVERIGN GRACE

"For the Word of God, and for the testimony of Jesus Christ",
(Rev. 1 v.9)

URBAN DIVINITY MINISTRIES

PROVIDING THEOLOGICAL EDUCATION BY

EXTENSION WORLDWIDE

"Study to show thyself approved unto God, a workman that needeth
not to be ashamed, rightly dividing the Word of truth",
(2 Timothy 2 v.15)

Other Published Works by the Author

1. **The Power, Passion and Purpose of Prayer**
   "Pray without ceasing",
   (1 Thess. 5 v.17)

2. **The Place, Role and Function of Women**
   In the Church
   In the Home
   In the Workplace
   In Society
   And
   In the World at Large

   Biblical Principles and Imperatives

3. **Reformation Today**
   Does the Evangelical Church need Revival?

4. **An Appreciation of John Calvin**
   500th Anniversary

5. **The Eighteen Fifty-Nine Revival**
   A Brief Overview

While stocks last, copies available from:

P.O. Box 55
57 Parkmore
Townland of Balteagh
Craigavon
County Armagh
BT64 2AE
Northern Ireland
United Kingdom

Other Theses and Dissertations by the Author

The Present Crises in Protestantism
A RETURN TO NEW TESTAMENT CHRISTIANITY AND THE SIMPLICITY OF
THE APOSTOLIC CHURCH

The Psalter: The Book of Praises
THE INSPIRED AND ORDAINED MANUAL OF PRAISE

The Atonement of Christ
THE BIBLICAL THEOLOGY OF APOSTOLIC PREACHING ESSENTIAL TO
TRUE RELIGION AND WORSHIP

The Biblical Basis and Practice of Worship
THE SUBSTANCE, STRUCTURE, STYLE AND SETTING OF WORSHIP

The Call, Qualifications and Work of the Christian Ministry
APOSTLES, PROPHETS, EVANGELISTS, PASTORS AND TEACHERS

Patrick: The Apostle of Ireland
THE MAN, HIS MESSAGE AND MISSION

The Church and the Means of Grace
EKKLESIA --- CALLED OUT --- THE BODY OF CHRIST

Biblical Protestantism and Roman Catholicism
Forever Apart
EVANGELICAL CHRISTIANITY AND THE DIVINE PRINCIPLE OF
SEPARATION

The Covenanters and the Revolution Settlement
THE CROWN RIGHTS AND ROYAL PREROGATIVES OF CHRIST JESUS
OVER CHURCH AND NATION

The Bible and the Reformation
SOLA SCRIPTURA: THE SOLE AUTHORITY IN ALL MATTERS OF DOCTRINE
AND PRACTICE

The Life and Times of Oliver Cromwell
THE MAN, AND THE TASK THAT LAY BEFORE HIM

Samuel Rutherford: The Saint of the Covenant
A MAN OF SPIRITUAL STATURE AND VALIANT IN LEADERSHIP